Somehow I Survived

A MEMOIR OF A LOST SOUL

Somehow I Survived

A MEMOIR OF A LOST SOUL

S.M. JORDAN

DORRANCE
PUBLISHING CO
EST. 1920
PITTSBURGH, PENNSYLVANIA 15238

Dorrance Publishing Co
585 Alpha Drive
Pittsburgh, PA 15238
Visit our website at *www.dorrancebookstore.com*

ISBN: 978-1-6470-2308-9
eISBN: 978-1-6470-2828-2

Contents

Introduction

It was early in the summer of 1977. My team was losing 5-4, with two outs in the bottom of the last inning. We had the bases loaded with the count at three balls and two strikes.

They all watched, family members and friends in the stands, my teammates on the bench. I knew they were waiting breathlessly, hoping and believing as the next pitch came hurtling toward the plate.

To become the game hero was all on me, 12-year-old Stephen Smith. I felt the pressure, every ounce of it. But determination coursed through my veins, it pulsed in my wide eyes. I gripped my bat tight.

I had to get a hit. I *would* get a hit.

The pitch came. It was way high over my head.

I swung…

…and missed.

Strike three. "You're out!" cried the umpire.

I slammed my helmet down in the dirt and trudged back toward the bench where my teammates were all kicking dirt and slamming their hats and gloves on the ground. The game was over. We'd lost, because of me.

My best friend Roland came running. "Stephen, you could have had a walk!" he pleaded desperately. "We would have won!"

I exploded at him. "I DIDN'T WANT A WALK! I HATE WALKS! ANYBODY CAN GET A WALK! I'D RATHER STRIKE OUT THAN GET A WALK! I WANTED A HIT!!!"

And that's what happened that day.

I wanted the greater thrill, the greater glory.

So, that game—little did I know back then—would turn out to be like much of my life. It was to become just one of many harrowing experiences, many setbacks and losses, that I would suffer in the years ahead.

When life throws you a wild pitch, swing high and swing hard. It just may be the only opportunity you'll ever have.

Somehow I Survived

A MEMOIR OF A LOST SOUL

CHAPTER 1

Willard Beach

A story for the Homeless of Hardship's caused by his unability to cope in society

The water was calm, the fog and light rain settling the mood on that very quiet Sunday afternoon in Maine.

I was alone, the only soul searching along the shore at Willard Beach.

My parents had warned me not to go near the water during a red tide. But I'd never been one to take their warnings—or take seriously anything anyone else said, for that matter.

At only the age of six, I'd already climbed the perilous steep rocks along Dana Cove by myself. Oblivious to my own safety, I'd prevailed, coming home with only my sneakers and pant legs soaking wet after searching between rocks for sea glass, shells, starfish, and sand dollars.

But what I'd always wanted most in my young and sometimes rebellious adventures was to catch a live crab.

Not to cook it up and eat, though. I could never stand the thought of eating or even breathing in the disgusting smell of seafood. It was just the challenge of catching a big crab alive that captivated me. Many times, I'd turned over big rocks in my pursuit, but the fast crawling crabs had always escaped out of reach before I could snatch them out of the water.

On this particular Sunday afternoon, I remembered how I'd often seen some of the older kids who did snag crabs get their fingers pinched angrily. The poor sea creatures had only tried to escape their captivity the best way they knew how.

And to my dismay, I'd watched those same cruel kids pluck off the crabs' claws and legs to smash them on the rocks.

I'd screamed, "No! No, don't hurt them!"

I'd just wanted to keep them as a pet. But it never happened.

At last, though, I knew *this Sunday afternoon* was the time. I was at last going to capture a pet crab for myself and take care of it. And surely enough, this time the task proved easy. A tiny wave rolled my crab, tangled up in seaweed, right to the shore. I pulled him out and set him on the steps nearby. He was moving very slow.

"He's alive!" I said, so excited that I'd caught a real live crab. I looked around and found an empty soda cup in the sand so that I could carry him home on my bike. I never thought about filling the cup with ocean water. The poor sick crab bounced around in that empty cup the entire time I peddled home.

When I arrived, I quickly filled a bucket with cold water from the kitchen sink, adding some table salt for my new friend. I noticed he wasn't moving anymore. I figured he was just sleeping as I set him out on the back porch.

I woke up early the next morning for school. After having a bowl of Fruit Loops cereal for breakfast, I decided I wanted to take my new friend to school for Show and Tell. I decided it would be better for him if I refilled his bucket with ocean water. And maybe he might like to eat some seaweed. So, I took a detour back down to the beach before I began my short journey to Dora L. Small School a little over a half mile away.

Now I was obliged to walk, and the bucket grew heavy as I trudged along carrying it. I had to keep switching arms, all the while knowing I still had to bear the same heavy load back home at the end of the school day. My determination got me there. But the tougher challenge proved to be trying to convince the entire class my new pet crab was only sleeping. While many of my classmates tried to argue that crabs don't sleep, the smelly ocean water bucket sat next to my desk until it was time to go home.

I carried the heavy bucket back home.

My crab died in his sleep a few days later. I sighed with sadness.

But I soon came up with another goal. This time, now at the age of 7, I was going to catch a real live bird. Playing out in the back yard with my family's dog named Phoebe, I made repeated attempts to trap or get one of the birds fluttering about us to eat out of my hand. For a while, as you can imagine, I had no success.

One morning, though, Phoebe was with me again and together we watched a whole flock of little birds landing in the yard. Phoebe ran into the midst of them, and they all flew away—except one. Phoebe nosed at the one little bird left behind on the ground, a beautiful little Pine Siskin. It may have been too scared to fly away. For whatever reason, it just stayed there.

I bent over to pick it up. I held this beautiful bird in my hand, the moment breathless. When I set the bird down and watched it fly away, there was joy in my heart. I had done it! I'd captured a bird!

I had to admit, though, being 80% deaf in my left ear and having 20% hearing loss in my right ear never made other things quite so easy for me. I only heard half of everything that was said to me. The fact that I didn't *want* to listen to anything anyone said to me didn't help much either. In 1st grade, I would often wander around the classroom mumbling to myself. Clearly, I was a regular disturbance to the rest of the class.

And if somebody heard me mumble the S-word or the F- word, some tattletail would let Mrs. Blanchard know. "Stephen just swore!"

"Well, then, Stephen can go back down to Kindergarten!!" Mrs. Blanchard would cry, charging at me as I threw my papers in the air, accomplishing nothing to distract my assailant. She'd grab my squirming body, kicking and screaming while two other teachers helped drag me across the hall where I would often spend the rest of the day sitting in the corner—or until Mrs. Blanchard thought I was ready to go back and sit with the rest of the class.

Aside from this sort of thing happening on a few occasions, I was mostly quiet either day dreaming or staring at the clock, waiting for that bell to ring so I could get out of there.

By the time I made it to 2nd grade, the school system thought they'd solved the problem.

They set me in the back of the class with a folding wall around my desk.

This is great! I thought to myself. *I have my own fort in the back of the room where nobody can see what I'm doing! In here, I can pull down my pants and nobody will even know what I'm doing! I can be standing here with my pants down, letting it all hang out!*

And, so, I did.

"Stephen, what are you doing behind there?!!!"

I turned around buckling my pants as fast as I could. "Oh, *nothing*," I answered, embarrassed that Mrs. McClellan might have come back to my fort and seen my private little thing.

But she only told me I would have these walls around my desk for the rest of the school year—and all next year as well.

Not true. After just a few weeks behind my private walls, I was very disappointed when they took them away from me. I had poked a few peepholes with my pencil and drawn faces all over my desk and the wall. I'm surprised the school didn't make my parents pay for all the damage I'd done.

What was more amazing was that I even survived those younger years, given the way I rode my bike to school. We lived near the top of the hill on Henry

Street which was usually pretty quiet, with very little traffic. I'd heard all the lectures: *"Stop and look both ways before crossing the street!"* But that never really concerned me. Every time I set out on my bike peddling hard and fast down across Willard Street, I never stopped to look. I thought, *what are the chances a car is coming at the same time I'm riding full speed across the street?*

And if a car had to come screeching to a halt, I thought that was funny.

Another thing. I once turned a corner so fast, I was suddenly heading straight towards a car screeching to a stop. My front tire slammed into his bumper.

I yanked my bike out from under his bumper and set out pedaling again, while the old man stepped out of his car cursing and swearing.

I rode away, believing the "accident" was his fault not mine.

Back in those days, my parents were very strict. It wasn't unusual for me and my brothers to get our butts whipped at least once a day. Things would just… happen. Like this.

My brothers and I were out with the rest of the neighborhood kids looking for something to do. We saw a clothes line with freshly cleaned clothes hanging out to dry. We decided to yank them all down, stomp them into the mud, then toss them in the bushes. How anyone found out it was us who had done the deed, I'll never know. But when those aggrieved neighbors came to our door that evening and told our parents what we had done, we got our butts whipped to a pulp.

Plus, that night we had to give our apologies in person.

Other crimes we perpetrated on other occasions included setting off the fire alarm, stealing money from the Cub Scouts fund, and digging up a neighbor's vegetable garden. With our reputation, sometimes we also got blamed for things we didn't do. (Which sort of made up for all the things we did do but never got caught for.)

Whatever the case, Mother made sure we repented of our sins each night before we went to sleep. Every night, we had to kneel before getting into bed and repeat "The Lord's Prayer." I repented all the sins my mother knew about during our open prayer. But I also said silent prayers for the sins she didn't know about.

In addition, attending church every Sunday was very important to our parents. Holy Cross Church is where I was baptized as an infant. Every Sunday afterward, we kept on attending until one Sunday when Mom told us we were not going to Holy Cross Church anymore. My older brother Rick got so excited he was ready to call all his friends and tell them, *we don't have to go to church anymore!*

But Mom toned down his excitement when she added, "No, I did *not* say we are not going to church at all anymore. I said, 'We are not going to *that* church anymore.'"

Mom always made all the decisions about which church we should be going to. So, from that day on, as long as we lived under our parents' roof, The South Portland Church of The Nazarene was a big part of our lives.

CHAPTER 2

Willard School

In the summer of 1973, when I was just eight years old, my brother Rick was ten, my brother Shawn five, and my youngest sister Lisa almost three. We four, along with our dog Phoebe and our beautiful black cat Midnight, were called upon to make a move to a new home. Soon we were adjusting to life in a much bigger house on Pillsbury Street, about a mile from our old house on Henry Street.

Even with more space to live in, though, my father Richard Smith and my mother Ruth Ann argued a lot. In spite of this, they managed to put forth the necessary effort to keep the house in general good order. Dad's work was as a Service Manager for a Pontiac dealership, while Mom stayed at home full-time making sure we all had clean clothes and dinner on the table.

I was actually excited about our new home and neighborhood. But the one thing I dreaded was the thought of attending Willard School, in an old brick building right across the street from our new house. Back on Henry Street, Small School had been for me a recently built facility with all new desks, a large play-ground, and a grass lawn, with each classroom having its own bathroom. Though I hated school in general, at least in those days I had a clean, newly constructed building to enjoy.

But now I was going to have to attend class in an old rundown building with broken glass scattered about the stretch of pavement which they called a play-ground. I begged my mom: "Please don't make me go there!"

She ignored me. And soon, as summer came to an end, school started. I had to face my fear and enter that dreadful old building.

Once inside, however, I looked up at the high ceiling, the beautiful hardwood floors, and the big windows. I also looked around at all the pretty girls in my class. And suddenly I thought to myself, *this isn't so bad after all!*

After just a few days of attending Willard, I knew I liked this school much better than my previous one. Except…

Mrs. Searway was our teacher. She was usually very nice, but I was often drawing or doodling on paper while she was trying to teach the class. One day, I drew a beautiful chopper motorcycle and was just about finished with my masterpiece when she grabbed the paper away, crumpled it up and threw it in the trash.

I was so mad. I felt I could never again draw such a beautiful motorcycle, no matter how hard I tried.

As you might already guess, I never paid attention very much in class even at Willard. Still, I got much better grades since this time I was repeating the 2nd grade. I knew all the answers before they were asked. Maybe I had learned a lot more the year before than they thought I did.

After just a few weeks at our new school, my brothers proved to be better at bringing home new friends than I was. Rick had met a fellow named JJ Ross. Shawn, who had just started Kindergarten, made friends with JJ's younger brother Eric Ross, who was his same age. The Ross family lived just three houses up from us. JJ was the oldest, just one and a half years older than I was.

Then there was Tracy Ross. She was a few months older than me and usually didn't like me. No big deal.

But the Ross's were all…well, a bit strange. I thought this to be true especially when I saw JJ riding a bike with no front tire, just a bent-up rim that rattled and clacked so loud you could hear it all over the neighborhood. As for Eric, he *always* had dirty hands. And he never seemed embarrassed about his filthy clothes and rude behavior.

Meanwhile, their father had a large stack of Playboy and Penthouse magazines he kept in his office in their house. All of us kids had access to them, young as we were. In spite of this moral problem, since they lived so close to us, we became close friends with the Ross's.

Things were inconsistent, though. Sometimes I was friendly with Eric, other times I'd fight with him. And I'd always side with JJ whenever he and Rick got in a fight, which they did that a lot. Eventually, JJ and I would form a close friendship.

I looked up to JJ because he wasn't afraid to do anything. We'd set up ramps for making bike jumps and talk about Evel Knievel and how we would own motorcycles and make great jumps one day. No matter how high we set the ramp, JJ seemed fearless when he flew his bike through the air. Sometimes he made a crash landing. But usually he landed safely. I respected him. And I felt that I could trust him to keep confidence with anything I said to him in private.

But! He loved to talk about girls and he already had himself a girlfriend. So, when I spilled it out that I really liked Alice, the most beautiful girl in my 2nd grade class, JJ wasted no time letting her know.

The next afternoon, upon returning home from Sunday church, I saw that JJ and Alice were waiting on my front lawn. I wanted to run and hide as soon as I got out of the car. But I couldn't. She was right there.

I started shouting, "NO, NO, NOT HER! NO, I HATE HER, NO!!!" I was so scared. She looked so beautiful, and I wanted to tell her I loved her. But I was just scared. Even with JJ there trying to encourage me, and Alice there still smiling—looking so beautiful and wanting to be my girlfriend—I chickened out.

(And just so you know, a similar incident would happen two years later when I was in 4th grade. I spilled it to my friend Roland that I liked Katy. He let her and the rest of the kids on the playground know it. She'd also said *Yes!* to the idea of being my girlfriend, but once again I got scared and denied aloud that I ever said I liked her—while the whole playground was watching and listening. From then on, I vowed only to ask out girls who were guaranteed to say *No!* to me.)

Anyway, returning to Willard the next fall for 3rd grade, we had a new Principal, Mrs. Emmons. She was the meanest—and the last—Principal that Willard School would ever have. I was living proof how mean she was. Whenever I didn't keep my head down on the desk, I acquired a few bruises on my arms where Mrs. Emmons grabbed me, digging her long fingernails into my arm and poking something sharp on the top of my head. This left deep scars in the skin over my skull. Mrs. Emmons once even slammed my head against the coat hooks.

Okay, so, I was probably asking for it that time. I'd stood up in class and said, "Shut up, Emmons!" She walked away for a moment but then returned to the classroom and said, "Stephen, come here!"

I got up from my seat and walked to where she stood in the hallway. "Stephen, what did you just say to me?" There was menace in her voice.

I answered back. "I told you to shut up!" I put a big smile on my face, showing I'd just accomplished another great goal of mine. I'd told that old hag to shut up straight to her face.

Wham! I felt her hand slap me hard across the cheek. Then she grabbed my hair and slammed my head against the coat hooks. Like I said, I got a few bruises out of the situation. But I felt it was worth it because I'd really told that old hag off.

Mrs. Black was my classroom teacher at the start of that school year. But she resigned at mid-year so that she could adopt a baby. Many of my classmates felt sad that she was leaving, but not me. I was glad she was leaving…

…until we all met our new replacement teacher named Mrs. Solack. She took over for the whole rest of the school year. We gave her the nickname Mrs. Sleestack, taken from the Saturday morning TV show "Land of the Lost."

We also gained a few new students in our class that year, including Roland LaChance. Roland was a short but tough kid who had recently moved to South Portland from Bracket Street in Portland. Our whole class ganged up on him for the first few weeks because he came from a rundown part of town. But after a few weeks of staying after school together, he and I became good friends.

The first time Roland and I stayed after school together, Sleestack left us alone in the class room with her purse sitting in the corner behind her desk. As soon as she left the room, Roland dashed across the floor, sliding on his knees straight for her purse. I saw what he was doing, and I ran up right there behind him.

This happened more than once. We only took about two or three dollars each time, so she never noticed the money was missing. We had a pretty good business going for a while, since we had to stay after school almost every day.

But finally, my mother noticed I was showing off all this money. She and Dad sat me down and asked where I was getting it. I just shrugged my shoulders and said, "Roland gave it to me."

Immediately, Dad took me for a ride to see Roland's stepfather. I sat in the car while Dad knocked on the door and went inside. I could see them all sitting at a table through the window. Roland looked a little nervous while my Dad and his stepdad were asking him questions. They were sitting there a long time while I was in the car feeling bad. Yet, I put all the blame on Roland. It was up to him to think up something to keep us out of trouble, and I really didn't think Dad would question the matter much further.

Dad finally came outside and didn't say another word as we drove home.

The next day, I asked Roland what he told them. He said, "I just told them I found it." And that was the end of it.

More about Roland. Like me, he had a big crush on Alice. But unlike me, he wasn't afraid to tell her so. Sometimes he'd go to her house then brag to me about how he'd kissed her. Other times, we'd go there together, and she'd tell us to fight on her front lawn and whoever won could have her. So, we did. And I would lose on purpose—but not because I didn't want Alice as my girl. It was because I was so afraid I didn't know how to kiss her.

By the time I was in 4th grade, a new blonde girl named Melisa had joined our class, and I could see Roland already had his eyes on her. But I could tell she didn't like me. When I asked her out, she proved it and said, "Noooo waaaaayy!"

Still, I asked her out many more times—just to get the same answer and have an excuse why I didn't have a girlfriend. I could truly say I was rejected.

Meanwhile, my younger brother Shawn asked Melisa's younger sister out, and she would invite him over to their house. But I stuck with my excuse as to why I didn't have a girlfriend, which made it so that I never had to admit I was afraid.

At Christmas in 1975, my parents gave me an AM/FM Stereo Record player, and I would find my escape from my personal frustrations and pain through music. It was a great year for music and Elton John was my favorite artist. Also, Dad gave me his collection of 45's with Little Richard, Jerry Lee Lewis, Elvis, and hundreds of other records. Every day, if I was at home, I was in my room jumping on my bed and listening to all this great music. Eric and JJ would come over, and sometimes we'd all be jumping around my room.

By this time, I also had a better way of earning money—helping my brother with his paper route. I'd save my earnings to buy many more records.

I missed a lot of school that year in 1976, going to hearing tests and visits to my psychologists. I didn't mind at all. I looked forward to any excuse to get out of class for a while. But after having a kidney infection and blood in my urine, the hospital was not a place I wanted to be. I feared being stuck with needles and taking pills. After spending most of my spring vacation in the hospital, I vowed I would never let anyone know I had any pain in my kidneys or blood in my urine again. I never wanted to be stuck with another needle again.

Only a few years later, I learned I could have avoided a lot of pain and suffering just by drinking fruit drinks and water.

Before that school year ended, another strange family moved to town, living right next door. Annie and Nathan Levine were the kids' names, and they even went to a strange school called The Waynflete School. I thought it had to be the coolest school in the world, though, from what Nathan would tell me about it. They learned how to build teepees and did lots of fun stuff like arts and crafts. They also had so many vacation days that Nathan would get his bike and ride it on the Willard playground during our recess time.

In fact, Nathan could get away with anything, and the Willard teachers couldn't touch him because he didn't attend our school.

Plus, I thought Nathan's mom was the coolest. She would listen to rock 'n roll on her radio in the kitchen while all of us kids played in the attic, listening to the music and jumping out the window to the roof below.

One day, Nathan and I were trying to hide some magazines in our little fort we built in the attic. Nathan's mom came up, shouting: "Nathan your hiding something from me!"

I thought, *Oh no! We're in trouble now.* But suddenly, to my surprise, Mrs. Levine's face lit up with excitement as she pulled a Playboy magazine out from under a blanket. "Nathan! I'm so proud of you, you're growing up so fast, I don't know what to say!"

I was shocked. My mother would have taken those books away and grounded me for a week. But Mrs. Levine worked as a psychologist and said it was perfectly normal for a boy the age of ten to read Playboy magazine. It was the only way he was going to learn.

Even though I was always so jealous of Nathan for having such a cool mother, he would often admit to me: "I wish my mother didn't allow me to do so much. You get to be sneaky and worry about getting caught. But nothing happens to me if I get caught." He said this with a regretful little laugh in his voice. Deep down inside, I knew, he really wanted to get his ass beaten the way everyone else in our neighborhood did.

And one day, it happened.

Nathan's mom had told him not to have any friends in the house while she was not home. But Nathan *always* had friends over when she wasn't there. And one time, he got caught while we were up in the attic playing the music loud and paying no attention to the time.

Suddenly, Nathan's mom came home without notice. She shut the music off. "Oh, Nathan you disobeyed me," she said with a not-so-mean tone of voice. "I'm going to have to spank you this time."

He just laughed and said okay. He laid himself down across her knee and she spanked him with only one slap of the hand.

"AH, COME ON, MOM!!!" he shouted. "STEPHEN'S MOTHER HITS HIM HARDER THAN THAT!!!" He jumped up and slapped his mother across the face. "Stephen mother hits him like this!!!" he said, slapping his mother repeatedly.

"Nathan, stop it!!" I heard her shouting as I turned around and ran home laughing. Nathan was grounded to his room for the rest of the day. But all his friends hung around outside his window where Nathan put his head out, bragging that he was grounded and couldn't go outside.

Nathan's sister Annie was very pretty, and most of us boys in the neighborhood noticed her. Of course, I never thought she would ever show any interest in me, but Roland, Eric and JJ weren't shy like me when it came to asking a girl out. I was the only one who was petrified and afraid of anybody knowing just how scared I was.

So, when the guys all got together, they would chase Annie around the backyard saying, "I love you Annie! You're beautiful!" and throwing kisses. I ran along with them, chasing her up to her back porch just for fun and to hide my fear and expecting none of Annie's attention.

But! She stood up there next to Tracy with a big smile on her face.

When we all shouted, "Will you go out with me?" and looked up at her in awe....to my amazement, with that beautiful smile she said, "Stephen! I want to go out with Stephen."

Petrified, I pretended to be excited as all us guys ran off—with Roland and Eric and JJ clearly feeling disappointed. But I couldn't fake my excitement for long, so I ran into hiding. I didn't even go to JJ for advice or encouragement. I just hid in fear.

Luckily, Tracy later talked Annie out of her preference for me. I knew Tracy hated me, and for that one moment in time, her hatred ended up rescuing me from love—which I feared the most.

CHAPTER 3

Mrs. Brailey

The summer of 1976 came to an end. Annie joined our class for the new school year of 5th grade because her mother thought it would be easier for both her and Nathan to attend the school across the street.

It was easy for me to avoid Annie in the classroom and on the playground, even though I still secretly liked her. I also liked Alice but kept on pretending to have my heart set on Melisa.

A very large, overweight woman, Mrs. Brailey was our classroom teacher that year. She made school a fun place to be, and for the first time I could go to school every day without it being a drudgery. She always gave us plenty of activities to do, whether it was arts & crafts or sitting around the record player playing records all day long. We could bring in our own stuffed animals, blankets, and pillows. At the back of the room, Roland and I were even allowed to have our own fort under a table using cardboard walls taped to the table legs.

We also put up on the walls some posters of Elton John, Farrah Fawcett, Fonzie, and many other popular celebrities. We had records and magazines and helped ourselves to the snack box that sat on top of the table. We had everything necessary to make school a fun place to be.

Since I had taken over my brother Rick's paper route during the summer, I always had plenty of money, and I knew about all the latest new music albums. Elton John was a favorite artist of mine from the beginning of the school year, but soon I would discover many more like Kiss, Alice Cooper, and The Eagles. I became more popular with my classmates since I was able to buy the newest releases as soon as they hit the shelves.

Every day before school, we'd all show off the records we brought in for that day. Even Mrs. Brailey added a stack of her own collection. So, we were always quite busy once class began, and we often gathered around the record player deciding whose record to play next.

Not all our classmates, though, were enjoying the fun we were having in school that year. There had been a lot of bullying going on the years before, and this year too we all got bullied at one time or another. For the most part, the rule was bully or be bullied.

Sometimes, in order stay on top, I had to join others who were on the bullying side—and keep it up. A few students had become easy targets starting as far back as 3rd grade.

It wasn't, as though, they were any different from the rest of us. In fact, in a lot of ways the bullied ones were a lot like me. For instance, one girl who peed her pants. Well, I knew I'd peed my pants many times too. And George was everything I hated about myself: awkward in his speech, clumsy with every step, etc. George and I had even been friends back in 3rd grade. I remembered walking with him going to his house after school, and we had made a promise to each other that we'd *always* be friends.

When the bullying had started this year, self-esteem had once again spiraled low for those being abused—which made them an easy target for even more hateful treatment. We showed no mercy. We played cruel games. If we brushed up to close to a bullied student, we'd say "Eeewwww! Get away from me!" Then we'd tag someone else and say *George's germ's, Jack's germs,* or *Lisa's germs!*

And we'd shut them out of the regular games we played, poking fun of the clothes they wore. Anything we could do to bring someone else down and make ourselves look big, we did. This was something that never bothered me. I never felt guilty about any of the things I'd done.

Until one day before school started...

A gang of us out on the playground watched as George's parents dropped him off at the corner near the end of the playground. As soon as he stepped through the gate, someone shouted: "GET HIM!!" And George took off running while we all chased after him.

He ran ahead of us up the steps to the school's front door. He pulled and pulled on the door handle, damn it! The door was locked! We had him cornered as he turned around then buckled over and burst into tears. His body was shaking as he sat with his head down to his knees. He cried so hard he was choking and drooling from his mouth.

All I could do was stand and watch his jaw shaking as the fluids just flowed from his face. Suddenly, for the first time in my life, I felt the pain of another human being. As guilt and shame sent sharper and sharper pain through my heart, I couldn't stand it any longer.

What did George do to deserve this kind of abuse? Just show up at school day after day? *This kid is no different than I am. He just has the guts to cry. I should be down there crying for all the pain and suffering I've caused. But I just never have had the guts to cry.*

At last, we all just slowly backed way. And from that day on, I thought twice before taking part in any bullying again. I even became friends with George once more, and for the rest of that school year. So, even if we never opened up a single text book, I can honestly say I learned more in that short moment before the start of Mrs. Brailey's 5th grade class that day than I had learned in all my school years combined.

With the coming of spring, baseball season arrived. Baseball was the game I'd hated since I was eight years old when I was the worst player for the last-place team. I'd struck out in three pitches every time I came to the plate for the first half of the season. The second half of the season my teammates told me, *"Don't swing at any pitch! Just stand there and watch the ball go by!"*

So, I walked after four pitches every time I came to bat for the rest of the season.

The Red Sox were in first place in early spring of 1977. I'd finally grown to love the game I once hated. My enthusiasm grew as I began to understand Batting Averages, E.R.A.'s, and all the other statistics that make up the game.

Even though I doubted I'd ever be a great player myself, in my heart I set big dreams that one day I *would* become so good I'd play in the Big Leagues. It was a bit like asking out only the girl who's guaranteed to say no. I'd made a career choice I could never achieve.

In fact, at twelve years old I was such a terrible player that I sat on the bench of a farm league team on which my younger brother got more playing time than I did. And the one day my teacher Mrs. Brailey came to see me play, I made the mistake of turning around to wave to her as she stepped out of her car. I was supposed to be covering 1st base and paying attention to the game. But the ball was hit down the 3rd base side then thrown directly at me—while I was daydreaming.

"Ouuufff!!!!" The ball hit me right in the gut.

"Pay attention, Stephen!" the coach shouted out to me from the bench. Those words I'd heard so many times in my life. *Pay attention!*

It was very sad to see that school year end. Even sadder, it was our last year at Willard School. The school was so old it never had another 6th grade class. And worst of all, while most of my classmates would be attending Small School the following year, I was not going with them.

You see, Mrs. Brailey, my parents, and the rest of the school board thought it would be better to separate me from the rest of my classmates. Even though two other schools were much closer to my house, they decided I would attend Brown School for my 6th grade year.

So, once again, I dreaded the thought of the upcoming school year and the school I would be going to.

However, Mrs. Brailey invited me to her house a few times over the summer so that I could use her swimming pool. Sometimes my older brother Rick came along. I could sense he felt a bit of jealousy that I had such a fun teacher. But I knew all the fun we'd had that school year was over forever and I had to face a real school teacher when the summer was done.

Like most summers in Maine, the summer of 1977 was very hot and muggy. But even in the heat, our neighborhood of friends always found plenty to do. We spent a lot of time near Willard Beach jumping off cliffs into the cold Maine ocean water. Sometimes, we'd hike along the rocky shore all the way to Fort Williams.

But wiffleball was the game that brought us all together one early evening on Nathan and Annie's front lawn.

Tracy was up to bat wearing just a bikini top and shorts. Suddenly Nathan called, "Time-out, time-out!" while waving his arms like there was some important game-stopper. He walked up to Tracy, pulled a bit of her top open, and peeked inside.

"Yup, they're real!" he said with a big smile on his face as he walked back to the field.

Tracy's jaw dropped. But then she broke out with a smile, laughing along with the rest of us.

Soon, the summer of 1977 was coming to an end and all the good times along with it. As much as I feared the start of the coming school year, the saddest day came about a week before school started, when our dog Phoebe ran out the door.

Phoebe was an all-around mutt of many colors who won every fight— even with much bigger dogs. She had already been caught by the dog catcher twice that same week and my parents had been stuck with big fines to pay. Phoebe was well known by the K-9 control and they wanted to take her to the pound rather than continue harassing my parents about fines they couldn't afford.

Phoebe had been with us for 9½ years, as long as I could remember faithfully present either by my or my brother's side. Whether we were delivering papers or just playing in the neighborhood, Phoebe was always with us except the times we were in school or church.

It was amazing we had her as long as we did, given the many times I'd seen her dash out across traffic chasing a cat and bringing cars to a screeching stop.

Another time she ran in front of a couple fire trucks with their sirens blaring. The lead truck had slowed down, the firemen hanging their heads out the side of the truck to shout: "Get outta here!" and "Beat it, mutt!"

Nothing ever stopped Phoebe, it seemed. She'd survived every dangerous situation. And I'd never seen her lose a fight.

But on one sad day, mother was in the kitchen when she said, "We just can't afford to keep her anymore." I ran outside where the K-9 van was parked. I took one last look through the back window at Phoebe and she looked up at me one last time. She didn't wag her tail.

The start of the new school year arrived. My attitude was that I was not going to like this school. I was not going to make any new friends, even though I already knew one from church, Billy. For a few years, he and I had attended Sunday School together at The Nazarene Church. We were both big fans of Kiss and talked more about rock 'n roll music than we paid attention in Sunday School.

But this time I made no effort to fit in with anyone, even when right after the first day, two cute girls named Lori and Terry came to me on the playground to ask if I was going to be in their class. I said I was going to be starting the 6th grade, and they showed some excitement that I'd be with them in their class. I couldn't figure out why they were so excited. I was prepared to be seen once again as the ugliest kid in the class.

Another thing. It was hard for me to adjust to a school where we were actually given homework. I hadn't carried a book home since 4th grade. But I had to learn my lesson fast. As soon as my mother saw that I had homework to do, she immediately demanded that I sit down at the table to do my homework. I couldn't go out to play until it was done.

So, after that first day of homework, I never brought another text book home again. Getting low grades or getting yelled at for not doing my homework didn't faze me. After being called a *scab* by a straight-A student, I felt compelled to look up the meaning in the dictionary when I got home. I was shocked to find that the meaning was "a worker who refuses to work."

Nothing could have been more wrong about me. I was always working, whether it was at chores around the house or out earning money delivering papers, mowing lawns, or shoveling snow. I was never a lazy worker. I just felt that the homework they gave us at school was a waste of my time.

I became very isolated in my own world that school year, even though Terry and Lori would often talk to me during recess. Mostly, I kept to myself. I really liked Terry and wanted to tell her so. But like with all the rest of the girls before, I was afraid.

And Lori was cute too. But she found out her mother was once my 2nd grade teacher, and now I was in serious trouble. The story had actually started when I was still in 3rd grade, when our class was learning to write formal letters. Most of the other students just wrote letters to each other and sent them through the mail. I thought that was a dumb idea since they were already there in the class room with each other.

Why would I want to write them a letter to send it through the mail? They were already there with me every day. If I had anything to say to them, I could just say it.

After having trouble trying to decide who I should write to, another student offered a suggestion. "Why don't you write a letter to your old teacher, Mrs. Searway?" That sounded like a great idea at the time, since she had gone to teach at another school and I thought I'd never see her again.

So, I wrote Mrs. Searway a short little letter, telling her what a great teacher she had been for me in the 2nd grade and how much I really missed having her as my teacher. I thought I'd get a passing grade for my letter and this assignment would be over. Mrs. Black even helped me locate the proper address and the letter was officially sent.

But now, three years later, that letter-writing was coming back to haunt me. Here's what happened. I met up with Mrs. Searway at a high school track meet and she told me she had saved the letter I'd written her. She still kept it as a cherished reminder of a great student. Lori and Terry, though, had learned about it too, and were now determined to tease me about that letter throughout the entire school year. My chagrin was unending—and the problem would continue in the years to come.

In the end, I made no real close friends with anyone during my 6th grade year. Since most of the other boys were stupidly excited about the new Star Wars movie, I saw no reason to take interest in anyone. Being away from Willard School, where I had felt confident and close to my friends, circumstances had now deteriorated my attitude to one of lower self-esteem.

Things would only become worse in the years to come.

In the spring of 1978, the Red Sox would have one of their best starts of any year in history. At one point, they were 18 games up on the Yankees. They would later disappoint us in the final game of the season, but the excitement of that 1978 season locked me into an isolated world of baseball and baseball cards.

I would care little about anything else for the next few years.

At the end of the school year, a notable thing occurred. Everyone got out of class a little earlier than normal at Brown School, and I remember running up the hill to meet up with Nathan, my brother Shawn, and all the other younger schoolmates for the final closing of Willard School. The Channel 13 News was already there waiting when we arrived.

The news cast was still setting up their cameras when we began jumping and screaming and trying to get on the news. The news cast asked us to go back *into* the building so that they could re-record them coming *out* of school. I decided to join in with the excitement and wait inside the hallways till they called us out. We had to keep doing retakes about 4 or 5 more times before the director called it a take.

In the end, Nathan was the only one of us who actually got a close-up on the Evening News. He'd walked casually, crossing the street in the marked-off cross-walk, while the rest of us were jumping and waving our arms and trying to be seen by the camera.

Before all of this, many of the residents had insisted that we save the old building and turn it into a museum—or remodel the inside to create condominiums, or at least divide it up into shopping venues. The City Council of South Portland, however, voted to take the old building down.

So, the construction workers had now begun their task with a heavy crane and dump trucks as dust filled the air. We all stood watching as the heavy crane gave many strikes before cracking the first layer of bricks of that well-constructed building. It was a sad sight to see that first hole in the side. But soon we all joined in throwing bricks and busting windows.

The beautiful bell tower, though, still hung way up high while the sides of the building began to crumble with each blow. Despite the fact that many wealthy people in the area were offering a large amount of money just to buy the bell tower, the crane swung with a mighty blow, sending the bell tower crashing down to the rubble below.

That was the saddest moment. We knew it would soon be gone forever, without a trace left behind.

The city could have saved the bell tower or auctioned it off to make a little money for the city. But no, they decided to smash it, wiping out all that remained, leaving just the sad memories.

Soon after the bell tower came crashing down, the ground began to shake with loud booms, like continuous bombs going off as the chimney came crashing down. This left the sky full of dust for many hours afterward. Only the old school's corner and the final wall remained, which the demolition crew spent over a week and a half to destroy. They were only knocking a few bricks off each day. They were obviously getting hourly pay by the tax payers' money and wanted to waste every dime of tax payers' time.

My father, like many other neighborhood families, backed his car up to the pile of bricks so we could fill the trunk with used bricks. We would later build a patio in our backyard with those bricks.

Mrs. Brailey called and asked if we could save her 10 corner bricks. We did, stacking them on our front steps where they stayed for a few months, all the while waiting for her to pick them up. But she must have forgotten about them. We never heard from her again.

I was hoping to retrieve the big bell that many of us thought might have come down from the bell tower. But no such bell survived the crash. So, I found the next best thing. Beside all that pile of rubble, the fire bell was still attached to a short piece of pipe from the sprinkler system. It was quite heavy, with a lot of pieces hanging out the side. But I managed to drag it across the street to set it up in my backyard. I figured out I could hook up a garden hose at full blast through the sprinkler pipe. It would ring that alarm bell so loud you could hear it all the way to Willard Square.

But I don't think my dad appreciated me filling the back yard with all that water. Still, I was sure proud to be the last person ever to ring the bell from the old Willard School.

After the demolition crew pulled all their equipment out, a still quietness about the big, ugly vacant lot left a haunting feel to us all. The most beautiful building in all of South Portland containing all our childhood memories had just been destroyed.

The city later turned the lot into a beautiful park. But that could never fill the hole in the hearts of all us who attended the old Willard School.

CHAPTER 4

JJ's Courage

I always looked up to JJ for his courage, his ability to talk his way out of any situation, and his never-say-*impossible* attitude toward any ideas that crossed our minds.

But most of all, I admired JJ for his musical ability. Whether it was an out of tune piano, a guitar with a few broken strings, or an old beat up set of drums, he could somehow make beautiful music out of it. Many Saturday mornings I'd be at the Ross's house while JJ was practicing his piano, playing songs like "Don't Let the Sun Go Down On Me," "Nadia's Theme," or "The Entertainer." He'd play while all our friends would gather around in amazement at how great he was at just thirteen years old. We all thought he'd grow up to be the next Elton John.

One morning, I ran up to JJ's house to find something to do for the day. JJ was practicing a new song the theme song to Laverne and Shirley, "Making Our Dreams Come True." He stopped for a moment and looked at me and said, "Hey, I was just thinking how much this song relates to us. *Never heard the word impossible…read a set of rules, we'll break it…we'll do it our way, yes, our way.* Every line of this song describes our friendship."

That's also exactly the way I felt about the way we did things every time I heard that song. Although it was mostly JJ's ideas and courage that carried the day, I was always there with him. JJ would always tell me, "*Never back out on a dare!*" And we dared each other to do some of the craziest stunts. Whether we were running through our paper route in under three minutes or climbing up the side of a building, we always met the challenge.

I once dared JJ on a freezing cold winter afternoon to climb up the side of Frank I. Brown School.

So, he climbed about thirty feet up the side of the building before his hands got so numb from the cold he could go no more. Nathan and I stood watching till we begged him to come back down. We could tell his hands were so cold he could barely hang on to the cold cement blocks. The school janitor, Mr. Stewart, just happened to be driving by and noticed the kid hanging on the side of the building. He quickly turned his car around and drove up onto the school playground with a mean look on his face—enough to scare JJ down a little faster. He quickly climbed down to about ten feet then jumped out into the snow below. He scrambled up and we all ran away, faster than Mr. Stewart could get out of his car.

The winter of 1977-78 was brutally cold, with so much snow that school even got dismissed during session. I remember being excited when the announcement came that we could all go home at noon. I walked nearly a mile up the hill in the blizzard, so happy to be out of that classroom. It was well worth the freezing cold wind in my face.

But when I got home, it was not yet time to get warm because we had to make sure the driveway was all shoveled out before dad got home.

The snow was so deep it took all three of us—my two brothers and myself—the rest of the afternoon to cut down the 7-foot snow bank at the end of the driveway. We shoveled enough for dad's car to fit in before he came home for dinner. We knew that after dinner, Dad would help us all clear out the rest, and make a nice wide walkway around both cars.

Mom would always have plenty of hot chocolate whenever we finally came inside to warm up, even if it took us late into the night before we had all the snow cleared out. I was always happy, too, because when a big storm like *that* came, school was called off for the rest of the week. The next day we could get up early, a group of us carrying shovels through the neighborhood door to door to make extra money shoveling driveways.

It was also JJ who taught us all how to endure the bitter temperatures of those freezing cold Maine winters. We'd all be at the bus stop bundled up with heavy coats and hats, shivering and keeping our arms and shoulders stiff, jumping up and down. Meanwhile, JJ would wear only a thin jacket and sometimes only a t-shirt, standing and looking so relaxed that the cold didn't bother him.

When I asked him how he could stand the cold with only a t-shirt, he said, "Just relax and let your shoulders loose and it will stop the shivering." So, I let my shoulders down and began to relax. He was right. I didn't feel nearly as cold then. And we all took our coats off and it didn't feel so cold.

We even decided to have a contest for who could stay out in the cold the longest. One evening at Nathan's house, Nathan himself took the challenge to stand outside barefoot in just his underwear on shear ice during a heavy sleet and rain storm. He placed himself under the gutter with water pouring on his head. He stood out there for almost 20 minutes, until he could no longer feel his legs. We had to carry him to the couch because he kept falling down.

We laid him on the coach while we dried him off with a towel, his whole body shaking. He kept saying, "I can't feel my legs!" JJ took a lighter and held it under his feet while Nathan laid there still shaking. "Can you feel this? Can you feel this?" JJ kept repeating as he moved the lighter around near the bottom of his feet. We were all scared for a while. We thought Nathan would never walk again. It took a few hours, but he eventually got his strength back, starting out a little wobbly-legged and finally walking again.

Between my brothers and me, we set some of our own challenges. For instance, one night when our parents were gone—and the temperatures reaching -3 degrees Fahrenheit—Rick and Shawn would see how far they could walk bare foot across the icy driveway. Then I'd show I could walk farther, remembering how JJ taught me to ignore the cold. Shawn and Rick once got a kick out of locking the door while I was standing out in the cold. I could see them laughing through the window while I was standing outside in my underwear. I decided I was going to set a new barefoot-on-ice record and started running down the street as fast as I could until my feet got so numb after about 100 yards that I turned around and ran back to the house and started pounding on the door till they let me in.

Fortunately, we always kept a fire blazing in the woodstove on cold nights. When I got inside I just laid on the floor raising my feet to the heat for relief. That woodstove kept us warm on most winter nights because Dad didn't like to run the furnace. It cost too much for heating oil. He would only buy fifteen gallons of diesel fuel every week to run the furnace for hot water only.

We were allowed to turn on the furnace about half hour before we planned to shower. This usually worked out well for all of us unless somebody forgot to shut off the switch. Then we had to take cold showers the rest of the week, which happened quite often. As for the rest of the house we relied on that woodstove.

It's a wonder we didn't burn the house down when our parents went out. We would load that stove up with tiny pieces of scrap wood, and we stuffed newspaper and cardboard into the roaring hot flames until the cast iron sides turned cherry red. Then we opened the door to stuff more paper in, causing a heat wave that sent flaming paper up to the ceiling then down on the curtains.

With Lisa screaming, Rick and I would quickly bat down the flames with a couple of pillows while Shawn ran to the kitchen for a pan of water, so that in the end, no harm was done. Still, the living room would be full of smoke and ashes which we had to clean up before mom and dad came home.

Between that wood stove and dad's cigarettes, then, the house always smelled like smoke. I don't think our parents ever suspected how close we often came to burning it down.

Standing outdoors in the cold Maine air was nothing compared to the cold water that JJ and I fell in one extremely cold winter day. After finishing up the paper route we both shared, we looked out over Willard Beach and saw huge chunks of ice floating. We were amazed at the size of those ice chunks, some of them ten, fifteen, even twenty feet wide, and all of them so close together we could step from one to another if we were careful not to rock them too much.

The bigger chunks were pretty sturdy. But as we worked our way out to the deeper waters, the chunks of ice got much smaller, more tippy, and spaced further apart, making it harder and more slippery when we jumped on to the next ice chunk.

Suddenly, that day, we found ourselves in a truly dangerous situation, with the tippy ice and water splashing over us with each step we took. The water made those small ice chunks so slippery we couldn't even stand up anymore. We tried to get up and leap back to the larger chunks, but the salty waters had splashed all over the ice, making it so slick I slipped and fell straight forward, face down to the ice.

Hanging on from my waste up—while from the waist down my legs were submerged in the freezing cold water—I used all my strength to pull myself up. It took everything I had, but at last I did it, then tried to run as fast as I could to jump on to the next chunk of ice, and then the next, tipping each one till I tipped one completely over.

Suddenly, I was completely submerged under water.

The water was so cold I thought there were lobster claws all over my body, biting my arms and legs as the cold water caused my muscles to cramp. Yet the fear of freezing in the ice-cold water kept me above the surface as I swam hard and climbed onto the next tippy ice, falling then swimming then climbing and jumping over, trying to run then slipping back through the icy cold water.

At last, somehow, I reached the shore.

But quickly I found it colder on my bones and skin as I stepped out into the frigid open air. Still, I had the presence of mind to turn around and look for JJ. I saw that he was still having the same trouble I'd had—repeatedly slipping into the freezing cold water as he tried running over the slippery ice.

But at last he made it to the shore too, and we both ran to a nearby apartment building we often used to sit in the hallway on cold days just to warm up. This time, though, we ran there with our pant legs and jackets frozen stiff until we got inside to thaw. It really was a matter of life and freezing to death.

Still shivering and dripping wet in the hallway, JJ stripped down to his underwear and tried to ring his clothes dry. I only took off my dripping coat. We had, it seemed, a chance to survive our ordeal. But suddenly a mean old woman came out of her apartment and threatened to call the police if we didn't leave. We quickly put our wet clothes back on and ran to Bathras Market about a half mile away. As we did, our clothes froze up again, but it was there that JJ was able to call his mother to come pick him up. I didn't dare call my mother. I just waited a few more minutes to warm up, then I ran the rest of the way home, my clothes frozen so stiff it made it hard to keep moving.

Somehow, I made it home alive.

Just a few months later, when it wasn't quite as cold, we were back in that water again. An early March snow storm had taken out a few fishing houses that had stood atop the ledge over Willard Beach. JJ, Nathan, and I were checking out all the debris washed up on the beach—an entire wall from the fishing house, plus a couple of large pieces of Styrofoam. We suddenly came up with an idea.

We took the two large pieces of Styrofoam and laid the wall over it. "You think it will hold us, JJ?" I asked. I could see JJ smiling, like he was thinking the very same thing.

Looking around for a few boards to use as a paddle, JJ found a couple flat boards about ten feet long. "Perfect!" he said.

We both stepped on. I don't know why Nathan just stood there and watched as we pushed our newly constructed raft into deeper water, using our long boards to push into the soft sand. Maybe he thought there wasn't enough space for him on our little raft. Or maybe he thought we had gone far too crazy with another one of our ideas. Whatever the reason, he only stood there on the shore.

I watched him get smaller and smaller as JJ and I pushed away with our long boards. We were both lying down, thrusting our long boards underwater, trying to feel for the bottom. "I can't reach the bottom anymore!!!"

I'd begun to panic. I saw Nathan still standing on the shore, getting smaller and smaller as we drifted out to deeper water. "JJ, we're drifting out too far!"

And I began shouting at JJ to do something about it. I stood up and JJ started shouting, "Don't tip us off balance! If one of these Styrofoam pieces comes loose, we'll both sink!"

Suddenly, I stood up and dove in the water, boots and all, leaving JJ alone and setting the raft off balance, the Styrofoam shooting out from under him. I swam hard and fast till I reached the shore, JJ right behind after sinking off his side of the raft.

"Why did you jump off!!" JJ screamed at me. "You set me off balance! And that Styrofoam shot about ten feet in the air!"

Then he told me how he'd almost had the whole thing under control until I dove in. He also said he saw me swimming so fast I looked like an Olympic swimmer going for a gold medal.

We were both shivering from the cold. Lucky for JJ he had on a wool sweater, which dried up almost instantly when he got out of the water, But I was wearing my soaking wet coat. I looked at Nathan in his dry clothes. "Give me your coat," I demanded as I grabbed it off his back. "You carry this." I handed him my dripping wet coat.

We three ran to our usual apartment building hallway to get warm. This time, no one threatened us. Then we made a run to Bathras Market for another warm-up before we ran the rest of the way to our homes.

When I got to mine, I entered through the garage and on in through the side door leading straight to the basement. Stripping off my soaking wet clothes and putting on some dry clothes, I threw my wet stuff in the dryer, water still dripping out of my coat. I let the dryer run an entire cycle. But when I pulled my clothes out, they were all still dripping. I reset the cycle several times during the night, hoping those clothes would dry before my mom found out what had happened. But when mom came downstairs to start the other laundry, my clothes were still soaking wet.

She saw them and started hollering at me. "How did you get your clothes so wet?"

"I got in a snowball fight, Mom." That was the only excuse I could come up with.

"It smells like salt water!" she screamed back at me. "You got that wet from a snowball fight?"

"Well, we were near the beach and somebody threw my coat in the water."

I had always been quick with a necessary excuse, and I never let my parents know the real danger I'd survived the day before. I don't know if Mom ever truly believed the excuse I made this time, but at least she never heard what really happened.

The winter of 78 finally ended. With warmer weather approaching, JJ and I were climbing rocks along the shore between South Portland and Cape Elizabeth. Suddenly, we looked up and saw a beautiful house with a well-kept lawn overlooking the ocean. An old row boat was resting in the garden. Perhaps, we thought, it was left there to rot into the landscape and become useful for a flower bed. But JJ and I wondered if we might fix the boat up.

When JJ knocked on the door to learn whether the owner was interested in selling the old boat, he did all the talking, as usual. I was too shy, so I only followed along with him. Anyway, we met Mrs. Eastman, an elderly woman who was very nice to us. She happily came outside and told us all about the boat her son had not used in many years. She said the wood was so badly cracked and rotted, the boat was beyond repairable condition. She would in no way feel right about selling it to us.

But JJ was so certain we could repair that old vessel he convinced her to give it to us, just to get it off her hands.

So, there we had our first real boat, an eight-foot wooden dinghy, though it was in bad condition. We had been wishing a long time for any kind of boat, especially all those times we'd climbed along the rocky shore, looking out over the ocean and talking about all the places we wanted to explore—all the nearby islands and lighthouses we had never been to. Most of all, I wanted to see Fort Scammel up close and walk through its dark caves.

We were excited and believed that for sure we could make our boat float. Together we carried that heavy old rotten thing over a mile to JJ's house, only to hear JJ's stepfather tell us we would be wasting our time and money if we really thought we could salvage it.

But he did give us a bit of advice—that we go to Tommy's Hardware on Congress Street in downtown Portland for all the boating repair supplies we would need.

We wasted no time. The very next day, using all our paper route money, we took the bus downtown to find this place called Tommy's Hardware. It was supposed to be a little past the downtown district across from Levinsky's clothing store. Sure enough, there it was. Tommy's Hardware was a place we'd walked past many times before and never noticed.

When we walked inside, we saw everything we would need. The salesman was very knowledgeable and showed us the right kind of sealer, calking, boat paint, oars and oarlocks. Everything was quite expensive. So, we started out with a good boat primer and some caulking. We worked on that little boat every day after school, and on every weekend after church, we were spreading another coat. We chose a beautiful dark blue color with white striping around the trim. We used many layers of sealer and paint to make sure all the rotting wood was covered. I must admit, our work made it look beautiful as it sat upon a couple of sawhorses in front of The Ross's garage. We had no doubt, it was ready to take out in the ocean.

After returning back to Tommy's for oars and oarlocks, we had almost everything we needed to set that boat in the water. Almost everything that was needed—except lifejackets. But that was ok with us. We were good swimmers, and we already had a half lifejacket that we'd found washed up on the beach a few weeks before. We decided to keep that in the boat, just in case.

It was just the second week of May. The weather was a bit cool and foggy, not the best weather to be out in a boat. After investing so much time and money in this boat, we couldn't wait any longer to see if it would really float. As soon as we got home from school, we were ready, with my brother Rick to help us. We three carried our newly painted boat all the way to Willard Beach. JJ toted the oars, wearing just his shorts and sneakers as he led the way, while Rick and I carried the boat along with the half lifejacket and two small pales for bailing water, just in case there was a little leaking.

Rick and I were dressed in long pants and a jacket, not expecting to do any swimming—or get wet at all—since the water was still quite cold that time of year. Meanwhile, JJ seemed as always ready to jump in the water whether it was warm or cold.

Rick and I set the boat down on the shore as the rough water began to rush around our tiny boat. We quickly jumped in and smiled with excitement. "It floats!" we cried, as the next wave very quickly lifted us up from the shallow waters and swept us toward the deep.

JJ hurried to lock the oars in place, and the next wave pulled us further into deeper water. The current was so strong that we instantly found ourselves being pulled deeper—now into rough waters.

JJ rowed hard. Rick and I bailed water as fast as we could. "JJ turn it around!" I shouted, beginning to panic.

But JJ was one who never showed fear, no matter how much danger we were in. "Just shut up and keep bailing!" JJ yelled back.

Rick and I bailed faster and faster. But the water was coming over the sides faster than we could bail. "JJ, turn it around!!" I screamed, dumping a pail of cold water over his head.

"Dammit !!!" JJ screamed back at me, "YOU DO THAT AGAIN AND I'LL JUMP OUT AND SWIM BACK, AND YOU TWO CAN ROW THIS THING YOURSELVES!"

As we argued, the strong current was pushing us far off course. We began heading toward the rock jetty that lead to The Spring Point Ledge Lighthouse. Soon, we were trapped in a little cove. There was no way out, other than to crash into the rocks.

JJ kept paddling hard. Rick and I kept bailing water as fast as we could.

Then, through the light fog, we suddenly heard the sound of a Coast Guard Helicopter. "JJ, we're in trouble now!"

I thought they would have us arrested for not having enough lifejackets in the boat. But now I was panicked for another reason. JJ had started paddling in a new direction, hoping he could bring us back over to the beach.

But the water was too rough. The waves slammed our boat along the walls of Fort Preble and into the corner of the rock jetty. Finding ourselves in a shallow corner, we all jumped out in knee deep water. I began to climb up the wall. JJ and Rick attempted to tip the boat on its side to let all the water out. I guess JJ was thinking if he could dump all that extra water out, he could row back over to set the boat back on the beach.

But no such luck. As he was attempting to dump all the water out, more waves crashed in, knocking them both down and filling the boat with even more water. Meanwhile, I had climbed to safety and was shivering from the cold when a man from the coast guard approached me, asking how many lifejackets we had.

I told him the other two lifejackets fell out of the boat in the high waves.

He yelled out for Rick and JJ to climb up. He wanted to have a talk with us.

We all got a good lecture as he took us for a ride in his truck. When he asked us to give him our name, we all made up a phony name.

He dropped us off up at Willard Square and told us the coast guard would tow the boat. We'd have to pay a small fee to get it back. But when we walked down to The Coast Guard base the following day to ask about our boat, they said the boat broke to pieces when they tried to tow it.

After investing so much hard-earned money, time, and confidence in our project, it was all washed out to sea.

Summer finally arrived—with scorching hot weather. Even though we didn't have a boat, after all, we enjoyed a lot of hot days jumping into cool waters of the rocky shores at Fort Williams, exploring the deep dark tunnels of the abandoned forts. If we weren't near the water, we certainly found other dangerous games to play in our own back yard.

We played with a fire we built, for instance. Rick and JJ tossed an almost empty can of deodorant into it, causing an explosion so loud that we all fell to the ground in shock.

We also made bows and arrows out of sturdy branches we found in the woods, using some strong string tied tightly. After whittling a couple of sticks for arrows, I suggested we pull the tips off JJ's dart set, attaching them to our little sticks then attaching the little plastic fins. We had ourselves some dangerous weapons as we set out for some target practice.

We started out targeting trees and random garages in the neighborhood, not caring whose property we might damage. But suddenly JJ shouted, "Lookout!!!" and launched an arrow that flew fairly close to my head, laughing as he did so.

And he talked us into playing a new game—one where we would see just how close he *could* come with his arrows, without actually hitting me.

"Lookout!!!!" Another arrow flew by, and I felt the slight breeze.

"Cut it out, JJ!!" I screamed back at him, even as I heard the thump of another arrow strike deep into the wood siding of the garage behind me.

I guess that one was too close, even for JJ. He turned to a better idea, launching the next shot for distance and hitting the roof of an apartment building. We'd lost one of our life-threatening arrows.

JJ launched the other arrow straight up. It disappeared into the sky.

Later that afternoon, my mom sent me to the store for a loaf of bread and a gallon of milk. While I was waiting at the crosswalk, I noticed a dart head stuck into the pavement. I smiled and thought how lucky nobody was crossing the street when that arrow landed.

CHAPTER 5

Rotten Tomatoes

It was just another ordinary afternoon for us. We had a good game of baseball going in the back yard…

… until JJ threw a pitch and I swung hard at what looked like a rubber ball.

"Splat!!!" The rotten tomato splattered everywhere. We all broke out laughing and soon tomatoes were flying everywhere in a big neighborhood rotten tomato fight. Quickly, we all started running through the neighborhood with rotten tomatoes dripping from our clothes and hair. We targeted anything and anybody, and people passing by knew to stay out of our way.

Even passing cars made a challenging target for us. So, when the Metro Bus made its routine stop and the door flew open to pick up waiting passengers at the corner of Chase and Pillsbury Street, Rick strategically launched a big old rotten tomato in that direction. It hit the bus driver with a solid splat on the side of his face. At this, he slammed the bus into park, leaving it right in the middle of the road and began to sprint after Rick all the way down Chase Street, leaving that bus full of passengers stranded.

Twenty minutes later, the driver returned, frazzled and exhausted and unsuccessful in his angry hunt. But who knows what he would have done to Rick if he had gotten his hands on him?

Clearly, we Smiths were the loudest and wildest kids in the neighborhood. Even though JJ was usually the instigator of all our pranks and misbehavior, it was always us Smith boys who gained all the attention. It was almost embarrassing, considering that our mother was a Sunday School teacher and Dad drove the church bus.

Every Sunday afternoon, that church bus was parked right in front of our house. Its big letters read, *South Portland Church of the Nazarene.* Everyone knew, then, what church we went to, and we were expected to behave like Christians. Yet Nathan and Annie—who came from atheist parents—behaved far more respectfully with their parents than we ever did.

At least, that was before they moved into our neighborhood. Before that, Nathan had never even sworn before. Nor had he ever stolen anything.

Nathan and Annie had always enjoyed a good relationship with their mother. Mrs. Levine one time had me over for dinner, and we all sat around the living room floor, enjoying good conversation in a very relaxed atmosphere—something we Smiths had never known in our own house. All of us had to sit at the dinner table and each of us say a prayer of thanks for our food before we could eat. Then, on top of that, if any conversation started at all, it would end up with a big argument. Even after church during our Sunday pot roast dinner, we would end up in some big verbal brawls.

Where was all the happiness people were supposed to find in accepting Jesus Christ as their personal Savior? Where was the love and peace I'd heard so many people talk about when they stood up and gave their testimony during church service? For years, our parents had been forcing us to go to church and say our prayers and be thankful we knew Jesus. Why, then, were we all so miserable in our own home?

Nathan and Annie had absolutely no church upbringing, no concern whatsoever whether God even existed. Yet, they had more happiness in their house than we ever knew in ours. I was always so jealous of Nathan and Annie for the freedom they had in their home. It was like they had no rules at all. They could swear, sit on the floor during dinner, listen to rock 'n roll on the radio during dinner, stay up as late as they wanted, even run through the house naked— which was something Nathan did quite often.

Unfortunately for me, though, Annie never did that sort of thing. Annie was always quiet, did her homework, and got good grades at school. And nobody ever forced her to do anything. Meanwhile, there were so many rules in our house. It was impossible not to break at least a few of them.

Nathan actually learned a lot of his bad habits from me, like stealing and vandalizing property or playing with fire—the type of thing his mother never found out about. I carried a lot of guilt inside, knowing God was watching over us, knowing everything we did was sin. If we were to die unrepentant, we'd be going to hell, for sure. At least, that was the way they used to make us feel during those long altar calls at church, calling us all for repentance as we cried at the altar while people laid their hands on us and prayed.

It grew so monotonous, it became just a game of getting attention.

I stopped playing that game at age of 12 and became very quiet at church. I'd realized just how ridiculous we all looked, week after week repenting of the same sins again and again. Still, we never made any changes in our home life. And Nathan never understood the rules we had to follow, like being home at a certain time every night so we could listen to Mom read us a Bible story and say our prayers together. And worst of all, I wondered, why did I always have to miss out on listening to Casey Kasem's American Top 40 Countdown Show that aired every Sunday while we were in church?

I felt like I missed out on so much of life because of my parents being so strict. I would often go to Nathan's house just to escape the tension I felt at home. I just liked being there because we could play the music loud and jump on the furniture and simply enjoy having fun—all the things I always had to wait to do at home till my parents went out of the house.

But I always felt a bit of guilt, and responsible for some of the other things we used to do. That is, until the day Nathan was singing a song by Andy Kim. *Rock me gently, rock me slowly, take it easy, don't you know, I have never been loved like this before.* He sang as loud as he could while we were walking up to "Jones's Drug Store" just a short way up Cottage road. But then Nathan began to sing a little louder, adding the F-word in place of "Rock," not caring who was listening while we were on our way to Jones's Drug Store to do some shoplifting.

Suddenly, though, I decided we shouldn't go there to steal anymore.

Nathan said, "But, why? They don't care. They don't do anything if they see us steal something. They just look the other way."

We'd been there many times before and stolen from them several times while employees were watching. They'd just looked the other way.

But I knew God was watching us. He saw everything we did.

I asked Nathan why he didn't believe in God.

He replied, "Oh, I believe in God. It's Annie who doesn't believe in God. I have always believed in God, and I always say my prayers after I eat."

"Why *after* you eat?" I asked. "My mom makes us all pray before we're allowed to eat, so God will bless the food we eat."

"But what if somebody comes and takes it away before I eat it. That's why I wait until after I've already eaten before I say a thank you prayer. I get down and pretend like I'm tying my shoes, so nobody notices I'm bowing my head to pray."

"So, why do you think it's okay to steal, if you believe in God?'"

"Why doesn't God just stop us?" Nathan laughed. "It's so easy and nobody in the store cares, so why not?"

"But God is keeping record of all our sins. We need to repent or we're going to hell when we die," I challenged him.

"Oh, I have repented of my sins," Nathan admitted. "I got down on my knees and ask God to forgive me."

Just as we approached the store front, Nathan looked at me and said, "You're right, we shouldn't steal things."

We turned around to start heading back home, and Nathan continued singing his song. He was always so cheerful and always had a song to sing.

Nathan even came to church with me once during Vacation Bible School. He said that it was his first time ever going to church. We were always encouraged to invite our friends to church, and a few of them did come once in a while.

But we never had to invite JJ. He would invite himself and joined in with every activity, whether it was the Youth choir, Bible study, or camping trips, JJ always took great interest in every gathering.

Nathan and Annie moved up to Skowhegan before the end of 1978. We only saw each other a few more times before they left, then I never heard from them again.

JJ was now attending South Portland High School, and I started attending Mahoney Jr. High. Everything changed quickly for me, and I had to make new friends. Most of my classmates never learned that I had a first name, because even the teachers had started calling me "Smitty." From the beginning of Jr. High,

"Smitty" became the only name I was known by.

Terry came and sat with me before class every morning as I hung out in my Home Room. Terry would slide her finger up and down my arm and ask me if I was going to the school dance. I would blush and use that slogan "Disco Sucks" for some lame excuse "… and they're probably going to play a lot of disco there." I actually loved Disco and danced at home in front of the mirror quite often. The truth was, I really wanted to go to the school dance. I was in Love with Terry. But I was still too shy to tell her so. I guess I was waiting for someone to come along and force me to go.

But even then, I would have probably turned around and run.

Before the end of my 7th grade year, Terry told me some news. She was moving to Scarborough. Expecting me to show some sadness, she seemed disappointed when I hid my feelings. But deep down inside, I was very sad. I'd held it hidden in my heart that one day I was really going to have the courage to tell Terry how much I loved her, how much I cherished the times she spent talking to me.

But I never got the courage to tell her how I truly felt—until it was too late.

If there was one teacher I had any respect for that first year at Mahoney Jr. High, it was Mr. Towle, even though most other students referred to him as Mr. Troll. I liked him, not so much for being a Social Studies Teacher and a great track coach, but for his teachings on positive attitude. He would lecture us on how important it was to be on time, to have good attendance and reliability, to be neat in appearance and be organized, and to always be prepared the day before and give 100% effort, whether we were running on the track team, doing school work, or working out in the world.

This was advice I could actually use. Many years later now, it still comes in handy. Mr. Towle also gave us great health advice, like how disgusting smoking is. This helped me make my decision not to take up smoking, which many of my classmates soon began doing anyway.

But the most important lesson I learned from Mr. Towle was to drink lots of water to clean my kidneys out. I remembered all the pain I'd suffered through elementary school with my kidney infection, all the unnecessary doctor visits and hospital stays, with all those painful needles and worthless pills that did nothing but give my parents high medical bills. All anyone had ever needed to do was say, *Drink more water!* and all the pain would have gone away.

Thank you, Mr. Towle, for your simple advice that may have saved my life.

From that day on I drank three or four tall glasses of water each day and never had any more pain in my kidneys again.

But in the early spring of 1979, just when I was starting to take on a new attitude of thinking positive and trying to get better grades at school, unexpected bad news came. My Father came home from work and said he had something to tell us. After dinner, we all gathered into the living room.

"I've been fired from my job," he explained.

We sat quietly, listening in shock because this message came so unexpectedly. Dad had always been a good worker. People would even come by our house and tell us so. How could this happen to someone like my Dad, who every week had his name in the newspaper? I'd seen his name there so many times. I actually ran out of space on the refrigerator, covering it with magnets and newspaper clippings.

Service Manager of the Year, Dick Smith! We were all so proud of my dad, who always had been well known in the Portland area for the great work he did.

"They loved you at the Ford dealership! Why would they fire you?" we asked him. We couldn't understand.

He went on to tell us how the dealership had been sold so his old boss could retire. And a new younger owner had taken over. As soon as he'd introduced himself, he'd gone over new plans to double the labor cost. My dad had agreed to the new cost plan, but when he'd proceeded to change the advertised price of $25 per hour labor, the new owner said, "No, I want you to leave the sign as it is. I just want you to double up all the labor cost." His demand had been firm.

"No, I will not," my dad had answered him back with a stern voice.

"You will do as I say, or you can hit the road!" The new owner was actually telling my dad to cheat his costumers—or he would be fired.

37

Their bitter argument continued, and then the new boss fired Dad.

It must have been hard for him to break the news to us.

As he left the house to do his weekly grocery shopping, mom had sadness in her eyes. I began to worry how long the food was going to last in our house, and how we would eat after the food was gone. How were we going to make the house payment? How many weeks would we survive after Dad's last paycheck ran out?

The following Monday, Dad went downtown to sign up for unemployment benefits, food stamps, and every other benefit the welfare system had to offer. But worst of all was the school lunch program. This meant that every day before school, my brother Rick and I had to stop at the office to sign our names to receive a free lunch ticket.

They had a special name for the free school lunches at Mahoney Jr. High. They were called "scum lunches," and anybody who ate these lunches had a special table in the cafeteria called the "scum side." This is where the kids who got bullied sat. This is where the kids whose parents were on welfare sat. This is the table I had once pointed to during lunch and said, "That's the scum side over there!" I'd even laughed at some of the kids who had to sit there and eat those "scum lunches."

And now it was my turn to sit at that same table. I was already skinny enough. Now I had to pick through the lunches that the school provided, paid for by the state. I usually ate only a banana or whatever fruit might be in the bag then drank the milk and orange juice that came in a carton. I didn't eat the sandwich or anything else that might have been made in the school kitchen. I threw the rest away. It disgusted me even to look at some of the stuff in those bags.

And worse than that, I was no longer welcome at the table with the popular group.

Suddenly, all my plans to start coming to school with a positive attitude had all been shot down—lower than I ever thought I could bear.

CHAPTER 6

Looking for a Job

One hot summer day in the summer of 1981, I was with my two good buddies, Wayne and Packy. I'd known Wayne since Willard School. Packy and I had become friends when he moved to our neighborhood around the same time we started attending Jr. High. Although we all used to argue and fight whenever the three of us got together, we still remained friends.

Packy and I ran on the track team together, while Wayne and I were taking Drivers Ed. together. We all worked part time at Sam's Italian Sandwich and Pizza store for a little cash under the table. But on this day, the three of us walked down to Mill Creek Shopping Center and collected as many job applications as we could, as if we were on a desperate hunt for a new job.

We collected applications from Shaw's Super Market, from Shop 'n Save Super Market, from the local McDonald's restaurant, from Welby's Drug Store, from Deering Ice Cream, and from many different gas stations and small businesses in the area. Then we went back to Wayne's house and spent the rest of the day filling them all out. We each must have filled out about twenty different jobseeker forms.

The next day, we all walked back through every store to return our completed applications. We were excited and willing to take any work that we could get. A few days later, I was more excited. I'd received a phone call from Shop 'N Save. They wanted to set up a time for my first job interview. After learning Wayne and Packy would be interviewed as well, along with a few others, we realized we were all competing for the same job in the cans and bottle redemption department. It was a dirty job but something we each had experience in from working for Sam's.

As things turned out, Wayne was the one they hired for the job. I felt a little disappointment for myself, but I was happy for Wayne and very grateful for the experience of my first interview. My second interview went much better, at McDonald's, since they had many positions available. They had a group of us potential employees sit in a waiting room. Then they called us in for our interview, one at a time. Billy Dolye was in the waiting room that day as well, and when I saw him in church the following Sunday, he told me they had called him the next day to tell him to start work next week.

But they never called me.

I couldn't understand. I thought my interview had gone so well. But, there was still no job for me, even at McDonald's.

Third to call me for an interview was Shaw's Super Market. I went there with certainty and positivity that this was going to be the job for me. Again, I felt the interview went well and went home feeling good about myself.

The following Sunday, though, I was coming out of Sunday school class and I heard a girl's voice. "Oh, Smitty, I saw you yesterday."

As I turned around, the girl said, "I wanted to tell you, that's a bad place to apply for a job."

I wanted to tell her that no matter what, I would be grateful if I got the job. But I just looked at her and said "Oh."

Again, I felt very disappointed that I didn't get the job.

But fortunately, Dad was doing well, making a little more money than before, working now as the Service Manager for a Buick deaership. But our family was still trying to recover from the shock and stress of the nine months of financial hardship we had endured during the time Dad was out of work. And I was determined never to have to face that financial hardship again.

My brother Rick was working at a Sunoco Station, pumping gas. He already had his first car, a 1974 AMC Hornet—a real piece of junk. Every time he gave us a ride anywhere he drove it so erratically, Wayne and Packy would get out of the car laughing at how crazy my brother drove. And I kept saying, "I'm never gonna drive like he does! No way! Never gonna drive like he does."

My search for a job ended when a call came from a member of the church. Ernie LaBelle was looking for someone to help with some yard work at his house. I was excited that I'd gotten work for the day. Soon after the call, around noontime, Ernie drove by to pick me up to take me up to his house in Falmouth. That's where he had a pile of firewood for me to stack.

After working hard to do that task, I also dug up a large area in his back yard to make level ground for his new above ground swimming pool. I worked all day in the muggy heat and didn't even take a break during the rain shower that came. My feet and legs were covered in mud, my shirt and hair soaking wet, when dinnertime arrived.

Ernie's wife had been preparing the evening meal and he invited me inside. While I was taking my shoes off by the door, he gave me a towel to sit on at the dinner table with his wife and kids. I stayed pretty quiet during dinner, and afterwards I worked a few more hours. Ernie was so impressed with my commitment to complete the job, he asked if I was interested in taking a dishwashing job at his restaurant.

"Yes!" I answered with excitement as he handed me a twenty-dollar bill for the six hours I'd worked that day.

Ernie smiled and said, "Great! You can start tomorrow."

By this time, I already had my driver's permit, so it worked out great that mom would let me drive every day after school up to The Spurwink Country Kitchen. It gave me a chance to practice my driving. Plus, Mom was always wanting a little more money to contribute to the house budget, so she made me give her $10.00 a week out of the money I earned. Now that I was working, she told me, I should start paying rent.

My new job had me working full time 11:00 am - 8:30 p.m. weekdays and weekends until school started. After school started, my part-time hours were 4:00 - 8:30 every night after school. Making $3.35 an hour, I was still earning about $75.00 a week even after school started.

This meant that I could start saving for my own car. Unfortunately, though, it also meant I had to quit the track team.

Packy and I had trained hard all summer to be in top shape for the start of the cross country season. Packy had always been a good runner and had placed first in many long distant races. Sometimes I had kept up with him in training, but never during an actual track meet. One time, though, I'd had a chance to win a race back in Jr. High during an indoor track meet. I actually held the lead in the 1000-yard run for the first five laps. With just two laps to go I had plenty of strength to hold that lead to the finish.

But with all the attention on me, I lost my lead to the second-place runner.

Then...Packy blew by both of us and took the win.

Thinking back, I know it was a race I could have won. But the stark reality of actually winning I couldn't accept. I told myself it felt good just coming in third place. It was certainly better than the embarrassment of coming in last place, which is something that has to happen to somebody in every race. It had happened to me only once, and I would never let it happen to me again.

After the race where I lost the lead and finished third, I was going to try to just finish somewhere in the middle.

But now I didn't have to worry what place I would finish anymore. I was done with track because washing dishes could put money in my pocket. Running track had become just a waste of my time. Making money and saving for a car was my only concern from that point on.

I worked as many hours as I could through the last two weeks before school started. Packy was mad at me for quitting the track team, but that didn't bother me because I was making money. I worked every day after school, and I saved every dollar I could.

It turned out, though, that I was only able to save $400.00 by the 1st of November, and unfortunately The Spurwink was a seasonal restaurant like a lot of small-town restaurants in Maine. They closed during the winter months. This left me on another job search.

But not for long. Within just a few days, I was washing dishes at The Seaway Restaurant in South Portland. It was just a short walk down the hill, just before the bridge, less than a mile from my house. At first, I thought this job was going to work out great since they were open till 10:00 pm weekdays and 11:00 pm weekends. I was hoping to work more hours and save more money.

I started the first day with a positive attitude and showed up early. But to my surprise, the kitchen was filthy. Still, I kept my positive attitude, knowing I was there now, and I was the one who was going to clean things up.

As soon as I started to work on some of the filthy areas, the head cook acted annoyed that I was in his way, making me feel he didn't even want me there. The atmosphere was so dull and cold, nobody ever smiled or even spoke to each other. It was a far cry from The Spurwink Country Kitchen where everyone was friendly, where we'd always had the radio on and sometimes we'd all been singing along to a good song. And every Saturday Night we'd have the radio set for Bill O'Neil's Oldies party. And sometimes one of the waitresses would call the station to request a song. It was truly a fun place to work even when it was busy.

Now, though, I was stuck in a dump of a restaurant where nobody appreciated me. From the moment I stepped in the door, I was just in the middle of things and unappreciated. Removing my Walkman headphones, I heard the owner order me not to wear them while I'm working.

"Yes, sir. I wasn't planning on wearing them while I'm working," I replied, thinking I could put up with such negativity for a few hours each night till I'd saved enough money to make me happy. And I started cleaning those pots and pans in a tiny sink, feeling cramped near the back door where deliveries were coming in. At the same time, the head chef was standing there signing papers and smoking cigarettes. He and the delivery guy extinguished their cigarettes in the sink full of soapy water I was using for cleaning those pots and pans.

I was disgusted with what I saw but didn't say a word. I just drained out all the water and started over again. This happened several times every night in the short time I worked there. Although I tried to keep a positive attitude it got harder each day. When I noticed the dishwasher wasn't working and nobody seemed to care, I washed all the dishes by hand. And the guys continued to extinguish cigarettes in the sink. I felt more disgusted each day.

Smoking was never allowed in the kitchen area at the Spurwink. They had a smoking room away from the kitchen or workers went outside to smoke. Everything was kept clean and I felt appreciated there. But now I was feeling completely disgusted, watching one of the chefs lift a big pot roast with two long forks and a cigarette hanging from his lips, ashes curled down to inches from the roast as he transferred it to the food warmer.

I tried to ignore what I'd seen. I kept myself looking busy cleaning dishes. Yet nobody seemed to care if anything in this kitchen gets clean at all. After walking home late one evening, I was feeling sick and tired and not wanting to go to school the next day.

I went to bed and laid there thinking about calling in sick the next day. But then I came up with a better idea. Instantly, I felt better, deciding I would call the Seaway Restaurant up and tell them, "I quit!" And I was going to do it just as soon as I got home from school.

I felt great waking up the next morning, knowing I wasn't going back to that dreadful place anymore. I headed off to school feeling great relief from the heavy burden I'd been carrying. It was finally going to be over.

As soon as I got home, I did call The Seaway and I did call them to tell them, "I quit!"

I don't think they were surprised or disappointed at the short notice. They seemed even more grateful for me to be gone than I was. After just three days at the worst place I'd ever worked, I was unemployed again. But I was so grateful not to have that dreadful job anymore.

Being without work gave my free time back to me again. I decided to join the indoor track team to pass the time after school during those winter months. Although I never put much effort into it, I finished each race somewhere in the middle.

All the while, I looked forward to going back to work at The Spurwink Country Kitchen in the spring.

CHAPTER 7

First Car and New Friends

In the spring of 1982, after being out of work for the entire winter, I was flat broke again. As you can imagine, I was glad to start back to work at The Spurwink Country Kitchen.

Having gotten a taste of what it was like to work in another restaurant, I felt even more appreciation now for my job at The Spurwink and for the fun people I got to work with. Plus, I'd just turned 17 years old and desperately wanted my own car.

JJ had joined the Army, and Rick was in his senior year planning to join the Army as soon as he graduated. Rick had already taken his beaten-up AMC Hornet to the junk yard, and he was now driving a pretty blue colored 6-cylinder Plymouth Duster. He said to me, "Hey, Steve I was thinking about giving you this car when I go away to boot camp this summer."

"Oh, really?" I said, surprised. "But, why?" I was wondering why he would ever give me anything. All he'd ever done was take things from me and break them. I never thought he would care enough about me to give me his car.

"Well, I won't need it anymore," he explained, saying how he'd need to get rid of it before he was gone.

"Yeah, that would be great!" I replied.

So, I was thinking to myself that the coming summer Rick would really give me his car. That would give a little relief for my desperately tight budget that made me pinch every penny. Trying to save for a car had left me with no money to spend on anything else.

Confident of the free Plymouth Duster that was coming, I began to spend a little more loosely, buying myself a new Toshiba Boom Box and loading up on a variety of blank cassette tapes for recording a lot of Rick's vinyl records. To make those recordings—of The Rolling Stones, The Beatles, The Who, Jimi Hendrix and Deep Purple—I'd simply crank up the speakers and place them in front of the boom box covered with a blanket. The result sounded just as good as store-bought tapes.

The new Police album "Ghost in The Machine" was the first cassette I actually bought at a store. Over-playing it, I soon decided I didn't like the Police anymore. I went on to stock up a collection with everything from The Beach Boys to Cat Stevens to Journey and Neil Young. I was into just about every kind of rock 'n roll. Except punk rock. I thought punk rock was meaningless and downright disgusting.

Music was the only real freedom I had in my life. If I wasn't working. I was in my room listening to music and day dreaming about owning my own car and better days ahead.

Well, all my hopes of inheriting Rick's car came to an end just a few months before he left for the Army. The Duster's old rusty frame broke in half underneath from corners turned too sharp and never slowing down. The front end leaned on the driver's side to just inches from the road.

Rick had no choice but to junk the car for scrap metal.

The one good thing that happened to me in my Sophomore year was, I failed most of my classes so badly that they gave me an entirely different schedule of new classes for the second half of the school year. The really good thing was, they never put my name on the attendance sheet in any of those new classes. This meant I could cut classes any time I wanted.

Usually, then , I took every Friday off to go to the bank and cash my check then eat a burger at McDonald's and walk around Mill Creek Shopping Center. But there was one thing I hadn't done yet that I'd been wanting to do for a long time. As much as I loved rock 'n roll music, I'd never been to a rock concert. Neither had my two brothers.

One day, I was enjoying my afternoon off just when Eric Clapton tickets went on sale. It was a good opportunity to walk all the way to the Civic Center to buy three tickets for the show. When I told Rick and Shawn I had tickets for Eric Clapton, they were pretty excited.

But this happened just before Rick's car was junked. So now we had to find a ride to the Civic Center the night of the show. We knew our parents wouldn't approve of our going to a rock concert, so one of my brothers let it slip that Eric

Clapton was a Christian singer. So, Dad gladly agreed to give us a ride to the show and pick us up after it was over.

(Wouldn't you know it? Mom found out later that Clapton was not a Christian singer and she was pissed.)

We had great seats for the show, sitting in the 18th row and close to the front of the stage—but still far back enough for us to see the whole wide spread of the entire stage. Packy and a lot of our friends from South Portland High School were there as well.

The Fabulous T-Birds opened the show. After their set, it was quiet for a bit as more people crowded into the Civic Center. Packy and all our friends moved closer to our seats, actually standing on the steps of the open aisle near us.

The lights went out for a few minutes. Then they came back on. To the roar of the crowd, Eric Clapton and his band started off the set with his new single "I've Got A Rock 'n Roll Heart." Everybody jumped to their feet—except me. Spellbound, I just sat in my seat and observed in utter amazement how a man with a guitar and a band could set off a crowd of people, stirring them up until they were almost out of control.

I truly wanted to get up and dance on my seat. But I was too shy to move.

Packy kept turning around and pointing at me, saying, "Hey, look at Smitty! He's just sitting there!"

I was afraid to let my excitement show, so I remained quiet through the whole show and took it all in as the crowd roared even louder at the first sound of the guitar rips from "Layla," which sent the security personnel back behind the barricade to stay clear of the out-of-control crowd jamming against the stage.

Then, when Clapton ripped into the first three chords of "Cocaine," the crowd went absolutely nuts. But I just remained in my seat, observing.

"Look at Smitty, he's just sitting there!" Packy repeated, pointing at me again.

I only sat there, wishing I could be the man on that stage, the man of fame who could change the whole world with just a song. That's what I wanted, fame—to be heard and seen by the world. No one had ever paid much attention to me in my life. Seeing this amazing man gain so much attention truly amazed me and filled me with longing.

After Rick left for the Army, I didn't have him to drive me around anymore. I needed to find my own car soon. And before the end of the summer, sure enough, I finally bought my own car. It was real piece of junk—a 1972 Mercury Comet that cost me just $200. But with a lot of help from Dad, we gave it a good tune up and kept that old piece of junk running.

My Comet had no radio, so I carried my boom box in the front seat next to me and cranked out tunes from The Doors, Led Zeppelin, or Jimi Hendrix. Suddenly, it seemed, I had a lot of new friends, including Mike Baxter who needed me to drive him around everywhere. I never did like Mike that much, but since we both attended the same school and same church, we always seemed to find ourselves hanging out together.

And now that I had my own car, we were almost like best friends.

Mike liked rock 'n roll music as much as I did. We used to skip out on church a lot together, hitchhiking downtown and walking around Congress street on a Sunday night. Problem was, Mike would always try to do stupid things like try to get into a bar or an X-rated movie. Fortunately, he never had any money, so I never had to go in any of those places with him. I was just happy to get out and walk around town.

I didn't like sitting in church together with him any more than I didn't like school. Mike was sometimes embarrassing to be around because he'd brag so much about the things he'd done. Some of the stories he'd tell were so over-exaggerated they sounded like lies, and the rest of them *were* nothing but downright total lies.

You see, he'd brag about the many girls he'd scored with, or about how much weed or alcohol he could consume. There was no doubt he'd smoked a lot of weed and drank a lot of alcohol. But some of those girls he said he'd scored with weren't much to brag about. Worst of all, sometimes I'd hear him bragging about the sports car or the Harley Davidson he liked to believe he owned.

Truth was, we had only my piece of junk to ride around in.

But riding around listening to AC/DC or Black Sabbath during the hours we were supposed to be in church didn't seem right to me. Still, Mike was my only close friend at that time, and I did like to get out to cruise around in my car.

At times, Mike could even be fun. He could play guitar, drums, or even the trombone. We often talked about starting a band together. Although Mike liked to talk a lot about music and seemed to have enough talent for it, the trouble was, he possessed virtually no motivation to get started with anything organized.

His laziness, then, played a big part in our friendship. He could never keep a job, and he often leaned on me for most everything. Having my own car made me a lot more popular at school as well.

During our Junior and Senior years, school was split into two sessions. We had our morning classes at Portland Regional Vocational School, then spent the rest of the day back at South Portland High. It took about a half hour bus ride to and from. Many guys liked to get high during the ride between schools, so my car was always full of smokers in the back seat.

As much as I hated smoking, those were the only friends I had. So, I let them smoke just as long as they kept the windows open.

Not everyone in my car was there for the smokes though. For instance, there was Jeanine. She was a beautiful blonde I liked a lot. I had her in a few of my classes and I knew she liked me. But I had always felt too shy to make a move on her. Now that I had my own car, though, she jumped right in the front seat and sat up close to me. It felt really good.

With those guys riding in my backseat, all I had to do was put my arm around her and she'd be all mine. But I suppose she got tired of me keeping both hands on the steering wheel rather than on her. After a few more rides, she gave up on me.

So now I was stuck with the guys smoking in my car for the rest of the school year.

Mike was always with me, whether it was before, during, or after school. Weekends as well. And when he wasn't bragging about all the times he'd cheated on his girlfriend Pauline, he had her with us as well. Pauline and I got along well. I didn't feel so shy the times when I'd hang out with her and Mike wasn't there.

But I'd often ask her whether she sometimes felt embarrassed when Mike acted so immature and told his bizarre stories.

She nodded agreement. "All the times I'm with him. But so, what? We always have a good time. Yeah, sometimes Mike can be real fun. Or at least, it's never boring when he's around."

I thought about how at a church function, he'd often brag about all his sins. Or if we were on Congress Street, he'd tell an old drunk that Jesus could save you from your sins. Mike was just unpredictable about what he was going to say next.

That old junkie Mercury Comet of mine brought me a lot of new friends. But trying to keep the thing running wasn't easy. It burnt so much oil, now and then the engine would start shaking. Too much carbon buildup on the spark plugs caused 3 of the 6 cylinders to skip. So once a week I had to pull all the spark plugs out and spend about five to ten minutes on each one with a wire brush and sandpaper to clean off all the carbon.

An old car with blown valve seals was usually ready for the junk yard. But my dad taught me to keep it running long after its time was up. It would run quite smoothly for a while after cleaning those plugs. But it was just a lot of extra work to keep up.

With the summer of 1983 drawing near, keeping my Comet running was not one of my priorities. I'd already spent more money on brakes, tires, and a new muffler than the piece of junk was worth.

One day, when we were out on the highway, Packy shouted from the backseat, "Come on! Let's see how fast this thing can go!"

"Yeah, let's see how fast this thing can go!" everyone else in the car echoed. "You barely keep it up with the flow of traffic, Smitty. Let's see how fast this thing can *really* go!"

So, I stepped on the gas pedal. "Poof-poof!" The car almost stalled. Then it let out a loud "Bang!" from the tail pipe. When we finally, slowly began to accelerate, there came another "Bang!"

At last, the car reached its top speed of 75 mph.

"Hey, how much did you pay for this piece of junk, anyway?" One of my backseat smoking friends posed the question like he was thinking I'd gotten ripped off.

"Two hundred bucks," I answered back, knowing that was less money than my friend spent on weed each month.

"Hey, that's not bad, not bad at all, for two hundred bucks."

Everybody agreed I got a good deal for two hundred bucks.

But sometimes I wondered if that piece of junk was even worth another gallon of gas.

CHAPTER 8

Smitty's Beast

During the summer of 1983, I worked a lot of extra hours.

I'd begun working with my dad at the Buick dealership in February to keep myself working and making money during the months that The Spurwink was closed. Then during the spring, I also went back to my dishwashing job, holding down two jobs and putting in a lot of hours.

Working for my father gave me a whole new level of respect for my dad. I always knew dad worked hard and was very good at his job. But from the time I started working alongside the crew of mechanics that labored under his leadership, I could see just how important dad really was.

He was the first to show up every morning. At the end of the day, he was the last to leave. He was responsible for every car that came through his shop. Sometimes he had to raise his voice to get things done on time, just like he did at home.

But I didn't think dad ever really wanted to yell at us kids at home. Looking back, I now see and understand the stress and responsibility dad had to deal with every day. Even Shawn noticed how important dad was in his workplace. Dad had hired Shawn so that he could pay off the fines and damage he'd caused after taking Mom's car out for a joy ride with no license.

It was Shawn's job to sort out papers and help organize Dad's work space. Meanwhile, I worked washing and waxing new cars, prepping them for the salesmen to show.

One time, Shawn looked up at me and laughed. "Hey, Dad's the most important guy in this place. Dad's the only one that knows what the hell's going on in this place."

"Yeah, I know," I answered with a smile. "Our dad really is an important guy.

I looked around the work place and realized there were only a few guys who even knew much at all of what the they were doing. The rest of them were just there for a paycheck.

I was truly glad it was *my* dad who knew everything.

So, I knew right then I never wanted to be some useless worker on a payroll. I felt I had to be important in everything I did, whether it was washing dishes, washing cars, or someday managing a large work place like my dad did. *Be useful on the job or get out*, was my motto.

Given all the hours I'd been working, I had my mind set on buying a better car. With all the money I'd been putting into that old Comet, it was hard to build up my savings. But I did manage to save up over five hundred bucks. Still, that was not nearly enough to meet the asking price of the 1970 Black Chevy Camaro I had my heart set on.

Sitting in the used car lot for a few months with the retail price of only $2600, it had a 454 cubic inch engine, mag wheels, and side pipes. With my Dad's connections, I could have bought the car for just $1400.

You can imagine that I was very upset when someone else bought it before I could.

But dad came through for me when he offered to sell me his 1972 Chevy Monte Carlo with its newly overhauled 350 cubic inch engine. For just $1000, this car was in mint condition, newly painted white with a blue top. Dad allowed me to pay $500 down and then make payments for the rest.

I immediately posted a For Sale sign on my junkie Comet in front of our house for just $150. It sold in less than an hour. Adding that toward the Monte Carlo, I only had $350 left to pay.

Feeling like I'd gotten a really good deal, the first thing I thought to do was drive around the corner to show off my new car to Packy.

"Alright, Smitty!!" Packy jumped in the front seat.

I took him for a ride around South Portland, glad my new car had its built-in AM/FM stereo cassette. I no longer needed my boom box beside me as we cranked up the tunes in my new beast that was a much smoother ride than my old Mercury Comet.

We took it out on the highway. Packy shouted, "Let's see what this beast can do!" as he stomped on my foot, throwing us back in our seats and making us accelerate towards 115 mph.

"Wowwww!! THIS CAR'S GOT BALL'S!" Packy shouted.

Meanwhile, I was trying to yank his foot off mine. "Come on, Packy, CUT THE SHIT!!" I screamed at him, trying to keep the car under control.

I smiled as the car slowed to a smooth 75 mph of cruising speed.

"Yeah, this car's got ball's!" I said, still smiling and feeling much better about the car I had to drive. I planned on keeping this car clean both inside and outside. I certainly wasn't going to allow any smoking in it, either.

I couldn't wait to show off my new car on the first day of school. We were now in our senior year, and I stopped to pick up Packy.

"Let's go!" he shouted.

As he jumped in and rolled down the window, I took off from his house, squealing my tires and cranking up the music. We headed down the road, reaching 80 mph on the open stretch along Highland Ave.

We didn't slow down till it was time to make the turn in front of the school. "Screech!!!!" My tires smoked, smelling of burnt rubber. The stench filled the air as everyone looked to see.

"Smitty's got a new car!

"Man, what a beast!!"

Suddenly, I had a lot of unwanted attention and a few more friends.

The thing I liked best about vocational school was it took up most of school time. And the reason I took the food service course was because I liked to eat. Our teacher Mr. Britten, though, used to tell me how much he hated me, and I didn't even know why. But, I liked *him*.

Anyway, I got away with everything in his class, especially on days we had substitute teachers. I once dumped a whole box of frozen sausages on a hot grill, sending a loud sizzling steam up to the ceiling.

"Smitty what are you doing?!!!" shouted one of my classmates named Frank.

"I made Frank mad!!!" I said later with a big smile on my face. I really felt proud of myself for making him mad that day. He'd been trying to act like the teacher because our regular teacher was out.

The one good friend I had from that class was Bob Mason, who was the younger brother of Steve Mason. Bob was the complete opposite of his brother, Steve, who liked to ride in the back seat and smoke weed. But now that I didn't allow smoking in my car anymore, it was just Bob and I. Bob liked fast cars and playing our music loud. We sometimes went out on Friday nights looking for girls together. But since I was so shy Bob did most of the talking while I did all the driving.

The one thing Bob and Steve had in common with me was we all like to eat. At the end of each cooking class, the three of us would sit and just pig out. There was no telling who could eat the most. We just ate and ate and ate till everything was gone. Unlike Bob, Steve and I were both thin. It seemed that the more we ate the skinnier we got.

But after the bell rang, it was Bob and I racing out to the parking lot, to "Smitty's Beast," as Bob would call it. Sometimes, I'd even let him drive, revving up the engine and squealing tires as we headed out on the road. We'd fight our way through the traffic on Washington Ave. until we reached interstate 295. Then we'd open it up to well over 100 mph, racing against another classmate, Don, in his 340 Plymouth Duster.

Although many of our classmates drove at excessive speeds, it was usually Bob and I who led the pack. Every day, the racing got more intense, at higher speeds and with more daring, passing cars using the breakdown lane. It had become so routine that I was feeling pretty comfortable traveling over 100 mph in the breakdown lane.

Bob didn't seem fazed about it either. Meanwhile, other classmates seemed to show no concern for the danger we were putting ourselves in or the showoff treat we were to the many innocent law-abiding drivers.

This went on for much of the first two months of that school year. Then one day I said to Bob, "You know, I think we should slow it down. Sooner or later, somebody's gonna get in a bad accident."

Bob just laughed. But then he agreed.

And when we left the parking lot, I drove the speed limit all the way down Washington Ave. It felt like we were crawling along the road.

But as soon as we reached interstate 295, a line of State Troopers sat waiting with their radar guns, ready to nab the next speeder. We just smiled and drove by at 55 mph.

Everyone else must have been thinking the same, because we all took our time driving back to South Portland High.

And for the rest of the school year, I did no more racing with that car. It took a lot of practice, but I really tried to start driving by the rules.

However, one day I saw blue lights flashing in my rearview mirror. *What?* I didn't believe it.

And I was upset.

After all my former speeding, though, I should have been respectful when a police officer actually pulled me over. But given all the stuff I'd gotten away with in this car, being pulled over for a little roll at a stop sign seemed so petty.

I argued with that cop a bit. I thought he was just being so unreasonable.

I was very lucky to get away with only a stiff warning. I'd been stupid, not giving one thought to how lucky I was to not have been splattered all over the highway for all the close calls we'd had in the months before. And I'd had no thought for injuring someone else and having to live with it.

How lucky I was that those Troopers didn't set up their speed traps just a few days earlier. They'd have arrested me and suspended my license for life.

It wasn't long before winter hit, bringing slippery roads and making it very difficult to keep that old car under control. Even driving slowly one day, my car slid straight into a ditch. There was nothing I could do to prevent it. My tires had no tread left on them from all the abuse they had taken in the months before.

"Crunch!!" I felt my car break through the snowbank and tilt its front end into the ditch, the rear wheels lifted up.

I'm stuck in here pretty good, I thought. *There's no way this car's getting out without a tow.*

I set out walking, hoping Dad would be able to help me when I got home. Of course, Dad could help. Dad could fix anything. But we'd have to wait till after dinner.

Finally, after dinner, Dad called a few friends with trucks and chains and we all headed back to find my car. Only this time we found my car even deeper in the ditch, with the rear bumper and tail lights all banged up. I was feeling upset, knowing somebody slipped off the road in the same place I did, slamming into the back of my car.

Watching them drag my car out of the ditch, I could see my car was pretty banged up. Luckily the person who hit my car left a note. *Sorry I hit your car.* He included in the note his name and contact number. So, I was able to collect a little insurance money for the extra damage they caused. And still able to drive it with a banged up rear bumper.

By early spring of 1984, my car's engine was running a little rough. And with all the dents in the rear, it didn't look so pretty any more. But I still managed to get around in it.

One Sunday night, Mike and Pauline decided they wanted to skip church with me. So, we all headed out to the Westbrook Cinema to see a movie.

What we saw in the parking lot nearly blew me away.

My old Mercury Comet was parked in the parking lot. We simply couldn't believe it. Still, we knew for sure that it was my old car. It had the same black paint I sprayed on the side panel to cover up some rusty spots.

We all laughed, in shock that the car I'd sold for just $150 was still in driving condition. When I'd sold it, I'd thought it might run for another month or two, at the most, before it would be sold for scrap metal.

And suddenly, it didn't seem so funny anymore, when I thought of all the money I'd put into that car.

Plus, in less than a year, my once beautiful-looking, smooth-running Monte Carlo now looked and ran like a piece of junk.

CHAPTER 9

School's Out

On May 1, 1984, we were all just six weeks away from high school graduation. Packy and I were on our way to the Honda dealership, excited because this time we were *not* going to just look around wasting a motorcycle salesman's time, as we'd done so many times before.

You see, I had just been approved for my first loan. My credit union was allowing me to borrow $1,600. I only had to keep $800 in savings for collateral.

"Wow, I'm feeling pretty excited," I said to Packy. "This is the most money I'd ever held in my hand." I couldn't believe any bank would ever lend me money. It was so easy. All I'd had to do was ask for the loan—and provide the required security money—and I got the loan!

And now we were on our way to the Honda dealership.

I'd only attempted to ride motorcycles a few times before. First, I'd ridden Packy's Yamaha 125cc dirt bike—but not so well. I'd lost control along the dirt road and wiped out. When I'd tried to get it going again, I'd screwed up the clutch so bad we couldn't start it.

Then there was the Kawasaki KZ 400 that Packy and I had put our money together for last summer. It had been our very first street bike. We each had paid $200, thinking we'd gotten a great deal.

After Packy had taught me how to ride, we'd taken turns every other week for riding time. That had worked out well for a few riding lessons. But then Packy had crashed into a car while it was backing out of a driveway. He'd suffered a few scrapes and bruises but walked away from the collision okay. Our bike, however, was all banged up and we had to retire it to Packy's garage with bent forks, a flat tire bent rim, and a broken headlight.

The cost to repair it would far outweigh the bike's worth.

Today we walked into the Honda dealership with big smiles on our faces. Although the salesmen noticed us, they just ignored us—probably assuming we were just there to look around again as usual.

But this time we were there for serious business. I started looking for bikes in my price range. There was a whole row of brand-new leftovers from 1981-83, all of them reduced to prices under $1500.

Quickly, I made my decision—for a beautiful maroon-colored 1982 Nighthawk 450. After I'd sat on it for a few minutes, a salesman decided to come over and talk to us. He was probably thinking I was just another guy who wished I had the money to buy this kind of bike.

But then I showed him I had cash in my hand.

His face lit up and we began to talk seriously. Within just a few minutes, I was signing papers in his office. Within the hour, they had my new bike all set up with the 10-day registration plate. I was feeling pretty proud, holding the keys to my very own brand-new Nighthawk 450.

Now I just had to learn how to ride it.

I handed Packy the keys. "Be careful. I'm still paying for this."

Packy was a much more experienced rider than I was. He liked to rev up the engine every chance he got. But not this time. He took it easy while I followed behind in my car. Once in a while, when we stopped at a stop sign or a traffic light, Packy shouted with excitement. "*All right*, Smitty! This is a nice bike! It rides and shifts so smooth!"

All the way home, the excitement was overwhelming for both of us. Arriving safely, we found my parents, my brother, and my sister all there waiting. They came out to see my brand-new bike lighting up the evening sky on the front lawn.

My parents clearly felt proud of me, but they were concerned I didn't have a helmet yet. Nor did I have any insurance. My folks advised me to keep my bike in the garage until I got those things.

But I decided not to be worried at all. I was so excited I couldn't even sleep.

The next morning Packy was at my house early. We couldn't wait to ride my brand-new Nighthawk to school.

"Woo-hooooh!!!" Packy shouted out as we cruised up and down Highland Ave. before school started, the time each day that we could do whatever we wanted.

But then the school day afterward seemed so long. I looked out the window every chance I got. Everybody was pointing outside, saying, "That's Smitty's new bike!"

Suddenly, though, everyone was asking why I had let Packy drive it but wasn't driving it myself. I felt embarrassed. I didn't know *how* to drive it yet.

Finally, school was out and Packy was out by my bike, waiting for me. I was ready to go, and it took patience to let the engine warm up. Packy was on the back seat, and finally I attempted to let out the clutch.

"*Poooff!*" The engine stalled with a jerk forward, nearly knocking us off balance.

Now, everyone was watching. I tried it again, the bike sputtering and jerking while I slowly let out the clutch.

And before I knew it, with Packy coaching from the back, we were cruising— all over South Portland. I was really beginning to get the hang of it.

"You got it, you're doing all right!" Packy shouted with encouragement.

We cruised on out to Fort Williams, where many of our classmates liked to hang out in their cars. We rode up to the parking lot, and I heard a few comments about how I couldn't ride my own bike.

Packy jumped off, letting me know he wanted to hang out with our classmates for a while. Since I was feeling pretty confident by myself, I set out to take my first solo ride, down to the Lighthouse. Then I'd turn around and cruise up the hill.

Again, everyone was watching, and I was feeling good going into the turn that would take me down the other side.

Suddenly, I saw a patch of sand ahead at the curve. I slowed down quickly, feeling panic, thinking I'd be unable to decelerate in time.

This is it, am I gonna crash and die! I will soon find out!

And that was my last thought. "Bam!!" My head hit the pavement. There was a sudden flash of light...then darkness...and finally I woke up to a crowd of friends all gathered around me.

I felt dizzy, a lump on my forehead. I saw my brand-new bike lying on the pavement a few feet away. In shock that I was still alive, I bolted towards it and Packy helped me pick it up off the pavement.

Everyone could see the damaged side. The shifter was bent all the way back, the turn signal lights were cracked, and a few deep scratches ran along the clutch cover case.

Still stunned, I watched my friends holding up my bike while another pulled hard to bend the shifter back in place.

Packy knew we had to give it a test ride to make sure it could still run.

"Come on get on Smitty, I'll take you home."

I felt badly depressed on the way home. I told Packy I'd be selling the bike. I couldn't do it. I'd wasted all my money on a bike that I couldn't even learn how to ride.

After I got home, I called a few insurance companies to find out if it was too late for me to buy motorcycle insurance. Quickly, I realized the cost of the damage did not exceed the cost of insurance.

In the end, though, I chose not to give up after all. It took a while, but with Packy's encouragement I was soon up and riding on my own again, racing up and down Highland Ave., learning to down shift and accelerating as I leaned into sharp turns, finally feeling truly confident.

It wasn't long before graduation day arrived. Riding in to school wearing a suit and tie and a big smile, Packy and I reveled in the fact that this would be our last day. I parked in front of the building putting on my cap and gown, getting ready for the big ceremony.

I was feeling a bit out of place, though, secretly ridden with guilt and shame for the wasted opportunities here at school that I'd shied away from. Having taken the easiest classes just to get by with passing grades, I knew I'd never feel like I truly deserved a diploma.

But even that feeling didn't come close to the guilt and shame I suffered for all the times I'd sat in the bleacher during school dances, afraid of asking a girl to dance—or the shame over the times I'd shaken my head so shyly when a pretty girl asked me to dance.

Why had I been so afraid to put my arm around a beautiful girl who jumped in my car and sat close to me? What had been wrong with me? I knew I might never have these opportunities again.

I finished putting on my cap and gown to step in at the end of the line—instead of marching side by side with a beautiful girl, the way the rest of my friends marched in. I was among the few leftover guys who had no one to march with and felt very foolish for even being here.

After we marched into the gymnasium, we sat listening to a few speeches before they started calling our names one at a time to receive our diplomas. Standing six feet two inches tall, I *felt* about four feet tall when my name was called to walk down in front of over four hundred classmates and an unknown number of family and friends looking on.

To end the ceremony, we all stood as a choir and sang "We May Never Pass This Way Again." Those lyrics had a lot of deep meaning to my life thus far, and I hoped not to let my dreams slip away much longer.

When the ceremony ended, I headed out to my bike, unzipping my gown so when I rode away it would flow in the wind as I zoomed away from the school and down Highland Avenue.

My friend Mike joined the Army Reserves immediately after high school. Having just a few weeks left before leaving for Army training, he wanted to ride to visit a few friends up in Cumberland. And, of course, he wanted to drive while I took the back seat. Cumberland was a small town where he used to live before moving to South Portland. Since he knew where we were going, I let him take the driver's seat.

I was enjoying the scenery as we rode down a long country road. Mike drove a little slower as we approached his old neighborhood.

Suddenly, he stopped at the side of the road and said to me, "Hey, Smitty, just to make it look good, let's say this bike is mine."

"Ok, whatever." I decided to go along with his plan so he could impress his friends, a few of which owned their own bikes. I knew Mike would look good riding together with them.

He started to talk himself up when his friends rode up beside us, which made me feel like a tag along while he showed off "his bike."

But all went well, his friends were very impressed, and we headed home.

A few days later Mike had a bad breakup with Pauline. It was the first time I had ever seen him cry. I couldn't figure out why he cried so hard, since he'd broken up with her so many times before. He'd cheated on her and abused her, over and over. But this time she was breaking it off with him.

As you can imagine, I had to do the driving that one last ride before he left for his Army training.

Pauline and I remained friends after Mike left for the Army. I often picked her up after school to give her a ride to the home of her new boyfriend, the one she would eventually marry.

Just before Mike had left, he'd introduced me to Greg Foster. Greg was an expert biker. He had the same kind of courage JJ Ross had possessed, maybe more. Greg could even ride a wheelie for the full length of his street.

Like Mike and me, Greg also had parents who brought him to church every Sunday. He and I developed a long-lasting friendship by the end of that summer, as we went biking every day, and he turned me into a true biker before the summer was over. He also tried to set me up with Penny Cash, a nice girl with a funny name. I pulled my first wheelie in front of her house. Greg, too, was showing off riding wheelies back and forth in front of her house.

"Oh yeah, watch this!!!" I shouted, as I wound back on the throttle and let out the clutch. "Varoooom!!!"

Suddenly, I was looking up as my headlights lit up the sky. "Bam!!" my front tire came back down, my heart pounding with excitement and fear. I'd almost flipped over backwards.

Penny was quite impressed with all the wheelies Greg pulled that night. But she said she liked mine best. Still, my heart was pounding the rest of the evening, and I never stopped talking about my very first wheelie.

Another cute girl I met that summer was Heidi. She was only sixteen years old, but one day I was out riding and saw her sitting near the bus stop. She whistled and waved for me to come over, so I turned around to get back to her. She smiled and asked me for a ride home that evening. But then I kept seeing her around and soon she was riding with Greg and me every day.

By the end of the summer we had spent a lot of time riding together. Heidi was fun to be around, and I should have stayed friends with her. But I was still more interested in chasing girls I couldn't have.

Another friend I'd known since Jr. High, we used to call him Snowman I'm not sure if it was because he was so bulky or if it was for all the cocaine he consumed. Once a straight A student whose grades had begun to deteriorate to just a few A's and mostly B's during his Junior and Senior years.

Snowman would often brag about taking exams in biology class while tripping on LSD and still scoring an A. He was a big guy who played on the football team and weighed well over 200 lbs. He washed dishes at The Merry Manor Restaurant at the same time I began washing dishes for the Snow Squall Restaurant.

The one thing that brought Snowman and me together every Thursday was payday. Snowman had lost his license after a drunk driving accident wrecked his Jeep Cherokee, leaving him with huge fines to pay. Not that he had any intentions on paying those fines off, but he couldn't afford collage till they were paid.

Every Thursday, Snowman would call my house wanting me to give him a ride up to The Manor to pick up his check. It was usually the only day of the week I still used my car. So, after I'd pick him up, we'd stop at the Snow Quall for my check then drive out to The Manor for his check.

After cashing mine, I'd make a payment on my loan, put a large sum in my savings account, and just keep a few bucks in my pocket for the week.

Then we'd go to Snowman's bank where he'd cash his check and pocket all the dough before going to the nearest convenient store. Snowman, at just eighteen years old, was so big—with hairy sideburns—that most any store clerk wouldn't question he was over 21. Snowman would come out with a case of beer that we'd put in the trunk before we drove up to Kettle Cove, stopping at the liquor store on the way. Snowman would usually buy a bottle of Peppermint Schnapps and drink it while riding in the front seat.

After that, we'd meet up with Greg, Heidi, and a few other friends out at the cove looking out over the ocean.

On one occasion, I was thinking that Maine had to be the worst place in the world to live, while I was barely finishing half a beer. Snowman and Greg had just about finished the case before it was even noontime.

"We need to get out of Maine before winter hits," I said. It's only early September and I'm already worried about winter. We need to plan a bike trip to Florida and stay there for the winter."

"Yeah, yeah!" they all agreed, as they were getting more wasted.

"Maybe we can load our bikes up in Greg's van. Then we can all go."

"Yeah, yeah!" we all agreed. "Let's all go together."

After the beer was all gone, both Greg and Snowman were getting a pretty good buzz on. Nevertheless, Snowman wanted a ride back to the liquor store before I dropped him off at work later in the afternoon.

I complied with his request. And after entering the liquor store, Snowman came out with a pint of Vodka. He finished it in less than an hour, drinking in a parking lot near The Manor.

Just before he was to return back to work, he stepped out of the car and ran behind a dumpster. When he returned, he had a sad look on his face. He climbed back in the car. "AH JEEZZ I PISSED MYSELF!" he said with a whining voice as he grabbed his apron, tied it around his waist, and headed off to work.

CHAPTER 10

Moving Out

Mike returned home after spending just four months training at Walter Reed National Military Medical Center.

It was early in January of 1985, and he had enjoyed the freedom of being away from his parent's house for those four months. Returning home was not going well for him and I'd been getting sick and tired of living under my parent's roof as well.

Mike set out on a job hunt to every hospital in Portland, looking for work in the medical field. With just four months of training, he felt he was qualified to be a doctor and wouldn't accept a position changing bed sheets. So, after he'd burned all his chances of working in a hospital, I took him to Manpower Temp Service on an early Friday morning.

I decided I might as well apply for a better job too, since we were there. I'd still been washing dishes at The Snow Squall, but I wasn't planning on making a career out of it.

Mike and I filled out our applications together, and a woman interviewed us. She actually hired us for a construction job to start early Monday morning.

"We both got jobs!" I said, excited and anxious to do anything except wash dishes.

Mike didn't seem as excited as I was, and I couldn't understand why.

Now all we had to do was find an apartment. Mike showed a lot more enthusiasm after we stopped at a motel on Main Street with winter rates of $120 per week. It had one bedroom, one full-sized bed, one cot, one bathroom, a kitchen for cooking, and a big couch in the living room along with a big black and white TV, cable service included.

"We can afford it if we both pay just $60.00 a week," I said.

We wasted no time and paid our two weeks up front. With a little help from Greg and his van, we got everything moved in before the weekend.

Greg looked at us and laughed. "There's only one bed."

"I'll be sleeping on the cot," I said. "I don't mind sleeping on the cot just as long as I'm out of my parent's house."

After unpacking all of our clothes, along with my bench and weight set and stereo system, records, pots, pans, and utensils we'd taken from our homes, we had everything we needed to survive.

Except, we needed to get some food in that apartment refrigerator.

Mike and I head out to Shaw's supermarket to load up on groceries.

Mike made sure we had enough beer for the week. I was more concerned about having enough food. We filled up the cart with enough groceries to hopefully get us through the week, and the total bill was $60.00.

In all, it was only going to cost us $30.00 a week to eat, plus the $60.00 in rent. All we each needed, then, was $90.00 a week and we had it made.

We finished off all the beer before our first weekend was over, but we still had plenty enough food left. Rising up early for breakfast Monday morning, the subzero temperature outside really woke me up as I swung open the door with no shirt on.

"Woooooh!!" I shouted, watching the steam rise up from the manhole covers a short distance away. "Wooooh!!" I looked at Mike. He didn't seem as excited about our new job as I was. "Are we ready to go?!"

He was a little slow to get started but ready to go.

I was truly anxious to get started. We arrived early, finding a place to park on Middle Street. A few minutes later, we saw some workers arrive, unlocking the vacant building next to Carbur's restaurant.

"This must be the place. Let's go," I said.

Mike and I walked over to meet the crew as we introduced ourselves. Mike did most of the talking. We signed a few papers and were ready to start. With freezing temperatures and no heat in the building, I knew Mike and I would be getting all the dirty jobs.

We started out tossing all the scrap wood out the 3rd and 4th floor windows, with freezing winds blowing some of the wood off target. Every once in a while, we had to run down the stairs and clean up around the dumpster.

Next, we were down in the basement carrying all the broken concrete up to the street and tossing it into the back of a truck. After about an hour, I was stripped down to just a t-shirt and loving it.

Meanwhile, Mike was making good friends with a few guys who'd been working there a long time. At lunchtime, they both came over to my car. We all crowded in to keep warm with the heater running while eating our lunch.

These guys started giving us a bit of advice. "Don't bust yourselves, just walk around looking like your busy doing something. Take your time going up and down the stairs. Do a little here, a little there. Then go sit on the can for a few and before you know it, it'll be time to go home."

Mike seemed to like that kind of advice.

After lunch, a truck load of long planks arrived. We spent the rest of the day lugging the long planks up to the 4th floor and I was feeling exhausted by the time we headed home.

After I got showered up, with plenty of food still in the refrigerator, I cooked us some dinner. Greg and his girlfriend Mary Kay soon arrived, coming over with some beer to hang out with us that night and watch TV.

Greg took a big swig of his beer. But immediately, he spat it out. "Urfoooo!!" He'd been using a half-full can of beer for an ashtray and had accidently picked up the wrong can.

We all laughed, watching him spit up a few cigarette butts.

But it occurred to me that the place was beginning to look like a pig sty. In just the first few days, our apartment was full of cigarette smoke and smelled like stale beer.

Plus, I was the only one who cleaned the dishes. Mike and all his friends only come over to make messes.

Our work routine went very well for the first week—until Mike came up with one of his brilliant ideas. He'd been doing the math, and as I've said, he figured it was costing us each $90.00 a week.

He mentioned how he could afford that just working three days a week.

So, while I was getting ready for work Monday morning, Mike decided to take the day off. I went into work without him, and no one really noticed he wasn't there.

When I returned home, Mike had been joined by Snowman and they were sitting on the coach watching TV. It was another one of Mike's brilliant ideas in action. Snowman had just been kicked out of his parent's house, and he worked just a short walk from our place. He'd been sober for over a week now, and the two of them had realized that if we three split the rent, that was only $40.00 for each of us.

"Yeah, that sounds like a good idea," I agreed. Snowman could sleep on the couch.

And since he worked nights, it did turn out great for a while. For the first two weeks, he paid his $40.00 in rent and paid his share for groceries. Our apartment space was a bit crowded, but things were still good…

…until the night our whole gang was together. Snowman was still keeping himself sober. Greg was with Mary Kay. Mike had a few young girls over and they *were* drinking. But Snowman just sat on the couch, keeping sober.

Greg, though, gave Snowman a little encouragement.

"Why don't you just have one beer? You don't have to go all out."

Snowman grumbled and looked down, apparently feeling like he was not fitting in well with the party.

"Let me tell you what you're doing wrong," Greg said. "You go all out every time you do drink. But we only have a couple of beers to relax and have a good time. Every once in a while, we go all out. But most of the time we just have a couple."

"Don't do it, Snowman" I interrupted.

Big Snowman grumbled again. "Yeah, all right. Just one."

After one beer for Big Snowman, there was two. Soon, he was becoming loud and obnoxious.

Now, Greg was giving me advice. "Throw him out, you gotta throw him out."

I argued, "You're the one who told him to start drinking again."

"Yeah, I told him to just have one," he said laughing. "I never thought he would get out of control."

The next morning, Mike and I returned to work. Mike was just coming back after taking off two days in a row. When the boss asked where he'd been the last two days, it didn't go well when he told them he only wanted to work three days a week.

"If you don't want to work forty hours a week for me, then your fired!" the boss said in a loud, stern voice.

I felt a little embarrassed that Mike and I had even rode in to work together.

They decided to keep me on at the construction work because I didn't mind doing all the dirty work and I showed up every day.

I handed Mike the car keys. "You come pick me up at the end of the day."

When he did, he'd already landed a new job.

This, however, made things a little more complicated. We now had to take turns with the car, dropping each other off at work every day.

Meanwhile, Snowman's heavy drinking was getting even more out of control.

After another week passed, Mike didn't pay his share of the rent because he spent most of his check on weed and beer, which Snowman consumed the most of. But I was still getting along fine with Snowman because at least he paid his share of the rent and pitched in for groceries.

One evening while Mike was out, I was in the kitchen cooking dinner.

Snowman started telling me how angry he was with Mike. "I think we should kick him out. I've never liked him and I'm sick and tired of his mouth."

"I know he can be a pain in the ass sometimes," I said. "And the bizarre stories he tells are downright embarrassing. But, remember he's the one who invited you to stay here. If it weren't for him, you'd have no place to live."

But that didn't seem to faze Snowman. Later that evening, we all got together, and Mike was running his mouth again, talking himself up and laughing, drinking, telling bizarre stories.

Snowman just blew up. "All right, Mike! Let me see how tough you are!" He slammed Mike up against the wall.

I'd never seen Mike so scared, as Snowman cocked his fist in the air, screaming, "LET ME SEE WHAT YOU GOT! COME ON, LET ME SEE WHAT YOU GOT!!"

Snowman's fists were like bowling balls and I'd seen what he could do to someone when he was angry.

Lucky for Mike, I was able to calm Big Snowman down. Snowman had always respected me, ever since we were in Jr. High when he used to do his Andre The Giant impersonation, using me for body slams. While most of the other kids had run away from him, I'd taken his abuse over and over again. I think he really respected me for that.

Mike kept quiet the rest of the evening. After Snowman passed out on the couch, things calmed down. I went to sleep on my cot, thinking about what I should do. This was not the freedom I'd been wishing for and not the way life had been at Nathan and Annie's house, with the laid back feeling of no worries.

This, in fact, was absolute torture, far worse than living under my parent's roof. And a thought hit me. Quickly, I had my mind made up.

This was my final week. I was done cleaning up behind those two lazy slobs. And I was tired of working overtime just to cover the rent and food and having nothing left in my savings.

I'd had enough, and I was moving out at the end of the week.

The next morning, I got up early and left for work before Mike and Snowman woke up. I felt much more relaxed that day working on a construction site than I had in the past six weeks living with those two idiots.

When I got home, I said nothing. In fact, I didn't say a word about my plans until the final day the rent was due.

I started loading up as much as I could fit in my car. I dropped it all off at my parent's house then went to get the rest while Mike and Snowman were just waking up.

Those guys didn't seem one bit surprised. Neither of them had plans to put any money toward rent, anyway.

Mike moved back in with his parents and who knew where Snowman moved to? I only saw Snowman a few more times after we'd all moved, and he still was holding his grudge against Mike.

I remained friends with Mike, though, despite our differences.

CHAPTER 11

Wheelies and Weddings

Showing up at work early every morning in subzero temperatures was taking its toll on me. But fortunately, I showed up at the right time on an early February morning just days after Mike had been fired—along with a few others who thought they could goof off during business hours.

I entered that freezing cold building with every intention to work another long, brutally cold day.

Suddenly, the foreman pointed at me and said, "Why don't you go along with them too?"

At first, I thought he was sending me home.

Then he said, "No, you go with them. We're starting another project down the street."

So, I followed a few guys carrying tools about four doors down to another building. We climbed up a flight of stairs just above an antique shop and set all our tools down.

"This is where you'll be working."

"All day?" I asked with a bit of excitement in my voice. There was heat in this building.

"All day and from now on until the job's complete," my new foreman answered.

I tried to hide my excitement. *No more working in that freezing cold building,* I thought.

Yes, I'd have work with Jeff Blanchard, a young skinny kid that nobody liked because he worked too slow and couldn't bear the cold.

But once we started working together, his attitude changed in just a few days. We were each given a sledgehammer and a couple of crowbars and told to knock down all the walls on the second floor. I tried not to get too carried away at the thought of getting paid to bust up all these walls. But it was just so exhilarating.

Jeff? He watched as I swung that sledgehammer like a wild man. And soon he was right in there with me.

So, together we were smashing walls and knocking out studs as filthy black soot filled our lungs and covered our faces and clothes. This was the best job in the world! We were getting paid to listen to rock 'n roll and bust everything up.

Jeff was quiet and shy like I was. But once we started opening up in conversation we realized we had a lot to talk about. Jeff was from Jacksonville, Florida, and he'd played guitar here in Portland in a punk rock band called Distrust. But its members had split up and had no intentions of returning back home.

Jeff and I also argued a lot – about music. We kept the radio tuned to WBLM, a classic rock station, and both agreed we hated Big Hair Glamor Heavy Metal bands. But Jeff also hated a lot of other bands I liked, such as Neil Young, The Grateful Dead and Eric Clapton. We both liked Alice Cooper and Led Zeppelin, but Jeff would talk about Black Flag, The Misfits, and Suicidal Tendencies.

Soon, I became more interested in these new bands and borrowed tapes to listen to at home. This was it. I'd made up my mind. This was what I wanted.

I looked at myself in the mirror, thinking. I was dull and plain, still listening to music from the 1960's. *You're so boring, I hate you!* I thought to myself.

I ripped the sleeves off my shirt and cranked up the music—the very music I thought I hated just a few years ago was now the music I lived for. And I felt the need to introduce this new music to the rest of my friends.

My introduction didn't go well with Greg. He still lived in a time warp of 60's music. Mike didn't jump into the new stuff too quickly either.

I said to them, "You've gotta give this stuff a chance! I didn't like it at first either. But then it just sort of grows on ya!!"

"The only thing that's gonna grow on me is what I've got between my legs!" Mike shook his head, showing absolutely no interest.

It took several tries, but eventually I found the right band and the right song to get him started. We were out riding in his car and I slipped a Black Flag tape in his tape deck. The song "Rats' Eyes" came on.

His face lit up. "Yeaaaah!! What a cool song!" he kept ranting on. "'*I see the world through rats' eyes, rats' eyes, rats' eyes.*' Whaaat a coooool song!!!"

He kept rewinding and playing "Rats' Eyes" over and over again. I would later gain his interest in other bands such as Dead Kennedy's, Minor Threat and The Sex Pistols. Soon he was hooked on this new shit for music.

Mike finally bought himself his own bike early in the spring. It was an old Honda 350 from Mr. Towle. But it didn't take long before he'd beaten it up beyond repair. Greg and I had beaten up our bikes as well.

Within a few weeks, the three of us had moved up to bigger bikes. I was getting tired of the same old routine, riding up and down Congress Street then parking up on The Promenade to listening to Mike's mouth still talking about Black Flag. It was all he'd been talking about for the past few weeks.

Mike and I were honored to be chosen as ushers for Greg and Mary Kay's wedding. The date was set for the last Saturday in June, which turned out to be a beautiful day. The three of us came riding into the parking lot of The First Baptist Church and parked our bikes for a few minutes just to assess how cool we looked in our tuxedos, giving each other the high five as we started singing the ZZ Top song "Sharp Dressed Man."

After we'd stood posing in front of our bikes for a few photos, it was still early, long before the ceremony started. Filled with the excitement of the three of us looking so sharp, we just couldn't resist the idea of showing off by riding up and down Congress Street before heading back to the church.

We attracted a lot of attention as we headed out on the road together. People were smiling, honking horns, and waving to us while crossing the bridge that headed downtown. I was thinking to myself, *I sure hope nobody does anything stupid right now. I don't want anything to happen to this rented tux.*

Suddenly, Greg revved up his engine and started riding a wheelie.

"Wooooooh!!" I heard Mike shouting as he saw Greg take off. "You've got guts, Greg!" And he went on shouting "Wooooh!!!"

Mike and I were just riding along as careful as we could, watching Greg take the lead. Another biker pulled up beside us and asked, "which one of us is getting married?"

"Him," we replied, pointing and laughing.

The biker waved and shouted "Congratulations!!" Then he rode away.

We all headed back to the church and arrived just in time to join the crowd. Greg looked his absolute coolest in his sunglasses and a tux, riding a wheelie into the church parking lot with all his friends and relatives looking on.

At the beginning of the ceremony, I was a bit nervous about my role as an usher. But once we got started, all went well. Walking down the aisle wearing my tux, I escorted ladies to their seat with a big smile on my face.

I even attracted the eyes of a bridesmaid who, after the ceremony, came running up to tell me how handsome I looked.

I just gave her a shy smile and said, "Thanks."

Mary Kay looked beautiful in her wedding gown. Greg looked very happy as they both recited their marriage vows.

After everything had gone smoothly, we all headed downstairs for the reception. I noticed Mike sitting close to Vicki, who was a close friend of Greg's. Vicki was taking to Mike's smile and charm. It wasn't long before they had really hit it off and began living together, within a few weeks after Greg's wedding.

Returning back to work after an exciting weekend, Jeff and I had absolutely nothing to do since we'd finished knocking all the walls down and had spent a few weeks cleaning up the debris. Now it was just down to sweeping floors over and over again till there was nothing left to sweep. We both realized we liked overworking ourselves—much better than trying to look busy with nothing to do.

Yet we still hung in there through the rest of the summer. Jeff had bulked up with a lot of muscle and he'd added a few tattoos since we'd started. While I still looked long and lanky, I felt weak without holding that sledgehammer. Sweeping is boring and I felt the need to swing that sledgehammer again to make me feel strong.

We talked about punk rock all day long and it was becoming very addictive for me. All that time Jeff had been trying to influence me, I wanted to show him I was as serious about punk rock as he was. I came in to work with a crew cut and an anarchy sign carved on the side of my head.

Jeff was blown away. "Man, you got guts!" he kept saying.

We started hanging out on Friday nights with other punk rockers and spray-painting anarchy signs around the city. Jeff showed me a few walls the members of his band had painted. *Love is wrong* and *Portland doesn't count!* explained its meaning and what his band stood for. *Punk rock is for people like us, people who just live without purpose, without love, without much money, and with no worries.* He went on to explain that he wanted to "just take life as it comes."

"Oh, but I want to find love and get married someday. And I want to make lots of money," I replied, trying to argue my case.

"You'll never find love in this world. It doesn't exist," Jeff insisted with a big smirk on his face.

I supposed that I couldn't prove him wrong. At least not yet, anyway.

With the summer coming to an end, Jeff was making plans to return to Jacksonville. He invited me to come with him. He thought I could be a good front man for his new band he'd be putting together. With my lanky body, a shaved head, the right drive and attitude, I would be the perfect fit for his band.

I thought about it but decided I'd wait till the end of September—after Mike and Vicki's wedding.

I would later regret not leaving with Jeff then. I never heard from him again.

Vicki had been complaining for weeks—right up to the time of her wedding—at just how immature the three of us had shown ourselves to be when we rode our motorcycles wearing tuxedos. She said, "you guys better not be doing that for my wedding."

Being the diehard biker that he was, Greg answered, "I don't know about you guys, but I'm gonna arrive in style."

Lucky for Vicki, though, both Mike and Greg wrecked their bikes pulling wheelies just a few days before the wedding. And since they weren't riding, I didn't want to be the only one riding with a tux. I rode in the back seat of my parent's car.

After the wedding, Mike and Vicki seemed very happy for about a week. But that was about the longest stretch of happiness the two of them would ever experience.

Mike spent a lot of time riding around with me in his car listening to punk rock while cursing and swearing at how he hated married life. I didn't doubt being married to Vicki was really as bad as he says it is. But for me marriage was the only way to happiness if I could just meet the right girl.

"You'll never find anyone!" Mike would say, always cursing and shaking his head at the idea of ever finding real love. Then he'd add, "We gotta get you laid. That's what you need. You need to get laid."

But Mike's advice was never an interest to me, I wanted a real woman one who takes real interest in me.

I was feeling pretty miserable at work since Jeff had left with the job winding down. I felt like I was just showing up for paychecks and had no real reason to be there. The early October mornings were feeling colder, and another construction project across the street had been in progress for a few weeks. I was feeling more useless everyday where I was, yet they kept me on just in case they had a dirty job for me. I looked across the street and noticed the truckloads of sheetrock being unloaded. I saw Packy among the large crew of workers entering the building. Packy looked over and waved. I smiled and waved back, trying to still look busy.

"Smitty!" he shouted when it was getting close to noon. Both of us needed to make a run to the store for a sandwich. "What's up?" Packy smiled as we met up, giving each other a high five. "What do they got you doing?"

"Absolutely nothing, and I can't stand it anymore. I just walk around with a broom, looking for something to do. I hate it. I'm thinking about quitting."

"Well, come work for us. We're hiring and we've got a ton of work for the next several months." Packy showed a lot of excitement, trying to recruit me to do the dirty work which he was doing. He wanted to move up to become a full-time finish taper.

So, quick as that, I returned from lunch to say I was quitting. The very next morning, I started working with Packy. Just as I suspected, he wanted me to do the dirty work that he'd been doing. I was now to be carrying heavy buckets up the stairs, moving sheetrock down the halls, tossing scraps out the windows with the cold wind blowing in my face, and—the worst job—stuffing itchy insulation in the walls.

All for just $5.00 an hour.

"I hate this job!" was all I could think.

I could tolerate this for just a few more months. Meanwhile, I planned to save as much money as I could.

I hadn't owned a car in nearly a year now and had no intentions on wasting money on another car. With winter coming, mornings were too cold to start my bike. I'd have to rely on catching a ride with dad every morning then ride with Packy—or sometimes even walk home—after a long day of heavy labor.

I was torturing myself by anticipating my life would sometime soon, in the next few months, be filled with happiness—if I could save enough money to get out of Maine.

CHAPTER 12

Big Jump for a Red-Haired Girl

By the spring of 1986, I had turned 21 and I'd managed to save well over $3000 from my construction cleanup work during the winter months. But I'd finally had all I wanted of dirty jobs and had no intentions of staying in Maine much longer.

I gave my resignation to Wagner Drywall, telling them that this would be my final week. I planned on packing as much as I could on the back of my Nighthawk 650 and riding as far away from Maine as my money would take me.

But as soon as company owner Chris Wagner heard I was leaving, he came out to the jobsite to talk me into staying. He promised me a big increase in my hourly pay from $5.00 to $6.50 per hour—with a lot of overtime during the next few months.

I couldn't resist his offer. It was more money than I'd ever thought I'd make. I decided to stay on the job a little longer, until at least the end of the summer. Who knew how much money I could save by then?

But as excited as I was about my raise, I was going to make damn sure my parents didn't find out about it. They'd ask me to pay a lot more than the $25.00 a week I'd already been paying them.

By keeping them in the dark, I'd have a real chance to save money.

Mike and Vicki were still struggling to keep their marriage together. I spent a lot of time at their apartment and often they would break out into a brutal fight.

Mike would storm out the door, then he'd jump on my bike demanding we get out for a ride.

He never had enough money, it seemed, to fix his own bike since he'd crashed it last summer. And now he was back to relying on my bike. I don't mind him chauffeuring me around, though, and he enjoyed the fresh air as we cruised around town.

On weekends, I often went to Geno's, a dark, disgusting basement bar that smelled like stale beer mixed with the urine odors escaping from the filthy restrooms. This was the one place in town where bands who couldn't get gigs anywhere else could play. Usually they were punk rock or other types of bands just starting out. Despite its smelly atmosphere, the dance floor was usually crowded with young beautiful girls.

The first time I snuck into Geno's, I was underage and sat by myself in the back. I didn't care much for the beer. I just wanted to check out the band. Looking through the smoky crowd, I saw the band on the stage, the freaky lead singer dressed all in black. With chains hanging from his boots, he was a wild man.

A few times after that night, I saw this same guy out walking the street, and one day I pointed him out to Mike. "That's the guy. I saw him singing for a really cool band at Geno's."

Mike wasted no time. He pulled the bike over to the sidewalk and began talking to him like he already knew him. "Yeah, I saw your band at Geno's. You guys were really great."

And he went on and on about some of the other bands that played there.

Suddenly, the freaky guy got all excited. "Well, if you like that band, there's gonna be a *really* cool band coming from San Francisco next week. They're into all that stuff Slam Dancing, Satan Worshipin'!! Totally hardcore! I can't wait. It's gonna be a great show."

I was sitting on the back of the bike, feeling tightness down my spine. I reached up and grabbed Mike on the shoulder, giving it a little squeeze. Sudden fear had overcome me.

Mike remained calm, finishing off the conversation. "Yeah, it sounds like a band worth checking out."

The freaky guy replied, "I gotta go now. I'll see you around."

Mike and I slowly rode away, gradually increasing our speed, both of us not saying another word for several blocks.

Finally, I leaned forward and repeated in Mike's ear, "Slam Dancing, Satan Worshipin'!!! Satan worshipin', Satan worshipin', SATAN WORSHIPIN', SATAN WORSHIPAAAAAAN!!!!"

Suddenly, Mike slowed down and pulled to the side of the road. He was breathing heavy and wiped his eyes. Then he let out a big "Whaoooooooh!!!! Man, that guy does a lot of drugs. That's what it is, a lot of drugs."

After Mike caught his breath, having accepted drugs as a legitimate explanation, we rode away slowly, heading back home.

Work was going very well for me at the start of the summer. I'd been working a lot of overtime and had become the company's best drywall sander. At least, that's what they were telling me. I was, in fact, the best they'd ever seen. So, in fact, I'd been declared the best at the worst job in the world.

But I didn't see it that way. I saw it as the next best thing to being a rock star. I could listen to rock 'n roll all day, work as many hours as I could stand, and the money just kept rolling in.

On the other hand, Mario Leal was one of the best finish tapers around, and he'd spent many months training my friend Packy until he became a great taper as well. Mario, a pretty easygoing guy, had a wife and kids who had recently relocated to Corpus Christi, Texas, and he gave me a lot work too, which I was able to do on the side.

While Mario had to stay and finish building a huge addition to his house so it could be sold, he offered to rent me a room in his half-framed house for just $25.00 a week and help with any projects on his house.

Finally, then, I was moving out of my parent's house. I now had the freedom I wanted and it wasn't costing me a whole lot of money for a place to sleep, shower, and eat.

Mike and I had been anxiously waiting for June 22. It was a Sunday evening, the night The Ramones would be playing at Hampton Beach Club Casino. We left around noontime, with Mike doing most of the driving down I-95 on an extremely hot afternoon. We found ourselves stuck in traffic, causing my bike to overheat. After taking several breaks to allow the engine to cool down, we finally made it to Hampton Beach where the cool ocean breeze helped keep us and the bike running cool.

Mike said to me, "I sure hope they don't ask for ID at this place because I didn't bring my wallet."

"What? Why didn't you bring your wallet?" I was thinking, *how could you be so stupid?*

"Vicki told me not to bring it. She was afraid if we got bumped around in the crowd, it might get stolen. I think I'll be alright. They probably won't ask for ID, anyway."

With Mike confident the ID issue wasn't going to be a problem, we continued to cruise up and down Ocean Boulevard, not giving the matter another thought until 7 o'clock.

When the doors opened and a mob of Ramones fans were pushing and shoving their way through the door, Mike and I were squeezing through the crowd wondering what was holding up the line. I looked up ahead and saw a man checking ID's.

My blood started to boil. I turned to Mike, furiously saying, "They're checking ID's!"

Now the line was moving quickly with a lot of pushing going on behind us. Mike reached the man holding a flashlight ready to check his ID.

I exploded. "HE BOUGHT HIS TICKET AND HE'S GET'N IN!!!"

Suddenly, before I finished demanding entrance, two big guys came out from behind the ID checker. I felt a hand on the back of my neck as they pushed us back down the stairs and out the door.

Now that we were both outside, we felt bummed out as we watched the line of fans grow smaller and smaller, each ID holder slowly passing through the checkpoint.

"How could you be so stupid, Mike?" I growled at him. "How are we gonna get in now? The show starts in half an hour."

We were both just hanging our heads, wondering what we were going to do.

Then suddenly, I thought to myself, *I don't have to miss this show, I have my ID.* "Mike you wait outside. You can use the bike while I go inside. I wanna see at least half the show. I've waited too long to miss out. I may never get the chance to see the Ramones again."

Mike looked up at me and said, "That guy won't let you through that door after what you did."

I pulled an extra T-shirt out of my backpack and changed my face to my nice boy image look. "See I look like a totally different person." Then I stepped in at the end of the line.

As I moved closer to the ID check, my pulse raced. The man gave me a dirty look of suspicion. But I politely showed him my ID, and he let me through.

The opening band Black Jack was just finishing their set when I entered the ballroom. The lights came back on as I walked around, amazed at just how fancy this place was. There were well-dressed waitresses, clean floors, and comfortable chairs with tablecloths. This was a far cry from the smelly basement walls at Geno's.

I walked to the T-shirt stand to buy one for myself, feeling bad for Mike for coming this far and not being allowed in. So, I bought a T-shirt for him too. I noticed the tension building up close to the stage. Fans were dressed in black leather and torn jeans, with wild hair.

Oh, how I wished I had the guts to fit in among them!

I sat by myself at a table near the back and ordered a beer. Suddenly, the lights got dim. A cloud of smoke covered the stage. Dee Dee shouted "1-2-3-4!" and I heard what sounded like a machine gun and a loud train passing through the silhouettes of the greatest sounding rock 'n roll band in the world. With Joey's voice sounding like a dog barking, the clearing smoke made way for the stage lights.

I was blown back in my seat as the crowd up front started getting out of control. I could see the club owner standing to the side, his face showing great regret he'd ever let these guys play at his club. The music was so loud and fast that it was almost hypnotic, with a driving force that was out of control.

I stood up on my seat, about ready to jump on the table.

The club owner looked at me. "SIT DOWN!!"

I quickly sat back down. I didn't want to get thrown out again.

The explosion of sound blasted out "Animal Boy" in just 45 seconds, then Psycho Therapy shot out even faster. Then the sound stopped for a few seconds. Joey's voice shouted out, "This next one's called, NOOO MOOOORE CRUMMYYYY STUFF!!!!" The sound exploded again—even louder and faster.

The show lasted a little over an hour, which I thought much too soon, considering it took Mike and me over two hours to get there.

Still feeling the excitement, I ran outside to meet Mike.

He was waiting on the bike. "I got you a T-shirt" I said, hoping to cheer him up a little. "You missed a great concert!! It was the loudest, fastest, most out-of-control show I've ever seen!! *We've* gotta start a band. We've just *gotta* start a band!"

I was still shouting from all the excitement as we cruised our way to find I-95 North. The evening air felt much colder for the ride home.

"Ok, you don't have to rub it in!" Mike shouted back at me while we continued cruising.

We definitely should have brought our jackets.

It was after 1:00 am when I got back to Mario's house. I thought that this was a good enough excuse not to go to work the next day.

But it wasn't.

Even though Mario and half his crew had taken the day off after going to a ZZ Top concert, The Ramones just didn't count as a legitimate concert to them.

Eric Ross had come back to Maine for the summer. He'd driven his little Datsun 210 all the way up from Florida, where he had been living with his mother for the past three years. Since his mother had remarried and moved to Florida, Eric had spent just a few weeks of his summers at his father's house. This summer, he was planning on staying up in Maine until the end of August.

At just eighteen years old, Eric still had his senior year of high school ahead of him and we wasted no time getting together. I told him all about the great bands I'd seen at Geno's. He told me about all the great night clubs he'd been going to with his fake ID. He'd sent away for a kit he read about in an ad on the back of a comic book. He told me how he'd pealed the plastic coating off his driver's license. Then he'd cut out the number of his date of birth and cut another number from his license, switching places. Using his laminating kit with a hot iron, he'd sealed his license back together. He never had trouble using it. He just showed his card and he was in.

I said, "That's great! We can go to Geno's this weekend. There's a great band playing there."

That Saturday night, Eric had no problem getting in when he flashed his ID and entered the front door at Geno's. Mike was already there, sitting at the table closest to the stage.

Bebe Buell and the Gargoyles were finishing up their set just as we arrived. We sat at the table with Mike and ordered a few beers, more people crowding towards the front.

Eric looked around. "What is this creepy place?"

I told him, "Just wait till The Gorehounds take the stage."

Eric chugged down his beer and ordered another while the band set up the stage.

The lights dimmed for a short session of poetry. The soft music and the voice grew louder, until…

…the music exploded. Eric chugged another beer down and smiled, watching all the girls dance.

Then, the pushing and shoving on the dance floor came close to our table, forcing us to move quickly. Eric and I ran to the next table, where we sat down and suddenly looked straight into the eyes of two beautiful girls.

They were a brunette, who seemed to take a liking for Eric, and a gorgeous redhead who immediately noticed the huge rip in my pants all the way up the side of my pant legs.

I said, "Oh, yeah," and ripped my pants all the way up on *both* sides. Now they were hanging by a thread around my waist.

"Did you need some attention?" she asked in her very seductive voice.

"I got yours, didn't I?"

She smiled and asked if Eric and I would like to dance with her and her friend.

"Sure!" I replied.

She grabbed my arm and led me to the dance floor.

This was my first time to dance in public. I was feeling quite awkward at first. But then, after finishing my beer, the redhead helped me loosen up. I was feeling great, a big smile on my face. She took my hands and brought them to her body and moved around real slow.

After we danced to a few more songs, we sat back down at our table. I'd made up my mind I wasn't gonna be shy anymore. I was in love with this redhead and I was gonna show those assholes how to treat a lady right.

"So, what's your name?" I asked her.

"Cheryl," she answered with her sexy voice.

"I'm Steve."

Suddenly, Mike was standing at our table and asking Cheryl to dance.

She said, "No, I'm dancing with Steve."

I jumped out of my seat and told Mike, "Get the HELL out of here!" I pushed him away.

That's the moment I knew Cheryl was crazy about me too, and nothing was going to come between us.

After the bar closed, Cheryl invited Eric and me to a party where we sat on the couch until she arrived.

"There you are," she said, climbing on my lap, running her fingers through my hair.

I was just smiling, and Eric smiled, watching.

We stayed for a while, but soon it was getting late. We had to go.

Eric kept saying, "Wow! She really likes you."

We were both smiling as I started up my bike.

After driving Eric home, I was feeling overwhelmed with joy, just thinking about that beautiful redhead Cheryl. Riding back to Mario's house, I was absolutely confident I'd finally found someone. This was my chance to show rest of the men in this world how to treat a lady right.

As the summer wore on, Mario had a lot of work to do on his house.

Having a great deal of extra space, it became a place for gathering after work. But soon another family was moving in. Larry Lane was a sheet-rocker who lived with his wife Sandy and their 3-year-old son in the Town of Bangor. Larry had been commuting the 140-mile trip for two weeks and he was looking for a closer place to stay. So, he'd worked out a deal with Mario to rent the upstairs and help with finishing a lot of projects on the house.

And there was Cecil. Cecil was a member of The Passamaquoddy Indian Tribe who appeared to be a good worker when they first hired him to work with me. We'd been working together for a few weeks when he told us how his roommate was kicking him out and he needed a place to stay. So, Mario let him stay on the back porch.

But then he had two more friends from his reservation, Chuck and Doug, also members of The Passamaquoddy Tribe. Mario gave them permission to pitch a tent in the woods behind the property. Soon they were hanging around the house and raiding the refrigerator while the rest of us were all working.

With a few other hired hands who stayed for a short time, as many as ten of us were living there. We all got along well at the beginning.

Larry had his Honda ATV 4-wheeler in the back yard while I was inside eating my dinner and watching MTV. Sandy came in shouting, "Hey, Smitty! Come on out here! Check out this jump we've set up!"

I quickly finished eating and looked out in the back yard. Larry was on the 4-wheeler racing toward the ramp set about two feet high. He went sailing through the air and landed safely as Mario, Cecil, Chuck and Doug all looked on, waiting their turn. After everybody made the jump safely, it was my turn.

I sat on that 4-wheeler and opened the throttle. I hit that ramp and flew four feet high, landing safely some twenty feet away. So, we all agreed to up the ramp a little higher, just a few inches—then even higher after we all made the next jump safely.

But after we'd moved it up again, and it was down to just Larry and me, even then we both jumped safely. Cecil looked and found a few more logs to shove under the ramp, raising it over five feet with a steep angle—almost 60 degrees.

"All right, let's see you make this jump!" Cecil was laughing while everybody was shaking their heads *no way*.

I sat on that 4-wheeler as far back on the runway as I dared, thinking about the courage of JJ and the courage Greg had. Most of all, though, I thought about the time Cheryl had called me a yellow belly because I got drunk after just one beer.

I opened up that throttle and hit that ramp at full speed, launching myself straight up fifteen feet in the air. When I came down, I landed on the front wheels, bouncing me back up and flipping me over. With my hand still holding the throttle, my leg caught under the rear wheel, twisting my body off the seat and under the tire.

Amazingly enough, I had but a few bruises and a tire burn on my leg. Somehow, I'd survived. "OK, now it's your turn!" I said, trying to hide the pain while I was limping around and looking at Larry.

Larry's jaw dropped. Knowing he was expected to do the same, Larry sat on that 4-wheeler staring down the runway and ignoring Sandy's plea. "Larry, don't do it!"

He took off down the runway, then hit the brakes—just before the ramp. He turned around to start again and stared down the runway. "Maybe if it wasn't so steep," he suggested.

So, Cecil and Mario found some more plywood and decreased the steepness.

Still, Larry stared down that runway…until he at last drove down the runway and slowly up the ramp—only to stop at the top.

He sat there looking over the edge, his jaw hanging open.

He stayed right there until the sun went down.

Finally, he gave up and came inside.

CHAPTER 14

The Road to Nowhere

"It's getting late, you guys! And we gotta get up early for work tomorrow!" I said, complaining from the back seat.

Eric and Cecil were sitting in the front seat.

"Yeah, we'll be ready to go soon." Cecil talked with so much confidence you'd think he believed it himself. "And we'll be ready for work tomorrow."

Suddenly, though, Eric was obviously feeling sick and stepped out of the car. His nose was running with eight inches of mucus mixed with white gunk.

Cecil yelled in a panic, "Don't waste it, snort it up!" If anything dropped to the ground, it would go to waste. He looked ready to scoop up what Eric was about to lose.

But Eric sniffed it all back up his nose. He held it in for a few seconds—till his face turned beat red. Then he puked.

"It's that hamburger you had at Geno's. I knew there was something wrong with it!" Cecil was clearly convinced that Eric's ingesting too much cocaine had nothing to do with it. "Here, take another line. It'll make you feel better."

"Come on, you guys!" I urged again. "It's almost three in the morning! We gotta be at work at seven!"

Another hour passed. The guys finally had enough and started heading home.

I looked for Cheryl every time I went to Geno's, hoping to sit and hold an intelligent conversation with her. I wanted to tell her how much I needed her to come with me, that we needed to get out of that place.

But again, she was not there when Eric, Cecil, and I came down to take in "Christ on Parade," one of the most radical bands we had ever seen. Eric and Cecil were so blown away, they had to keep running out to the car to snort another line in between sets.

I didn't know if they were blown away more by the music or by the cocaine. For me, it was the music.

I'd been slacking off a lot since I started working with Cecil. I'd had enough of his attitude. He talked his way out of everything. He somehow managed to show up in the morning, disappear all day, then show up at the end of the day so it looked like he'd been there all day.

And for a while he managed to fool our arch rival, Dirigo Drywall, into believing that he was showing up on their jobs sites as well. Somehow, he was receiving paychecks from both companies without accomplishing anything on either jobsite.

He'd show up at one jobsite and make some excuse to run an errand, only to go make a few cocaine deals then show up at the other jobsite just in time so a supervisor would see him there. He got away with it for several weeks until Dirigo caught on to what he was doing.

They fired him.

But he was still getting away with it at Wagner Drywall.

We finally arrived back at Mario's house just before 4:00 am. With just a few hours of sleep, we headed back to work. Cecil snorted another line before we started sanding.

I was feeling a bit tired after only two hours, but I'd worked under such conditions before and planned on working the full day.

Cecil, though, was feeling down. He'd used up his "supply" and couldn't deal with the reality of actually working. "Come on, let's go!" he said, pleading with me to take him back home.

I was beginning to feel even more tired with him dragging me down. Finally, I gave in, leaving all our tools behind. We hopped on my bike and rode away without a care in the world. I had well over $10,000 in the bank and felt no reason to keep working all the time.

But suddenly, after leaving the jobsite, I didn't feel so tired anymore.

So, we just rode around wasting the day away.

When we arrived back at Mario's house later that afternoon, Mario came storming in the house. "How come you guys left without finishing the job?" Wagner had been back charged for not meeting the deadline, he told us.

At that moment I felt guilty. I was failing at the only thing I'd ever been successful at. It was time to make some changes in my life.

By the end of September, Eric had returned back home to Florida to finish his senior year of high school. Evenings had been getting colder, and Mario's house had gotten more crowded. Cecil, Chuck, and Doug were now sleeping on the living room floor—against Mario's wishes.

Larry's family had taken over the entire second floor and I had to move to a small space on the first floor, where I slept on a thin mattress surrounded by piles of broken plaster and insulation. I kept a few clothes and a metal box which I hid my money in. I wanted to keep my life simple. Everything I needed to survive was here in this little space.

I sold my motorcycle to Chuck for just $200. Even though it was worth much more than that, I wanted to get rid of it. I was tired of the responsibility of owning a vehicle and giving everybody rides.

But then I did buy my very first guitar, for $350. It was a 1956 Les Paul in mint condition. Determined to learn how to play, I paid up front for three months of lessons. But with all the chaos at Mario's house, I only managed to make it to a few lessons.

However, I did learn the opening cords to "God Save the Queen."

My diet consisted mostly of peanut butter sandwiches and beer. Understandably, then, my health deteriorated. I was losing weight and breaking out with acne all over my back. But I continued to believe I still had a chance to win the love of my beautiful redhead girl Cheryl.

Meanwhile, stress and tension were growing among all the members of the household. Cecil blamed Doug for all the money, drugs, and food he'd been stealing. Mario finally had had enough of it all and wanted everyone, except me, out of his house.

When Cecil came to tell me that he'd gotten us a place to stay, I was pretty sure he was expecting me to help pay the rent. So, he became extremely upset when he found out Mario wasn't kicking me out.

Chuck and Doug found a room to rent upstairs from Chappy's bar, just down the street from Mario's house. It offered shared bathrooms.

Cecil, without me to help pay rent, decided to sleep in his car out in the parking lot of Chappy's, because he didn't want to pay any rent.

I continued my friendship with Doug, despite the tension he'd caused. Soon, though, I felt hatred for Cecil, who always dressed nice, wore cologne, and kept himself clean. With his charm, the girls always seemed to like him.

Chuck and Doug didn't bathe so often. They took whatever girls they could get. On the good side, Doug would often stick up for me, and maybe that's why I stayed friends with him in the many years to come, even though he stole from me. He admitted to it and tried to pay it back.

The Red Sox had finally made it to the World Series. This was after many mediocre seasons following 1978—which featured the greatest team in Red Sox history, only to be spoiled by a Bucky Dent home run.

I had just about given up and hardly watched a single game all season. Finally, here they were in game 6, just one strike away from winning their first World Series since 1918. I was holding Mario's portable TV set on my lap while he drove through New York City on our way to Corpus Christi, Texas. I'd started taking great interest in my Red Sox again, when suddenly they gave up a hit, then another hit, a wild pitch, and a slow grounder through the legs of Bill Buckner.

At that very moment, I was truly convinced they'd lost that game because I'd taken great interest again.

I shouldn't have watched game 7, either.

After taking turns driving all night, we saw the sun rising to the east. We'd reached warmer weather in Tennessee. We pulled the truck over to remove the glass sunroof and enjoy the feeling of summer again. With the warm wind blowing through the cab, I was loving it, thinking how great life could be without ever worrying about another cold winter.

As far as I was concerned, Portland, Maine, was the worst place in the world to live.

I didn't mind, then, that Mario wanted me to move down to Texas with him and help him start up his own drywall business, though he had me in mind to continue doing his dirty work.

We continued driving late into the night. Somewhere in Louisiana, we had to stop and get some sleep. I slept well on the tin mattress in the back of the pickup. Mario slept in the cab. We woke at sunrise to continue our journey through Houston down to Corpus Christi.

It was late in the afternoon, with the temperatures up around eighty-five degrees, when we finally arrived. Looking around, we saw all the beautiful green lawns and the one level 3-bedroom, 2-car garage homes that all looked the same.

"I love it here," I said. This was the kind of laid back, worry-free place I wanted to live in. And I'd made up my mind. All I needed to do was convince my beautiful redhead girl to move down here with me. She was the only thing in the world I really cared about now.

We spent the first few days at the beach. I was hoping the warm sunshine and salty water would help clear my skin. Just getting away from all the chaos and being able to relax was what I really needed.

After a few afternoons on the beach, Mario took me around to look at a few houses for sale. I could easily meet a down payment for just about any house in this neighborhood that had an average price just under $40,000.

I was giving it some serious thought. But the one thing on my mind was whether I could convince my redhead girl to come with me.

The following weekend, I rode with Mario's family up to San Antonio for a wedding. I met the rest of Mario's extended family, including two female cousins from Mexico. They both took great interest in me and took turns dancing with me during the reception. Although they couldn't speak English, they had an uncle encouraging me to consider what a great wife either could be. They were both very pretty and I probably should have taken his advice.

After returning back to Corpus Christi, Mario took me to a motorcycle dealership. He was hoping I'd buy a bike to keep in his garage—so as to guarantee I'd return back to Texas with him once he sold his house in Portland.

The salesman talked me into test driving the Interceptor 500. It felt so good to be on a bike again. And with that warm Texas weather, I couldn't resist. I pulled the cash out of my pocket and the bike was mine.

With just a few days left in the warm Texas weather, I couldn't stand the thought of being over 2000 miles away and having left my new bike behind. Mario was a little surprised, laughing, when his relatives were saying in Spanish, "He's got guts." I'd told them I was gonna ride my new bike all the way back to Maine.

It was still quite warm in Texas early on the morning that I hit the road, following close behind Mario's truck. We made one last stop at Walmart before leaving the state because I needed to buy a helmet before crossing the state line. I found one that didn't fit too well, but it was the cheapest I could find.

After getting back on the road for several hours, my helmet's tightness on my forehead and pressure on my nose was taking its toll on my achy body. We rode late into the night, taking short breaks along the way. With Mario driving by himself, he was getting tired as well.

When we pulled into a rest area just outside Little Rock, Arkansas, he suggested we stop for the night. I felt relieved that he suggested it first. I didn't want him to know just how truly tired I was.

That night I slept in the back of his pickup while he slept upfront in the cab again. I was in so much pain from my arms and shoulders and my stiffening back, I was beginning to doubt I could make it all the way to Portland. This was the longest trip I'd ever taken and the pain I was experiencing was beyond anything I could have expected. I'd been praying most of the way that I could make this entire trip.

If God helped me make this entire trip, I would know He was with me.

Before going to sleep that night, I continued my prayer that I would make this entire trip back to Portland. And if I could make the trip alive, I also wanted Cheryl. "God," I prayed, "please help me convince Cheryl I truly love her."

This was my prayer. This was what kept me going.

After getting a good night's rest, I was feeling very confident that I could make the rest of the journey. We set out early, enjoying much cooler weather and cloudy skies. I continued to pray and had no doubt God was with me through the increasing pain.

The weather continued to get colder. After riding a few hours, I was beginning to have blurry vision and trouble keeping up with Mario in his truck. When we were several miles outside of Nashville, the pain got so enduring I just kept praying, believing that if I could make it all the way to Portland God would answer my prayer.

But I was beginning to hallucinate and doze off. I kept praying and convincing myself I could do it. I kept myself alert for a few more miles, wondering how much more I could take with so many miles to go.

Then a sudden idea hit me. If I saw a U-Haul Center somewhere off the highway, I'd take it as a sign from God to rent a trailer and tow it the rest of the way.

That very instant, I looked up. And there it was—a U-Haul sign high in the horizon straight ahead.

I opened up the throttle, riding up to Mario's truck and pointing to the next exit. The part of me that felt like a quitter was overtaken by the cold and pain and fear I might pass out and crash.

After hitching the rented trailer to Mario's truck, we loaded on the bike. I fell asleep in the back of the truck and slept all the way to Virginia.

When we finally arrived back in Portland, the weather was extremely cold even for early November. What kind of fool had I been, thinking I could have ridden all the way from Texas in this freezing weather?

I was lucky-blessed that I saw that U-Haul sign when I did.

I spent the next few weeks riding around Portland in freezing temperatures and praying for a sign from God. Should I move down to Texas? Or should I waste any more of my life here in Portland? I knew I wanted to leave Portland. I hated it here. But my thoughts were on Cheryl, my little redhead girl. If I couldn't take her with me, I wasn't going. She was all I had been thinking about for the past six months.

Tension was soon building up between me and all my friends. My metal box I'd kept in my little space had been stolen. And Mike was upsetting me because he kept telling me I was wasting my time with *that* redhead girl.

"You don't understand," I argued with him. "I know she loves me by the way she rubs her fingers through my hair and talks to me I can just feel it she truly loves me."

"She does that to every guy she meets. I know the type!" he shouted back.

Not anymore. I'd made up my mind I would be her one and only. And

I didn't need to listen to any further negative advice from Mike.

Doug was the only friend I trusted during that time, even though he wasn't very trustworthy. He was all I had.

It was the last weekend in November, and Doug and I were down at Geno's, drinking a few beers and listening to the band Baton Sleeze. When Cheryl came down to sit at our table, I tried once again to start up an intelligent conversation with her. I wanted to tell her how I felt about her and how we could buy a beautiful house down in Texas.

Either she didn't feel like paying much attention, though, or the music was too loud. She just finished her beer, grabbed my hand, and took me out on the dance floor.

Another night on the dance floor, with her rubbing up against me.

But my thoughts were, *This is it. She loves me. I just know she loves me by the way her eyes glow every time we see each other, and by the way she rubs her body all over mine. She even takes my hands puts them on her tits while we dance a slow dance. She smiles with lovestruck joy every time she sees me. There is no doubt in my mind. She loves me.*

After the band finished, freaky guy jumped on the stage and shouted through the microphone. "Party at the Gorehouse tonight!!"

I knew I had to get up early for work the next morning, but I didn't want to miss this party. Doug and I followed the crowd up the stairs to the apartment. I knew Cheryl would be there, and I was hoping to find a quiet corner to talk with her.

But she was such social butterfly, she pretty much ignored me.

Doug walked around looking for anyone who might be passing a joint around. Meanwhile, I just stared around at all the people, feeling strange and out of place.

Suddenly, Cheryl came up behind me and said, "Steven are you okay?"

I slowly answered, "No. I'm not feeling well." Sharp pain was running through my chest. I felt that my whole body was ready to collapse on the floor.

Cheryl offered to give me a ride home.

I was feeling so out of place that I truly needed to find Doug and give him the keys to my bike so that Cheryl could take me home.

Cheryl helped me to the car. She asked if I wanted her to take me to the hospital.

I answered her slowly, staring out the window while she drove up Forest Ave. "No, I just want to go home."

The pain was still stabbing through my chest.

"I'm worried about you, Steven. I really care about you."

She'd actually made it sound like she really did care.

But then she went on to tell me why she never wanted to get married and never wanted to be tied down.

So, I never even got the chance to ask her to come go with me to Texas. She'd already known what I wanted, and she'd only played me along.

At that moment, I finally realized, *I'm just a joke to every girl who has ever touched me. They all were just playing me, making a fool of me. I wanna die tonight.*

When Cheryl stopped in front of Mario's house, I slowly got out of her car and mumbled a sad, "Thank you."

She asked if I needed any help.

I said, "No, I'll be alright." But I knew damn well I was not going to be all right.

I went inside the dark house. No one else was home.

I got undressed without turning on the light, trying to think of a way to kill myself.

I laid down on my little mattress and tried to make myself cry. But I couldn't.

Then the thought came to me—just as I was about to pray. *That's what my problem is, trying to be a Christian. That's what gets in the way every time I try to move my life forward. Why didn't I think of this a long time ago? I have to stop believing in God. From now on, I'm just gonna have a good time and let nothing get in my way.*

Then I lay down to sleep, still feeling that sharp pain going through my chest. I fell into a deep darkness, with a feeling of horror upon me and hearing sounds of babies crying.

I stared out into the far distance at a very bright light, so bright it was almost blinding. Yet it did not light up any of the darkness around it. I felt the horror of loneliness and rejection beyond anything I'd ever felt in my entire life. And it was all in a constant space in time where time didn't exist.

In fact, I couldn't tell whether a million years passed or just a few seconds. But the time was certainly not something of earth.

Suddenly, I felt my inner soul pleading. I wanted to come back. I opened my eyes with morning sun shining through the windows and the sound of the phone ringing. I staggered to the phone, not sure if my soul was completely back in my body, and barely heard my own voice saying, "Hello."

"Smitty! Smitty! This is John Campbell!" the voice on the other end kept repeating before I realized I was alive. "How come you didn't come in to work today?"

"Oh, I couldn't get a ride. I lent my bike to a friend." I said still trying to pull myself together.

"I'll come get ya! I got a small job you can help me with." After John hung up, I started getting dressed and ate some breakfast while trying to figure out what had happened last night. I'd either died and gone to hell and then come back, or I'd sold my soul to the devil.

Or maybe it was just a bad dream.

Whatever it was, I was still going to keep my vow to myself. *I don't believe in God anymore.*

All that day I worked with John, feeling like something had been ripped out of my chest.

CHAPTER 15

Highway to Hell

Mario was disappointed when I decided not to go back to Texas with him. I'd made my choice based on the high unemployment in Texas and the offer of $9.00 an hour to stay in Maine. My savings had dropped below $7,000, and I was afraid it would all be gone if I moved down to Texas without a job.

So, I rented myself a tiny one-bedroom apartment with a small space heater. The rate was fairly cheap at just $75.00 a week.

But there were problems.

Because the rest of the building was unoccupied, my living space was extremely cold during the night. I had to drag my mattress from the bed to the living room floor next to the heater to stay warm. And I was bored out of my mind every time I came home to the place. I had no TV and no one came to visit. It was too cold to go outside, and I was always freezing, just staring at the ceiling. I spent the entire weekend huddled next to the heater merely listening to my little clock radio barely loud enough to hear unless it was up close to my ear.

I became lazy and depressed. Dirty dishes piled up in the sink. I hadn't shoveled the driveway during the last snow storm, so my car was towed by the city for leaving it on the street. I didn't care. I didn't want it anymore. I'd only paid $100 for the piece of junk and it wasn't worth the $100 towing fee to get it back.

This was how I had to live in order to save up money this winter. At the same time, though, I wasted money faster than I could earn it.

Mario finally sold his house in mid-January. After he'd worked on it late into the night during the final two weeks of construction, his house was beautiful when finished, with new carpeting and fresh paint.

Why couldn't we have fixed it up much sooner so we could have lived in it when it was like this?

The new owners, of course, were very happy when they arrived and saw their beautiful new home all cleaned up.

So, we'd finally finished up all the work we should have been doing sooner while staying there in that big house. Larry and his family moved back up to Bangor. I don't think he'd ever given it a thought that the free ride would soon be over. All that time, he'd been partying his money away. Falling behind in his own house payment—on a house he had only paid $16,000 for, with monthly payments just a little over $200.00 a month. Larry was one of the best drywall hangers I had ever seen, working piecework all last summer he was taking home over $1500 every week. How he ever fell behind on his bills, I later found out was due to heavy cocaine use and all the hookers he snuck in the house whenever his wife was out.

I would later hear stories of Larry beating his wife—something I never knew was happening during the time we all lived together. I'd spent too much time working, and the rest of my time invested down at Geno's, to know anything about it. I'd only been at the house to eat, shower, and sleep.

So now, here I was lying alone and freezing cold, bored out of my mind.

Suddenly, the phone rang.

It was my very first phone call since I'd moved here two weeks ago, and it was Larry asking if he could stay here a few nights a week to save him time and gas on his two hour commute each way. I'd been so bored and lonely that I was willing to let *anyone* stay there just to have someone to talk to.

I said to him, "Okay. That's cool."

So that following Monday after work, Larry stopped by, bringing his own little mattress. The place was a mess, with just one chair to sit in.

"There's not much to eat." I was hoping Larry would pitch in and pay for a few groceries.

Instead, he ate what little food I had. Then he sat up half the night complaining about everything. He was angry at Mario and blaming everybody else for everything that was going wrong at work. After working 60 to 70 hours a week for the past six months, we were now just barely getting 40 hours a week. I'd been so depressed myself, listening to Larry only made me feel I wasn't so alone.

"If only we weren't so far behind on our bills," he said, "we could go out to California and work for my brother-in-law." Larry went on with a desperate hope in his voice. "Yeah, that sounds like a great idea—if we could be guaranteed a job when we get there."

I answered back, with a little encouragement in my voice.

Then Larry went on with all the stories of his younger years when he'd hitch-hiked all the way to California on three different occasions before he was even 21. His brother-in-law had taught him the drywall trade and now owned a business in Orange County, California. He had plenty of work out there.

The more Larry talked about California, the more exciting the idea sounded to me. "Let's just do it. We won't tell anyone where we're going. We can load my bike in the back of your truck." Suddenly, I didn't feel so depressed. Our idea escalated in my mind.

"But what about my house? It's ready to be foreclosed on!" Larry was plainly feeling desperate and pleading for a solution. "And what about my wife and son?"

He was so far behind on his bills that the banks were ready to take everything.

Still, the excitement of moving to California was overtaking me. We stayed up late complaining how bad it was living there in that dumpy apartment.

"That's it! Let's just do it!" I said. "I'll loan you the money to get caught up on your house payments. Then, at the end of the week, we'll load everything in the back of your truck and just go. As soon as we get settled, your wife and son can move out there as well."

The idea sounded better and better. I'd be helping Larry save his house and credit. And I'd be getting out of Maine.

Larry called his wife the next morning to tell her the good news. He also learned the figure of his total debt. All he needed was $1500 to be all caught up on all his family's bills.

"That's it, then," I said. "I can take out $3000 from my savings, plus we each can use our final paycheck from Wagner Drywall to pay for the gas and food along the way. That should be plenty enough to find a place to live when we get there. Then you can pay me back $100 a week once we start working out there."

This was going to work out great for everyone, we both agreed.

Larry headed back home to Bangor the next morning, while I stayed isolated in my apartment for the rest of the week. I was so anxious to go, I packed up the few things I was taking with me, which were already stacked near the door. Larry returned that Thursday night. We'd be ready to leave early Friday morning.

After barely getting any sleep that final night in my apartment, we loaded a few boxes onto Larry's truck. Then we drove to Wagner Drywall's office, collecting our final paychecks before making one last stop at my parent's house to load my motorcycle in the back of the truck.

I wrote my parents just a short note. *Moved to California.* I left it on the kitchen table with a few hundred dollars I owed my father for work he'd done on the car I'd left behind.

Then we were off to cash our checks and withdraw money from my savings. I handed $3,000 cash over to Larry and thought nothing more of it. I was just glad to be getting out of that depressing situation I was in.

It was another freezing cold day that last week of January, anyway.

That made it all the more easy on my conscience, to be leaving everything behind.

When we finally started down the highway, it seemed the first hour took the longest before finally we were out of the state of Maine. The excitement grew with every great song on the radio.

"Woo-hooooh!!!! We've made it out of Maine. There's no turning back now!" we said together.

Larry drove all through the night, bringing us all the way into Pennsylvania by late in the evening. Then we headed west all through the night—with Larry still doing all the driving. I was mostly concerned with only tuning the radio to keep finding a good station in every town we passed through.

Larry continued driving into the morning without stopping to rest. As we approached Indianapolis during rush hour, I thought of the opening theme song to the TV show "One Day at A Time." I began singing the song as we passed the Indianapolis highway exit, *This is it. This is life, the one you get, go have a ball.* I was trying to catch a familiar feeling to a familiar place I'd never been to before, only seeing it on TV.

As we exited from I-70 onto I-44, we hadn't even begun to open up and do much talking to each other. The only talking we'd done up till now was argue about what songs we wanted to hear on the radio. Every time Bon Jovi's "Living on a Prayer" came over the airwaves, he insisted on turning it up, knowing I couldn't stand that band.

Larry liked him, though, because the lyrics reflected his own relationship with his wife Sandy. He went on to say how he and Sandy had stayed together through extremely difficult times during their seven years of marriage. Even though he'd cheated on her many times, he still believed he and Sandy had something special in their marriage that other couples didn't have.

"When we get there," he said, "I'm going to start being more responsible. I'm gonna stop cheating on her. I'm gonna quit smoking weed and other drugs." Then he looked at me and added, "You should set some goals for yourself too."

"I do have goals," I replied. "I want to start eating a little healthier. You know, give up red meat. Make some better friends. Maybe get a better job than just drywall."

Larry lost it. "Give up red meat! That's the stupidest thing I ever heard! You gotta eat meat or you'll *never* be healthy."

Things got quiet again. I just gazed out the window, thinking about the first time I'd met Larry. It had been just a few months ago, during the summer. He'd been working with his nephew hanging sheetrock and I thought of him as just another redneck with a bushy beard and long blonde hair. He spoke with what I thought was a southern accent. But later I'd learn he came from the Town of Millinocket, a small town in northern Maine. That accent I was hearing was just one of those Hillbilly voices you might find in some of those northern towns. I never thought the time would come when this guy would be the only friend I would have left in the world. I never thought of him as smart, but he was one hell of a hard worker and I'd spent many months late into the night working behind him and Mario. Mario even said he was the best he'd ever seen. So, I did have a great deal of respect for him before planning this trip.

Larry continued on doing all the driving without taking any rest all the way through Oklahoma. We caught Interstate 40 coming into Oklahoma City and I finally found a good radio station after many miles of nothing but country western. A classic rock station was playing "Shooting Star" by Bad Company, a song that set me dreaming as I gazed out the window, watching the downtown city lights disappear in the side view mirror.

Larry had been quiet for the past several miles, his eyes staring straight ahead into the darkness on the never-ending road. His jaw hung open with a sense of worry on his face.

"Are you all right, Larry?" I asked. "If you need me to drive for a while, just say so."

"Nah, I'm okay," he insisted and kept on driving, staring into the highway lines and reflectors flicking by us, surrounded by darkness.

It was becoming hypnotic for me just to stare out from the passenger side. How Larry kept going, I didn't know.

After finally reaching Amarillo, Texas, he decided to stop. Renting a room to us at nearly 5:00 am, the motel manager gave us a deal of $16.00 for just a few hours of sleep, as long as we checked out by 10:00 am.

The room only had one full-sized bed. I looked at Larry and said, "We ain't sleeping in the same bed."

"No," Larry said, dragging the mattress to the floor. "Which one you want, the mattress on the floor or the box spring up higher off the floor?"

Without hesitation I answered, "I'll take the mattress."

"But don't you want to be up off the floor?" Larry sounded disappointed in my choice.

How stupid did he think I was? Would I actually choose a hard box spring over a mattress on the floor?

I slept well for those few hours, while Larry laid on that hard box spring.

We both took quick showers before we hit the road again. Larry continued doing all the driving. I sat gazing out the window, seeing the desert for the first time, feeling a whole new world around me that was so very strange. I wanted to jump out of the truck and explore every small town we passed through. I saw a softball game being played off in the distance and thought, *Wow, it's the last week of January and it's warm enough to play softball.*

Larry stopped at a McDonald's just outside of Albuquerque, hoping that he could get me to eat some red meat.

I ordered a chicken sandwich instead. I said, "One day, I'm gonna give up all the white meat as well, once I learn how to eat all vegetarian."

"What?" Larry was clearly starting to get upset at this point. He told me he would make sure that every place we stopped to eat had nothing but meat on the menu.

Every time we stopped for gas, though, I managed to find a microwavable bean and cheese burrito.

All was quiet again while Larry continued driving after the bright sun set beyond the horizon. I cranked up the radio, listening to Bob Seger's "Hollywood Nights" and feeling the reality of the Hollywood night life that I would soon be experiencing. I looked over at Larry. He had a worried look on his face again.

I turned down the radio after the song was over. "What's wrong, Larry? I thought you liked Bob Seger."

"I do. It's just, I want to hurry up and get off this road."

"What's the matter? Aren't we on the right road?" I was thinking maybe he made a wrong turn or something.

"Route 666. I don't know about you, but it sure scares me!" Larry's eyes stare straight ahead into the darkness. "It seems like it just goes on forever."

"I like this road," I said, showing no fear of the Route 666 sign we just passed.

"Well, aren't you scared?"

"No, it's just a road. I ain't scared of any of that mark of the beast stuff or hell fire."

"*That* doesn't scare you?" Larry asked, raising his voice. "GOING TO HELL? DOESN'T THAT SCARE YOU?!"

I calmly answered back, still gazing out the window. "No, it doesn't scare me at all."

"WHAT? YOU'RE NOT SCARED? HOW COME YOU'RE NOT SCARED!!!!??? IF ANYBODY SHOULD BE SCARED," he said, getting even louder, "IT SHOULD BE YOU!!! THE STUFF THAT YOU DO, HOW CAN YOU NOT BE SCARED!!??"

"I don't know. I just ain't. I just don't worry about it, that's all."

"AH, MAN! I THOUGHT YOU WOULD UNDERSTAND!!!"

In a few moments, Larry started to settle down, apparently feeling a little relieved. He said, "Well, I guess if you're not scared, I shouldn't be scared either."

Then he turned and looked at me. "But I would be scared if I was you."

"Nah," I said, still gazing out the window. "The reason I ain't scared is because I already know I'm going there."

"WHAT?!!" Now, Larry was starting to really freak out.

"Yeah, I had a dream that told me I was going there—and it wasn't that bad."

"AND YOU'RE NOT SCARED?!! I WOULD BE PETRIFIED IF THAT EVER HAPPENED TO ME!! YOU'RE NOT EVEN SCARED A LITTLE? I DON'T BELIEVE THIS! HOW CAN YOU BE SO CALM ABOUT IT?"

"I just told you. It ain't that bad. It might even be better than heaven."

Showing no remorse with my words, I remained calm and confident.

"WHAT? HOW CAN HELL BE BETTER THAN HEAVEN?"

"It just is. I just know it is," I replied.

"AH, NO! THIS TIME, I THINK YOU ARE WRONG! YOU ARE SO WRONG! IF YOU ONLY KNEW JUST HOW WRONG I THINK YOU ARE!! YOU ARE WRONG-WRONG-WRONG!!!"

"How do you know I'm wrong? I'm the one who had the dream and I know I'm right."

"I WISH I COULD BE SO CALM AS YOU ARE RIGHT NOW. I SURE HOPE YOU'RE RIGHT!"

"I know I'm right."

"BUT I DON'T THINK YOU ARE!!!"

Again, Larry calm down a bit, but went on arguing. "I wish you were right. But I don't think you are!"

"I know I'm right." I kept saying it with so much confidence, Larry just couldn't win the argument.

He continued driving, staring ahead into the darkness with a stunned looked on his face.

I added to his fear. "Just think! If this truck crashed right now, both of us would be going to hell for sure.

"Eck!!!" Larry couldn't argue anymore. He kept on driving, his jaw hanging open with many miles of darkness ahead of us.

It was getting late into the night. We were halfway through Arizona, and Larry had done all the driving up to this point. He pulled over to the side of the road to take a rest, with a little over 300 miles to go.

He decided to let me drive for a while, so he could rest.

But he couldn't get much rest, it appeared, sitting up in the passenger's seat and worrying about all the things we argued about.

I drove for about ten miles. But soon my eyes couldn't stay focused on the road, staring into darkness and seeing nothing but the reflectors from the roadside flicking by. I couldn't go any further, so I pulled over to the side of the road—Interstate Highway 40 in the middle of the desert.

Too tired to go any further and with not enough space to sleep, Larry got out and pulled a folding mattress from the back of his truck. Laying it down on the cold ground, he went to sleep.

I had stretched out and taken a little nap in the cab of the truck, coming back awake after only two hours. Larry awoke too and felt a sudden burst of energy. Ready to go, he jumped back in the truck and drove non-stop, our excitement growing after we'd crossed the California State Line.

Soon we could see the lights up ahead of us spread out along the hills and valleys. We were getting closer, and Larry was getting even more excited.

I only stared out the window, amazed at how many millions of homes were all around us for hundreds of miles in any direction. I thought of all the opportunity out there.

We finally arrived at a beautiful house in a beautiful neighborhood in Diamond Bar, California, and Larry's brother-in-law woke up to welcome us at 5:30 am when he saw headlights through his bedroom window.

He quickly came out to show us a place on the living room floor where we could spread out for another hour of sleep, which was just about long enough for us to fall into a deep sleep…

Suddenly, we were awakened by the song "Walk of Life" by Dire Straits. It was only Larry's brother-in-law showing off his stereo system.

I'd had all the sleep I needed, though, and I was looking forward to getting out and exploring California. Stepping outside into the beautiful warm sunny weather on the last day of January, I just knew I was going to love it here. I couldn't wait to ride my bike and never have to worry about cold weather again.

Looking round about me, I saw all the beautiful houses, so close together and with cactus plants and rocks along each tiny front lawn. The backyards were so steep that you had to look straight up about fifty feet to see the neighbor's house. These yards were far different from the beautiful green lawns with lots of open space I had been familiar with when growing up in Maine. I realized I should have been more grateful for what I'd had back then.

Larry's sister and brother-in-law showed us great hospitality, taking us out for Sunday brunch and paying for our breakfast. But as soon as we looked at the menu, Larry started getting on my case.

"Why don't you order some bacon or sausage to go with that omelet?"

Then he added, "Don't be so fuck'n fussy!"

I was suddenly feeling very out of place, sitting quietly at the table, like I was just Larry's tagalong.

CHAPTER 16

Learning Not to Smile

When Larry asked his brother-in-law if he had a paying position available for Larry in his business, he never mentioned that I was coming with him and needed a job too.

Nor had Larry made any plans for where we might stay. So, after enjoying our Sunday brunch, Larry and I set out looking for a place to rent. After seeing a few dumpy roadside motels and passing some No Vacancy signs, we finally found and settled for a very clean, full-sized one-bedroom apartment in Fullerton for only $200 a week. It was part of a huge complex that had many families moving in and out at every hour of day and night.

Larry paid two weeks' rent for us, using the money I had loaned him.

After unloading the truck, Larry took me out for a ride to show me all the places he remembered. After he had left here seven years ago, many things had changed. But Larry still knew his way around. The traffic was heavy, no matter which direction we were going, but I didn't mind. I was feeling great riding along with the windows down.

After taking our first little tour of the neighborhood, we stopped at the grocery store to stock up on food for the week. With Larry still holding the largest portion of my money, he made sure he bought a lot of red meat and junk food.

I didn't complain about anything, though. I was excited about being away from Maine and was looking forward to all the new opportunities, places to explore, and the freedom to ride my bike all year long.

The very first thing I did on the Monday morning after breakfast was set out looking for a job. Unfortunately, I didn't have much luck in my search. I hadn't brought proper clothing for most of my interviews. Jeans and tee-shirts were all I had ever needed in drywall, so they were all I ever wore.

The following day I tried a temp agency, hoping to have better luck. But most of their jobs were office jobs and required proper dress too. They did, though, keep my name on file in case an industrial or warehouse job listing came in.

Actually, I wasn't in the least bit worried about finding a job soon. I knew that, with the money Larry already owed to me and the money in my wallet, I could make it a few months before I needed to find a job.

I decided to take a cruise up to Hollywood to check out the scene. The traffic on the freeway, however, was beyond anything I could have prepared for— with traffic moving nearly bumper to bumper, and sometimes at speeds up to 85 mph with six lanes of highway in each direction. At times, all the traffic slowed down to less than 20 mph, moving in only short distances before speeding up again.

I felt very small surrounded by all those cars and trucks.

And it took over an hour and a half of stop-and-go traffic for me to reach Hollywood, all that time having to keep extremely alert following close behind fast moving vehicles changing lanes and having to constantly watch out for what was coming up behind me.

When I finally arrived safely, I took a walk down Hollywood Boulevard wearing my black engineer boots and a Ramones tee-shirt. I instantly felt a welcome atmosphere, and a man approached me with a camera to ask if he could take my picture. He even asked my name and phone number. He said he was looking for the right face to make a Ryder Truck commercial.

I told him I didn't know the phone number to the motel where I was staying, and he was clearly disappointed. But he said he'd keep my photo on file before I walked away.

I thought of it as another blown opportunity.

I walked further along, feeling a close connection to the streets and sidewalks. It felt like home. The sidewalks were crowded with more than just tourists. Homeless men, women, run away teens, even pregnant women and families lined the storefronts asking for help—but being ignored.

Why doesn't God do something? was all I could think. *There must not be a God. If there were, he'd do something.*

I swore right then that someday I would be rich, and I would do something about the situation. Every person in the world would have a home and enough food to eat.

I spent a good part of the day walking around and enjoying the energy of the place and the warm southern weather. I walked into a barbershop where I let a gay man cut my hair. I came out with a beautiful spiked hairdo. (But that was the last time I ever let a man cut my hair.)

I did walk around showing off my new look, passing a dollar to every homeless person who approached me.

Then I headed back to Fullerton.

The same heavy traffic and crazy driving I'd faced before on my way to Hollywood faced me on my way back to Fullerton. Plus, I got lost trying to find my way back to the motel. It was early evening by the time I walked in the door—only to find the kitchen a mess.

I started to clean the kitchen counter off before cooking up something to eat. Suddenly, the bedroom door swung open and Larry was standing there naked, smiling and saying, "You want anything, she's all paid for."

A naked girl was lying on the bed, waiting for a double take.

I just said, "No thanks." I couldn't stand the thought of paying someone for sex and, even worse, the thought of Larry's leftovers.

Larry looked at me in a puzzled way, clearly surprised I was showing no interest in the girl. He turned around and ran back in the room for a second round.

I popped a couple of frozen burritos in the microwave then laid down on the couch, trying to fall asleep while those two were running back and forth from the bathroom to the bedroom. I heard her say, "Hey, Smitty! Are you sure you don't want to come join us?"

"Nah, I just don't feel like it."

I really didn't want to hurt her feelings, but I thought she was ugly.

The following morning, I woke up early to continue my search for employment. I left the apartment before Larry even knew I was gone. I spent hours riding around trying to find every job agency I could and filling out applications for any position available.

Losing my way through the densely populated county, it took several hours before I found my way back to the motel.

Once again, the kitchen was a mess. A jar of mayonnaise was left uncovered, meat slices were left unwrapped, and an open container of milk was left on the filthy counter. After cleaning up the filthy mess and throwing out all the spoiled food, I laid down on the couch. Feeling tired and depressed, I laid there watching TV.

When Larry came home, he started yelling at me. He accused me of being lazy and very negative. "Why don't you do something with your life instead of just lying there?"

Larry was just too stupid to argue with, so I sat quietly staring at the TV while he went about complaining. I never mentioned the number of times he'd borrowed my motorcycle without even asking. Nor did I mention the fact that he'd used my money to pay the rent for this place.

The next morning, Larry was in a better mood. He had a few days off before the start of the next big construction project he was to work on. He suggested we spend the day at Disneyland.

"But what if I get a call for a job?" I replied.

"You're never gonna get anything lying on the couch." Larry went on to insist we get out for a while.

I decided anything was better than lying there feeling depressed and waiting for the phone to ring.

So, we were off to Disneyland for the day, wasting another twenty dollars each to enjoy waiting in line for every kiddy ride Disneyland had to offer.

It was late afternoon when we returned to find a note on the front door from the motel manager. The note said there was a phone call for me, and they'd left their number. I ran down to the phone booth to make the call. It was a warehouse job.

But in the end it was given to someone else—because I hadn't returned the call in time.

What a bummer. If only I'd have laid on the couch all day instead of going to Disneyland.

The next few days I spent riding my motorcycle around, feeling discouraged and wanting to ride out to the beach. But I stayed close to the motel because I was too afraid of missing another phone call.

Meanwhile, tension was already growing between Larry and me after only a week had passed. It didn't get any better when a man came by our door inviting us to a Bible study. I argued with the man for a while. I told him I used to believe in all that stuff. But now I just wanted to live long enough to have a good time.

"Then, I'm just gonna go to hell when it's all over," I added.

He pleaded with me to come and listen.

Larry stood watching.

I turned and said, "Okay, I'll go. But only if Larry goes."

"What? I don't want to go!" Freaking out, Larry started up again our old argument he couldn't win. He shouted, "I DON'T SEE HOW YOU FIGURE HELL'S BETTER!!"

Then he stormed out the door.

Soon, Larry decided that he needed to move in with his sister and brother-in-law. He wanted to save money so his wife and son would be able to fly out soon.

He told me this on the very last day before the rent was due.

I said, "That's fine. Just help me move my stuff with the truck, and I'll find a place in Hollywood."

The next morning, we loaded a bag of clothes, my electric guitar, a few boxes of records, some tapes, and my boom box. We tied them all down under a mattress in the back of Larry's truck.

I followed close behind on my motorcycle while Larry led the way. Heading down the freeway was crazy, as I tried to stay close enough behind while Larry constantly changed lanes and cars came in between us, slowing down and increasing the distance between us. I had to swerve and zigzag through the traffic to keep the necessary close distance.

Then, just as I caught up behind him, I noticed my mattress coming loose in the back of the truck. I swerved to the right and watched the mattress fly up out of the truck high above my head. It landed just to the left of me.

The massive traffic only kept moving, and I took a quick glance in the mirror to see the mattress catch the bumper of the car behind me. Traffic briefly slowed down behind us, but nobody stopped for anything on the Hollywood Freeway. The gap behind us filled in quickly with cars changing lanes.

I stayed very close behind Larry for the rest of the way. I spotted a dumpy looking motel near the corner of Sunset and Highland. It looked like it might be fairly cheap. I pointed in that direction, indicating to Larry to turn into the parking lot.

With Larry waiting outside in the parking lot, I walked into the office. The place had a slight odor. But I figured that if the place was cheap, I could tolerate it. The Manager said he had two rooms available with a weekly rate of $140. It was probably the cheapest rate available, and I didn't want to ride around searching for something better.

I took the room with the least odor, and Larry helped me carry my belongings up to the room. He noticed the slight smell of the place too. But I think he was just happy to be getting rid of me so quickly.

And I was just as glad to get away from him for a while.

After he left, I took a walk down Hollywood Boulevard to check out all the cheapest places to eat. My motel had no kitchen, so I would have to eat out every day until I could find a better place with its own kitchen.

Handing a dollar to every beggar who approached me on the sidewalk, I reminded myself I didn't even have a job yet. One beggar, though, told me that there were lots of jobs here in Hollywood.

That's great, I thought. But why didn't *he* have one?

On my way back to the motel, I turned the corner and four beautiful girls appeared in front of me. "Hi," I said with a smile, hoping to strike up a good conversation.

"Our car just ran out of gas," said the blonde who was leading the pack and holding out her hand. "Can you help us out with a few bucks?"

I handed her two dollars. They all smiled and said, *Thank You.*

I turned and watched them walk away. *Wow!* I thought to myself, hoping to meet more beautiful girls like those four again soon.

But little did I know, that would be the only time a beautiful girl ever talked to me in Hollywood.

The very next morning, I set out early in my job search. To my surprise, I didn't have to look very far. After finding a little café in which to enjoy breakfast, I stepped outside and there they were—recruiters standing at nearly every street corner and passing out business cards as they shouted, "Jobs here! We have jobs here!"

This is great, I thought. *There are so many jobs available, they're sending recruiters out into the streets. I should have no trouble finding one.*

But I couldn't figure out why all the homeless people were sleeping outside on the sidewalks. If there were so many jobs available, why weren't they jumping at the opportunity?

I wasted no time, reaching out to shake hands with a finely dressed gentleman who gave me his card. He gave me directions to a building and suite number on Sunset Boulevard. I walked with a skip in my step, for about eight or nine blocks, all excited about my potential new job. I found the right building, took the elevator to the 3rd floor, easily found the suite number, and walked in to a large office where a receptionist was there to greet me.

"Hi," I said, "I'm here looking for a job."

"Oh, yes, we have many jobs available here. Come right this way."

I followed the receptionist to a desk in the back where I was introduced to Jose. He was a very polite, neatly dressed man who seemed to offer great promise in every word he spoke. After giving me a few papers to fill out, he gave me directions to another location about eight miles away. I felt great excitement again as I left his office, and I hurried back to the motel parking lot to start up my bike.

But it took over an hour of searching for streets to find every correct turn in the heavy downtown Los Angeles traffic. And all the while, I was wondering what kind of job I'd be applying for. Jose had sent me, plainly feeling confident that I could do the job, but I still didn't know what the job was to be.

After finding the place at last, I went inside to fill out papers for what I thought was another job application. Then I took an exam with multiple choice questions. I didn't understand a single question on the exam and thought I had failed for sure. But then when my interviewer told me I did well on the test, I thought maybe I'd made a few lucky guesses.

He told me to return the following Monday to start classes. That's when I realized I had just enrolled in school to become a telecommunications network installations man, or something like that. If it involved some type of work installing telephones, I had absolutely no interest in the school training program nor in a career of installing phone lines.

I was a bit confused after all that riding around looking for what I thought was a job interview only to find out I'd just enrolled in school. The next morning, I rushed back over to see Jose again. "I thought I was going there for a job interview. I had no idea I was supposed to enroll in school."

Jose just sat at his desk listening to my confusion. Then he gave me another address to an office suite in downtown Los Angeles. I found my way there and met Kathy Jarvis, the owner of K.J. Enterprise. She was a middle-aged woman who sat behind a desk. She never could say my name right. She was always calling me Stefan. But she seemed to always be glad to see me every time I needed to walk into her office. She'd always say, "You should be a model, you have such a handsome smile!"

I would always simply sit and smile, while she'd feed me all her positive attitude speeches.

Still, I hardly heard half of what she was saying to me. The batteries had died in my hearing aid. She never knew I was half deaf. I just sat smiling while her lips moved.

And she sent me to a few other places, searching all over the city and filling out papers every place I went.

Later, I finally found out I was only signing up for financial aid. I had no idea what I was getting myself into.

Although each time I actually thought I was filling out job applications, I finally decided K.J. Enterprise was wasting my time.

I had no intentions of going to school and I wanted a paying job soon.

So, I tried every restaurant in Hollywood, asking if they needed a dishwasher. Still no luck.

Walking the boulevard by myself every afternoon, then, after having spent most of the morning searching for work, was becoming quite monotonous. In just a few days, I'd become just another familiar face in the Hollywood crowd.

Seeing the same people passing by, every hour I walked up the right side of the street, crossed over, then walked down the left side of the street, only to turn around and walk back up again. I could look through the record stores whenever I wanted, but I found myself only looking and wishing for a job.

I met all kinds of strange people in just that first week, and I learned quickly not to smile anymore. In one incident, I was walking along and minding my own business when a man came charging at me and looked straight up into my face, demanding. "WHERE CAN I EARN SOME MONEY? TELL ME WHERE CAN I EARN SOME MONEY!!"

He was a short guy, only a little over five feet tall and probably in his late twenties. But he looked a lot older with his rotting teeth and scruffy beard. I tried to ignore him and kept right on walking. But he insisted, talking up into my face. "YOU! WHERE CAN I EARN SOME MONEY?!"

I just shook my head and said, "I aint got any money."

"NO, I *SAID*, 'WHERE CAN I *EARN* SOME MONEY?!'" His voice became even more demanding as I tried to walk around him. "YOU TELL ME WHERE! WHERE I CAN EARN SOME MONEY!!"

There was real desperation in his voice.

But I just looked down at him and said, "I don't know. Get a job."

His voice grew even more full of angry tone as he shouted in my face. "NO! YOU DON'T UNDERSTAND, I SELL MY DICK, I SELL MY DICK, WHERE CAN I SELL MY DICK?"

"What? I don't know, man." I pointed randomly to another guy passing by. "Why don't you go ask that guy over there?"

He quickly charged over to the guy passing by and demanded the same.

I continued walking up the sidewalk but soon saw the weird guy again—in the back of a police car.

Walking the boulevard alone everyday left me an easy target, but not for the muggers. I knew how to defend myself against them. No, it was the seemingly friendly people I'd meet while out walking in the crowd that gave me trouble.

For instance, a young man walking with enthusiasm up ahead of me pretended like he was lost. He turned around and asked, "Hey, can you tell me if this is the right way to the beach?"

"Yeah," I replied. "This is the right way. But it's about 10 miles from here. You'll be walking a long time."

Having started up the conversation in a friendly way, he suggested we stop to buy a few beers and go up to his apartment to listen to records. I was just hoping this guy could be a new friend, someone to hang out with, someone to listen to records and drink a few beers with. I hoped maybe he'd introduce me to some of the girls in this area.

But the fellow didn't seem interested in any of that. Instead, he showed me where he lived, in a large rundown building with many tiny apartments. The rent, he told me, was fairly cheap, under $400 per month.

I asked him who his landlord was and if he had anymore apartments like this one.

He said, "Sure. I'll introduce you to him."

But first he had us sit in the tiny space between his stereo and his bed. A stack of records over four feet long leaned against the wall. He was flipping through his records, showing off some really weird bands. I, though, was admiring the tiny 2-burner stove and tiny refrigerator with a space of only about two feet for

110

standing or walking to the bathroom where the toilet was so close to the wall you had to step over it to get to the shower.

This was perfect. I wanted an apartment like this, with everything I would need to survive in this tiny space.

While I was checking out his apartment, I realized my new friend was checking me out. He put on one of his favorite albums from Sigue Sigue Sputnick. Then he sat closer to me on the floor. He seemed to take a lot of interest in the little bleach spots on my jeans.

Suddenly, he moved his face a little closer. "That's really cool. I like that little design on there," he said, moving his face even closer.

"Let's put another record on," I said, quickly trying to distract him.

Suddenly his hand moved up to my crotch.

I quickly pulled away. "Hey! Cut it out, man!" I jumped to my feet.

He looked up at me and mumbled, "So you don't fool around, huh?"

"No, I don't do stuff like that."

And before I had a chance to say anything else, he shouted, "THEN GET OUT! GET THE HELL OUT!!!"

I left that place in a hurry.

From then on, I tried not to smile anymore.

CHAPTER 17

A Man and His Dogs

It was a Saturday afternoon. I had one more day left on my first week's rent at that sleazy motel. I had applied for jobs every place within walking distance. But the job I truly wanted was to be the lead singer of a punk rock band. I'd seen signs on every post on every corner…

Lead singer wanted. No experience necessary.

I thought about giving it a try but chickened out. I didn't think I'd be good enough without some close friends to encourage me.

Many other posters were for movie extras. I wondered if I might give it a try. I thought it probably didn't take much talent to be an actor. I knew if I had the chance at the right part in the right movie, I could make it big.

So, I answered a few ads and met with a few agents. The first question they asked me was, "Would you be interested in doing pornography?"

I answered *No* and didn't get any parts. A few others took my name and the number to the motel where I was staying. But no one seemed to be interested in anyone who wasn't willing to take their clothes off first.

I was about to give up hope, sitting on a sidewalk bench with my head hanging down. I felt cold and depressed, with damp weather moving in.

Suddenly, I heard a voice. "Sir, are you looking for a job?"

"Yeah, I've been looking for a job," I replied, with a bit of excitement in my voice. I turned and saw a man with a patch over one eye. He sat down next to me and told me about the motel just up the street on Highland Ave. The place had caught fire a few months previously and he was looking for a young laborer to clean up the scattered pieces of burnt material. I'd be able to live with him in the manager's unit, which had a full-size kitchen. And he'd be paying me an hourly wage depending on how hard I worked.

"Oh, I'm willing to work real hard. And I'll need a place to stay."

Suddenly, I was feeling a whole lot better.

We walked up the street a few blocks so he could show me the place.

It was just like he said, a roadside motel with most of the units burnt up and piles of burnt wood and furniture scattered about. This was great. This was just the type of work I'd been looking for, and I wouldn't have to drive far to get to it. I wouldn't have to pay rent anymore. I could start saving money again.

He wasted no time hiring me. He seemed to like my attitude and willingness to take on the dirty work. We took a ride in his van back to the motel where I was staying to load up my belongings. Then I followed him on my bike to my new live-in employment home.

He asked me if I liked dogs.

I said that of course I liked dogs.

As his small white curly-haired dog came out to greet us, he said, "You can pat *him*, but you can't pat *them*." He was referring to the two pit bulls standing guard nearby.

I continued to pat his little white dog, knowing that as long as those pit bulls saw that I was friendly, I'd have nothing to worry about.

And it looked like everything was going to work out for me.

After we unloaded the van, the patch-eyed man took me out to eat. We each had very large portions while we sat and talked at an all-you-can-eat buffet.

He said he liked to be called Patch. He'd lost his eye at the age of fifteen playing with a BB gun. He was now in his mid 50's, and he had worked in the past as a radio DJ and therefore knew a lot of folks in Hollywood.

After we finished eating, he showed me around, introducing me to several different people. We met up with the leader of a biker group who bragged about being the most used biker gang for movies. He showed off their flyer "Rent a Gang," with a picture of all his biker friends posing with their Harley's. He poked his finger in my chest, giving me a stern welcome warning. *As long as I didn't screw anyone over, I'd be OK with them.*

I couldn't tell whether he was threatening or protecting me.

Patch would later tell me not to worry. The biker leader was a nice guy—as long as you stayed on his good side.

We walked back to the motel where his three dogs were waiting.

The pit bulls showed a lot of excitement when he came through the door, and I respected his warnings to keep my distance from them. He had them trained to protect him. When he stayed at that motel alone, those dogs were all he had.

Patch and I stayed up late into the night, sipping on hot bowls of soup and watching TV. Patch talked about his days on the radio and the people he'd interviewed on the air. We talked about the music we liked and I showed him my guitar, which I still hadn't learned to play yet. He said he knew many musicians in the area, and he was willing to help me in any way he could.

It really did seem like everything was going to work out here.

I couldn't wait to start work in the morning. I wanted Patch to know I was willing to work hard as long as I was here. But there was still one thing we hadn't talked about yet, and it was getting late, a little after midnight.

We were both sitting up straight on the one full-sized bed in the room. I was beginning to feel tired and I was wondering where he expected me to sleep.

He stripped down to his underwear and slid under the covers.

He said goodnight, turning off the TV. It was almost pitch black in the room, and his two pit bulls were on the floor near his side of the bed. His little white dog was at the foot of the bed.

Meanwhile, I was still sitting up straight and wearing my sweatpants. I was ready to fall asleep, but Patch hadn't yet mentioned where he expected me to sleep. So, I just laid on top of the covers, keeping my sweatpants on and using the blanket I'd brought with me. I stayed as close to the edge of the bed as I could.

Trying to get some sleep, I felt anxious to start work the next day. I stared into the darkness. But I was even more worried about what this guy was expecting me to do here.

Patch started snoring really loud, which fortunately I could tolerate. Hours passed, and I continued to stare into the darkness, unable to sleep.

Then suddenly, Patch rolled over and flopped his arm over the top of me. My whole body stiffened up. *What can I do?* I asked myself. *This guy's on top of me.*

I slowly started to slip out from under his arm, planning to take a few pillows from the bed and spread them out on the floor.

"What are you doing?" Patch asked. He'd woken up sounding all confused and upset that I had slipped out from under him.

"I can't sleep with you lying on top of me." I was trying to find a comfortable spot, feeling around the floor in almost total darkness.

"Well, you can't sleep on the floor!" Patch demanded in his still half- asleep tone. "The dogs have got to be able to get to the door quickly if someone tries to break in here!"

I answered, "I can move out of the way quickly if anything happens."

His voice got a little louder. "No, you can't sleep on the floor!"

"I can't sleep next to anyone," I answered back.

Patch's voice sounded a little angrier. "No, if that's the way you wanna be, then there's no reason for you to be here!"

"I'm only here for the job, sir, and nothing else. I didn't come here to make trouble." I could sense those two pit bulls knew there was some tension between the two of us. "I'll have my things out of here first thing in the morning, sir."

After our little dispute had toned down, Patch fell back asleep.

I found a place to lay on the floor and stared into the darkness for rest of the night.

When the morning sun peeked through the shades, I could hear one of Patch's dogs licking something. I just laid there on the floor, afraid to move and still staring upward in the dimly lit room. I was afraid Patch might know that I was awake, and afraid he might be aware that I suspected he was allowing one of his pit bulls to lick him. I didn't move. I didn't say a thing. Until Patch got out of bed and walked naked to the bathroom.

I got myself dressed while Patch was still in the bathroom. He came out while I was gathering my bags together. He seemed to be on friendlier terms with me after he came out and finished getting dressed. He told me if I still wanted to do the work for him, I could rent one of the other units and clean up the debris from the fire.

But I said, "No thanks. I've decided to go to school."

So, as it turned out, there were no hard feelings between us. Patch even helped me load my bags back into his van.

I found another motel, a much cleaner place that cost a little more. I was counting on Larry to pay me some money soon.

After I called him to tell him where I was staying, he came out to see me that same afternoon. But he didn't have any money for me. Instead, he came over with a few beers and we rode around Beverly Hills in his truck then took a ride up to Santa Monica Beach. On the way, I told Larry I'd almost had a job but then the weirdo wanted me to sleep in the same bed with him.

Larry snapped back and said, "You gotta be careful who you talk to. There's a lot of weirdo's around here."

I got out of the truck and walked along the beach. It was quiet and cold in the middle of February. I could imagine this beach covered with beautiful girls during the summer.

When we were riding back to the motel, I reminded Larry about the money he owed me. He promised payment by the next week.

I went back to KJ Enterprise that following Monday morning. Kathy was happy to see me and glad I decided to enroll in school. She helped me find a paying job working the loading docks for a trucking company making $5.00 per hour. The job consisted of a lot of heavy lifting, operating a fork lift, and sorting out packages to be loaded onto trailers. My work hours were all arranged so I could leave early to attend classes.

I started school with a positive attitude. I was planning to keep up with the rest of the class. But given my work schedule and the traveling through the heavy downtown traffic, I became very exhausted in just a few days. Trying to force myself to be interested in becoming a Telecommunications Technician wasn't as easy as I thought it would be. I began to fall behind the rest of the class in just the first week. Our class instructor informed us the school had a 90% dropout rate, but I was determined to prove that I was no quitter.

Larry came to see me again the following weekend, and I reminded him once again about the money he owed me. "I just paid for one more week's rent," I said. "I have barely enough money to eat this week and I'll need gas to get to work. I won't see my first paycheck until the end of next week."

Larry snapped, "I can't believe how stupid you are! Why don't you have a bank account?!!"

"Because you haven't paid me the money you owe me to start a bank account."

"Why do I have to do everything for you?" Larry asked, freaking out. Then he got back in his truck and sped away.

That would be the last time Larry would see me.

I tried to call him a few days later when I was almost totally out of money. But his sister answered the phone. She insisted he didn't live there anymore. I would later find out that his brother-in-law had kicked him—along with his wife and son—out of their home.

When Larry did come down to try to see me, he was hoping to borrow more money. He'd been broke when I'd asked him earlier for my money, and that's why he'd freaked out.

It had been a long, stressful week. I had my first paycheck in my pocket but couldn't cash it because the bank was closed on Saturday. I'd barely had enough to eat all week.

A very heavy middle-aged man wearing overalls and a big smile on his face stood next to me on a street corner. He asked me how I was doing.

I said, "Well, I haven't had much to eat today."

His smile got a little wider as he seemed to think up an opportunity to ask me about. "So, ah, do you hustle at all?"

"No, thanks. I'll be all right."

"Well, let me know if you change your mind!" His smile got wider.

I walked away, trying not to stay in one place too long.

I saw Patch walking along with a group of his friends. He nodded his head, like a friendly hello.

I just gave a half-smile and a partial wave as we passed by. I kept walking till I became so tired and hungry I had to sit down. I watched people passing by, people eating and laughing while I sat there and starved. That's when a thought hit me.

Ever since I'd stopped believing in God, it had seemed like my whole life had gone to hell. Maybe this was it. Maybe I was in hell. I couldn't stand it anymore. I wanted to go where there was fire. I preferred a place where there was real fire and brimstone.

As I sat there feeling depressed for a while, a young man with long hair and baggy clothes sat down next to me. He asked me if I was hungry and pulled a sandwich out of his backpack.

I said, "Thank you."

Then he offered to pray with me.

I said, "This sandwich isn't going to feed me tomorrow."

He went on to lecture me about faith and how God was providing for me today and would provide for me tomorrow as well.

I said, "Thank you for the sandwich." But what I would have liked to say to him was, *I'd like to go out and earn my own money instead of sitting on a bench waiting for a handout.* I'd been so hungry I'd eaten that whole sandwich before I realized it was a ham sandwich.

There went my plans to be a vegetarian.

Later that evening, I was wandering the sidewalk picking up pieces of a torn up one-dollar bill. I collected most of the pieces but not enough.

That's when an older gentleman asked me what I was looking for.

I said, "I'm trying to find the rest of the pieces to this dollar."

He reached in his pocket for a dollar and handed it to me. He asked me where I was from, and from there we started up a good conversation.

Since I had nothing to do, was bored, and hadn't held an intelligent conversation with anyone in a long time, I took up the man's offer when he invited me up to his apartment. He lived in a very nice clean building for senior citizens. His apartment was about seven or eight floors up. With a view from the window, we could see the Hollywood lights and heavy traffic down below. Off in the distance, the downtown LA skyline and city lights stretched out as far as we could see.

The fellow said his name was Flash Riley. He told me that he was a retired actor who had had a few guest appearances on shows such as "Good Times" and "Sanford and Son." He seemed like a nice enough guy, probably just a lonely old man needing someone to talk to. He started telling me his life story while he heated up a couple cans of soup.

I told him I thought anybody could be an actor.

Flash argued back, saying you have to go to school, and it took years of training to be an actor.

I said, "No, anybody can do it if they're given the right part." Then I did my Robert De Niro Taxi Driver impersonation.

The guy looked at me and said, "Hey, you do that pretty good. Do you want to be an actor?"

"Like I said, anybody can do it, if given the right part."

He said, "No, I think you do that pretty good. I could set you up with an agent if you want."

"Yeah, that would be cool if you could do that for me."

While sipping our soup, we watched a Billy Joel and Ray Charles video on VH-1. We talked about the music we liked, and he said that Ray Charles was one of his favorites.

After we finished our soup, he showed me his profile folder and gave me a lot of information about show business and how it worked. He said,

"You need to find a good agent."

He also gave me his phone number and told me to call him.

I had already intended to call him as soon as I figured out where I was going to be living in the next few days.

It was getting late. We sat up watching TV, and I was beginning to doze off on his couch. Flash began to softly comb his fingers through my hair. I heard him say in a sad tone, "Oh, Stephen," still combing his fingers through my hair. He noted aloud how skinny I was and the scars on my back, which I'd been trying to keep covered.

I quickly got up off the couch and said I should be going. He didn't believe me, that I had a place to stay. But I told him I still had one night left at the motel where I was staying.

He asked if I would come back to see him again, his look kind of sad.

I left his apartment and never thought about returning again.

When the rent was due, I tried desperately to find out where Larry was. But his sister said she didn't know.

I stayed in my motel room until late in the afternoon, when I heard a knock on the door. With the motel manager standing at my door, I pleaded with him that I would have the money soon.

It didn't work. I had no money to pay and by three o'clock that Sunday afternoon I was out on the street. But the motel manager allowed me to store my guitar and other belongings in an empty storage unit.

I tied a blanket, a pillow, and a change of clothes to the back of my bike. I rode off the property and parked in front of a nearby church. I didn't have much gas and couldn't ride very far. I left my bike and just started walking. It was getting cold and I was feeling hungry.

With no money, I walked into a Denny's Restaurant, sat down, and ordered a meal. Feeling like this could be my *last* meal, I ordered a second helping and ate it slowly, enjoying every bite. I sat as long as I could, keeping calm, knowing I had no money to pay for the meal. I just ate.

Finally, I got up to use the restroom then made my getaway.

I just slowly walked out the door, and as soon as I turned the corner, I ran a few blocks, turning another corner. The restaurant was out of sight.

I felt extremely guilty and vowed to myself that one day I would return and pay for that meal.

But I never did.

I walked back to the church where my bike was parked. I decided to sit in the back pew of the church and listen to a long boring sermon. I was willing to do anything just to have a warm place to sit, hoping the sermon would go on a little longer because otherwise I was back to wandering the lonely streets when the sermon was over.

Soon, I was walking up and down the Boulevard again. A few times, I returned to the church after the lights were out.

Finally, I spread out my blanket and pillow behind the bushes near the front door, feeling very safe, lying where nobody could see me.

CHAPTER 18

The Oasis

As soon as the sun rose on Monday morning I was up and out of the bushes. I walked around, anticipating the time before the bank opened.

Finally, after cashing my check, I was able to eat a good breakfast, fill up my gas tank, and ride downtown to KJ Enterprise. I met Kathy in her office and told her about my homeless situation.

She was very helpful and told me not to worry, she'd helped many of her clients find housing. KJ Enterprise, she added, had a good reputation of finding homeless people, enrolling them in school, and helping them find housing. She made a few phone calls, and within a few minutes I was on my way to the Hollywood YMCA for temporary housing.

When I arrived, I learned I had to sign in at the front desk by a certain time every day. And it didn't take long to get all set up for their program, which also provided me two free meals a day. They gave me a tiny room with a black-and-white TV and a small bed—all I needed to survive until I could find permanent housing.

Later, I walked back to the motel I had just been evicted from the day before. The manager was very nice, and he allowed me to take back my belongings. It took several trips, but I managed to carry my guitar, a few bags of clothes, some dirty laundry, and some boxes of other belongings up to my room.

And now it was late in the afternoon. I was exhausted from moving everything up the stairs, and I just wanted to eat one of my two free meals of the day. What they gave me was a hamburger for dinner, with eggs and bacon to come for breakfast.

I didn't complain. That was all I had available to eat. But I always got negative looks when signing in for my daily meal, which gave me a feeling of shame I couldn't ignore.

But the worst part about staying there was having to take a shower down the hall. The showers were open and shared by all the other occupants. So, I usually waited till the whole area was empty before taking my shower, because I also felt ashamed when anyone did notice the acne scars on my back and how skinny I was.

Most of all, though, I feared the presence of any homosexual that might be in the shower area. I always wore my swimming shorts and showered as quickly as I could to avoid any risk of being seen.

One night, however, I came home late and needed to clean up before going to bed. Two guys were already in there showering. I waited a long time, but they didn't come out. So, I kept my shorts on and kept my business to myself while I stood under my hot shower trying to clean myself up as quickly as I could.

One of the fellows reached over and shoved me on the shoulder. "Hey, you're that guy on that special housing program," he said.

"Yeah," I answered, hanging my head as I tried to rinse myself off and get out of there.

Both fellows gave me threatening looks as I dried myself off.

I was out of there in no time.

When I'd stayed at the motel, I'd always had a safe place to park my bike in the motel parking lot. Unfortunately, the YMCA didn't have any parking lot at all and finding parking on that side of the street wasn't easy, even for a motorcycle.

Still, I continued to ride my bike, exhausting myself every day for the first week, getting up early for work and then going to school in the evening. That Friday morning, I expected to receive another paycheck. But when I looked outside my window to where I knew I'd parked my bike the night before, it was gone.

I ran down the stairs and out to the street. I looked up and down the road, but my motorcycle was really gone. I started to panic. I had no way of getting to work.

I ran to the police station, but there wasn't much they could do. They just had me fill out papers.

Then I called KJ Enterprise, and they had me take the bus in to their office. I sat around for half the day. They finally offered me a bus schedule with about five different transfers each way. It looked so complicated I only took the bus back to the YMCA.

I had almost no money left and no way of getting to work. Plus, I had only one week left on my temporary housing. I was back to walking up and down the boulevard with my head hanging low, trying to think up a better plan.

I walked past a happy-faced Jesus-loving freak passing out invitations to come join his group for Worship and Praise. They even offered free food to all who attended. I'd walked by this guy many times over the past few weeks, laughing each time I'd passed by.

"Ha-ha-ha! I stopped believing in God when I stopped believing in Santa Claus!!" I shouted at him and kept right on walking.

But this time, I was feeling hopelessly lonely.

And the free food at last made me willing to check the Jesus offer out.

The Oasis looked like a small night club on Cherokee Ave. with a neon sign over the front door. When I walked in, there was a crowd of about forty people, most of them homeless and hoping to get a free meal. A Christian rock band was setting up on the stage.

I saw a table to the side, loaded with trays of thinly sliced sandwiches and burritos. I grabbed a few burritos and sat in the back. The band started to play, and the people lifted their hands in praise. I continued eating my burritos, enjoying the music, while more people continued to come through the door.

A young woman sat down at my table and began to show great kindness to me. She laid her hands on me and said a prayer. Meanwhile, the band played just a few songs before a young Hispanic pastor in his mid-30's and full of energy took the stage.

I sat and listened to him for a while. He wasn't some prosperity speaker, filling us all with false hope. In fact, this guy was really telling it like it was, the world was a terrible place and it was only going to get worse. He went on to talk about AIDS and other diseases. Then he spoke about earthquakes and other natural disasters. He went on to say, "And the Bible says it's only gonna get worse."

After our heads had been filled with fear, the band came back up on stage to play some softer music. The young pastor carried on in a long dragged-out prayer, pleading for all to come forward. In much the same way that I remembered had happened in the Nazarene Church, the people came forward, weeping at the altar. But I stayed seated to avoid all the attention.

The Oasis did, though, become a regular hang-out for me. It was open every day of the week, offering help to the homeless and needy families. Besides receiving the free food, I felt I was in a safer place than out walking the sidewalks.

On Sunday morning, a larger crowd gathered in the Hollywood High School gymnasium. I sat in the back observing as an older woman walked through the crowd and layed her hands on people who stood in a long line. The woman called out, "The Holy Spirit is telling me that there's somebody here with stomach ulcer!"

A man came forward and she laid her hand on his forehead. He collapsed to the floor.

Then she called out, "The Holy Spirit is telling me somebody here has just been diagnosed with cancer!"

Another person came forward, and she laid her hand on their forehead. They collapsed to the floor too.

The woman continued to call out a word from The Holy Spirit—for those with many diseases, family crises, aches, and pains—reaching out her hand to touch them on their forehead. Every person she touched collapsed to the floor. Another group of people walked around with white towels, spreading them over all the bodies lying on the floor.

I myself had a tremendous pain in my left ear, which I could barely hear through. I couldn't wear my hearing aid, it hurt so bad. I was afraid I was going totally deaf on my left side. Well, a young black kid—he might have been about 18 or 19 years old—came in and sat next to me. By the way he was dressed, I assumed he was into rap music. He looked at me and pointed to the front like he was encouraging me to go forward.

But I stayed in my seat.

Then I heard the woman cry out, "Someone has a terrible pain in their left ear!" I didn't move.

She looked through the crowd and repeated the very same words again. "Someone here has a tremendous pain in their left ear!"

Then, as she walked a little closer to me, she went on to say, "Someone in here has a demon spirit in them!"

The kid beside me seemed to already know me. He kept saying, "You wanna go forward."

His encouragement and the pain in my ear got to me. I began to walk toward the woman.

As I drew close, she reached out her hand and said, "You. You have a terrible pain in your ear. Come, come to me."

Suddenly, a crowd circled around me, with two guys standing behind me, waiting to catch me.

She laid her hand on my forehead. I felt a little push and a wave of peace and kindness come upon me.

But I did not collapse.

She laid her hand on me again.

But I remained standing.

She tried a third time, only to leave me still standing. So, she moved on down the line and resumed touching other people's foreheads.

All of them collapsed at just one touch.

When I left that place, I wasn't sure why all those people had collapsed on the floor or who the kid was who had encouraged me to go forward.

But suddenly, I noticed that the terrible pain in my ear was gone.

I couldn't remember when the pain had stopped. I just noticed that—sometime after I left that place—my ear didn't hurt anymore.

Every morning after eating my free breakfast at the YMCA, I walked down to the police station. I hoped each time to hear news about my bike, only to leave feeling disappointed.

I went back to walking up and down the boulevard with my head hanging low.

A man approached me and asked if I was okay.

I said, "Yeah, I'm okay."

He offered to buy me lunch.

I said, "Okay."

We went in a restaurant and he ordered up two meals.

I ate up fast, sensing he wanted a little something in return. So, I made some excuse to go to the restroom.

Quickly, I was out the door. But…

I did what I had to do to get a decent meal while out wandering those streets.

The Oasis always seemed like the safest place to go after they'd opened their doors late in the afternoon. Many of the homeless went there seeking help or just to sit around the tables and talk. I sensed that most of them wouldn't take a job if it was offered to them. Many were just attention seekers who cried at the altar after every sermon, asking God to help them even though they'd never do anything to help themselves.

I often felt out of place because I was not there for any of those reasons. I enjoyed going there to escape the freaks and the weirdos who seemed to target me, no matter what.

One evening at midweek, around 9:00 PM the Oasis was getting ready to close after a time of music and praise. This was when many of the homeless usually took their time exiting the door. Since it was pouring rain outside, many were still hanging out under the awning just outside the door.

I still had my room at the YMCA, but I was hoping for the rain to lighten up a little before I made a run for it.

That's when I met a taller gentleman holding a Bible.

He held a big, beautiful King James Bible with shiny gold-edged pages. He looked like a real Bible scholar, and he said he was going out for a late-night brunch and to lead a Bible study.

I was welcomed to come along, and I was willing to do anything just to get a little extra food in me.

So, we made a quick run through the rain to get to his car, a little Ford Festiva, and his head nearly touched the roof. His long legs could barely fit without his knees hitting the steering wheel every time he let out the clutch.

I sat quietly on the passenger side, looking forward to arriving at wherever he planned to take me to eat and hoping to meet other people at the promised late-night Bible study.

As soon as he put the car in gear, he made a rude joke about how skinny I was. Taking me by the wrist, he said, "My, you're skinny."

Then, with a little chuckle and a grin, he added, "My dick is bigger than that."

I pulled my arm away, looking out into the pouring rain, wondering why a true Christian would make such rude joke like that.

Then the man started to talk about Adam and Eve, putting his hand on my knee. He kept talking when I pulled his hand off my knee. He said, "You see Adam and Eve didn't know they were naked until they were sinners." He put his hand back on my knee.

"What?!" I quickly shouted back at him, confused, as I knocked his hand off.

"It's easy to understand," he continued to explain. "You notice, as I start down *here* it's okay." He placed his hand down near the top of my boot then slid it up my leg past my knee.

Suddenly, I punched his arm off my leg, wondering what this guy was talking about.

"You noticed," he continued with a big grin on his face, "it gets warmer right about in this area right here."

Bam!!! I slammed my fist down on his arm, before he got any closer.

"You're a beautiful boy, Stephen, and you learn fast." He still smiled, sliding his hand up my knee again.

Bam!!!" I slammed my fist down on his arm again just as he was stopping for a traffic light. I jumped out of that car in the pouring rain, slamming the door so hard it rocked his little Festiva and shaking him inside. I pounded on the hood screaming, "Faggot!!! You Faggot!!!" until the light turned green and he sped away.

I felt so much anger and hatred at that moment that I truly wanted to get back in that car and kill that man, had he not sped away.

With just a few days left before I would be homeless again, I had only a few dollars left. But for some reason, I decided to go to a coffee shop for a cup of hot chocolate. I was sitting quietly at a table near the back when a well-dressed black man walked in. He was very polite and good-looking. We instantly struck up a conversation.

He said that he didn't usually come down to Hollywood. But for some reason, he'd made a wrong turn down Hollywood Boulevard this morning and decided to stop somewhere for a cup of coffee. He said he believed everything happens for a reason because he also believed there was a God.

The man's name was James, and he was an attorney on his way to the LA County Court House that morning. He gave me his business card and wanted to meet up with me that same evening.

I told him my situation, explaining that I was staying at the YMCA.

He said he would meet me there at 6:30 P.M.

The one thing he said—*everything happens for a reason*—would be something I kept in my own belief system for many years thereafter.

After wandering up and down the boulevard for most of the early part of the afternoon, I went back up to the YMCA to get cleaned up and dressed before James came by to pick me up. When I was ready, I sat in my little room watching TV until about ten minutes after six then went downstairs and sat on the front steps.

James showed up at about 6:25 PM in a light blue Chevy Cavalier, and I quickly stood up as soon as he saw me. He stopped just long enough for me to get in the car and quickly insisted that I buckle my seatbelt.

I said, "I don't usually wear a seatbelt." But I buckled up anyway.

James indicated that he thought it crazy to ride in a car without a seatbelt.

The inside of his car was very clean. I could tell he was a very organized, reliable person, much like I always had been when everything was going right. James explained that his BMW had been stolen a while back and was only driving this Cavalier until the insurance money came through.

"Still a nice car," I said.

James drove us up to a very nice restaurant in Santa Monica and was very polite when we met the hostess. He said, "A table for two."

I noticed his hands wave down. That was my first indication that he was gay. But I didn't want to be too quick to pass judgement.

We sat down to look at the menu, and he told me to order anything I'd like. He seemed to be taking serious interest in me and said I could make it in LA. I just needed to know the right people. He also said he believed I was the right person with the right ambition.

I told him about the school I'd enrolled in, and I mentioned how I felt I'd been swindled into taking out a student loan.

James knew all about the student loan scandals and how many homeless people were victims of these kinds of scams. "You think you're applying for a job. Then you realize you've enrolled in school, taking a course you have no interest in. Most of the victims drop out within the first couple weeks. The school keeps the money while the student falls victim to the debt of the loan. The school continues to enroll more victims every time another dropout leaves an empty seat."

Then he told me he could help me get out of that situation.

After we ate our meals, we took a ride to the beach where we sat in the car listening to a classical music station. I watched through the window, seeing the waves roll along the shore. James went on telling me his life story, about growing up in Indiana and being raped when he was in the Air Force. And he talked about his lifetime goals.

Then he said, "I want you to know I like you a lot."

I'd told him very little about myself, yet he'd insisted he liked me a lot? And I was wondering if this was supposed to be some romantic setting. Yet he'd made no attempt to lay his hands on me.

I worried that part was coming soon.

He turned up the radio and said, "I wrote this song, by the way." He looked over at me like he was trying to impress me.

I showed him nothing but disbelief that I should believe anything he might tell me after that. The radio just happened to play that classical piece he supposedly wrote? On the very night we were sitting in the car together?

When he asked me what kind of music I liked, I told him I liked Bob Dylan and The Grateful Dead. I didn't dare tell him my real passion was for hardcore punk.

We both sat quietly for a while, tilting our seats back and enjoying the view of the ocean while the soft music kept playing on the radio.

James turned to me, smiling, and said again, "I want you to know I really, really like you a lot." He reached out and laid his hand softly on my arm.

I quickly set my seat back up straight.

It had gotten late, and he acted as if he knew we had to go. He started up the car and continued talking with a mixture of confidence and disappointment in his tone. Driving me back to Hollywood, he made one last attempt, asking me how I could ride a motorcycle. "They're so dangerous."

I only stared out at the street lights through the side window and told James I was a good rider. I stayed in control, and I could stop or swerve around any dangerous situation.

"But your legs are so long," he said, laying his hand on my knee.

I leaned a little closer to my window, not saying a word.

His tone began to sound desperate and disappointed. He kept saying, "I want you to call me tomorrow, no matter what you decide. Even if your answer is no, I want you to tell me why."

And those were the last words he said to me before dropping me off in front of the YMCA.

I never called James. Never even gave it a thought. But he'd treated me with a lot more respect than most of the women I'd met in my lifetime.

My temporary housing opportunity ended, leaving me back out to wander the streets at night again. Somehow, it didn't seem so hard this time. I carried with me a blanket, a toothbrush and a tube of toothpaste. I made sure I brushed my teeth and washed often—every time I found a clean public restroom.

I'd gotten so used to wandering up and down the boulevard, I'd given up all hope of something better and was ready to accept it as my life's destiny. Sleeping in the bushes wasn't so bad. The worst part, though, was not having an address or a phone number to be able to fill in on a job application.

After my second morning of waking up homeless, I remembered how quickly my life had deteriorated. Just a few months earlier, I'd had over ten thousand dollars in the bank. Now I was sitting here with just a blanket and a toothbrush.

And I realized that everything in my life had begun to crumble when I'd stopped believing in God.

Maybe if I started believing in God again, I could pray again and maybe God would help me.

So, I said a little prayer right there on that sidewalk bench.

Then suddenly an idea hit me.

I hadn't checked with the police department in a few days to find out if they had found my bike yet.

When I contacted them, I found out—to my surprise—they had indeed found my bike.

Thank you, God.

And suddenly I was thanking God all the way to find where my bike had been kept in a large parking lot full of other stolen vehicles. But I would have to pay a fee of $60.00 before they'd release it to me—with the fee increasing $20.00 each day that it stayed on the lot.

Once again, I prayed, then I went for a walk. I came to a car dealership and entered straight into the garage and asked a couple of mechanics whether any of them might want to buy a bike real cheap. Instantly, one of the mechanics showed a lot of interest and walked over to the storage lot with me during his lunch break. He took one look at my bike—with its ignition wires hanging out and the gas tank completely empty and there being no way of knowing whether the thing would even start.

I'd been hoping he'd give me at least $500.00 for it. That would be just enough so I could rent a place for a while and maybe get back on my feet again. I said, "Look, I paid over $2000.00 for this thing."

But the mechanic just shook his head and said he'd only give me $200.00 for it, just as it was, minus the $60.00 storage fee to release it.

I had no choice. Either I could take the money now or risk having a $20.00 increased charge for every day my bike stayed in storage while I searched for another buyer.

I took his offer.

With $140.00 in hand, I had a thought—one that hadn't crossed my mind since I'd been there. *Why don't I just go back home to live with my parents? And how much would a bus ticket cost to take me from here to Portland, Maine?*

Suddenly, the idea began to grow into a reality. I started walking to find the Greyhound Bus Station. And instantly, I started to feel better about myself, saying another quick prayer.

When I found the station, I prayed yet again. *If the ticket I need costs less than the $140.00 I have in my pocket, I am definitely going to take it as a sign from you, God.*

I walked up to the ticket window and asked, "How much does a one- way ticket to Portland, Maine, cost?"

"That will be $138.00."

It was a miracle from God. But it left me with just $2.00 in my pocket to buy food for the entire trip.

After buying my ticket, I had a two-hour wait before departing. The thought of calling my parents had not even occurred to me until that final day. I decided to use my waiting time to make that collect call.

My mother was very surprised and happy to hear from me. She had been worried, with good reason. Before that day, I'd had no intentions of calling *anyone* back home. But Mom had been praying for me, and on that very day she knew her prayers had been answered.

After boarding the bus, carrying just a blanket with my toothpaste and a toothbrush, I made sure I got a window seat. I wondered how far I could make it before spending my last $2.00. I wondered what I could possibly buy with just $2.00 from a bus station.

I sat watching the city of Los Angeles fade away through the window. I started looking through my wallet, going through all the phone numbers and business cards I'd collected during those past few weeks. There was a piece of paper with Flash Riley's phone number, and there were business cards from K.J. Enterprise and James the attorney who'd taken me out to eat. Plus, there was a card for a free vegetarian meal, which I regretted never having used.

Then suddenly, to my surprise, I found two twenty-dollar bills folded up and stuffed between all those business cards and paper.

What luck! I thought. *Now I'll have enough money to eat during the long trip!*

I must have hidden that money there then forgotten all about it.

Thank you, God.

I truly believed God was watching over me now.

CHAPTER 19

A Condo on the Beach

I arrived at the Portland, Maine Greyhound Station on the morning of March 24, 1987, two days after my 22nd birthday. It had been just eight weeks since I'd left Portland to go to California, but for some strange reason I felt like I had been away for years.

The weather was warming up and the streets were wet from the melting snow. Whenever spring arrives in Maine, it comes with a burst of energy and it's a new beginning—a time to set new goals.

I called my mother from a phone booth as soon as I got off the bus. When she arrived to pick me up, the sun's glare was so bright reflecting off the wet pavement that I barely recognized her car as she turned into the parking lot, splashing through the puddles. But the moment I saw and recognized *her*, I realized that I scarcely recognized myself. I felt ashamed, returning home like a failure holding just a blanket and a toothbrush. I'd left with no intentions to even call again.

I sat in the front seat and asked Mom if she could buy me a new set of clothes for my birthday. The clothes I had on, which I'd been wearing for almost a week, were all I possessed. And they were beginning to smell.

Mom stopped at the surplus store before heading home. She bought two of the cheapest pairs of pants on the racks and the two cheapest shirts, along with a pack of underwear and socks. When we got home, I took the long hot shower I needed badly before trying on my new clothes.

But I was already bored before I could even sit down and relax. I quickly got on the phone and called the one place I knew I could count on whenever I needed a job fast. And sure enough, I quickly learned Wagner Drywall had been desperate for sanders ever since I'd left them. They were overwhelmed with backed up jobs just waiting to be sanded. I told them I was willing to be there first thing in the morning, but I had no car.

During my time away to California, my parents had finally filed for their long-awaited divorce. All we kids had expected it many years sooner, growing up with their arguing and constant threats of divorce.

This time there was no more threatening. Dad had already moved in with his new girlfriend.

So, life was now much quieter, with just my brother Shawn and sister Lisa still at home. I slept on a couch in the basement. Dad encouraged me to start paying my mother $75.00 a week for rent to help her keep up house expenses, but I didn't like my situation at all after being out on my own for a little less than a year. It actually seemed lifetimes away that I'd last stayed in my parent's house. And while I'd been away to California, every other word that had come out of my mouth was a cursing swear word. Now I had to adjust to living in a house where swearing wasn't allowed.

Plus, with all the scars on my back and my body so skinny, I was simply un-recognizable to those who had known me before.

I had to depend on mom to give me a ride to the office of Wagner Drywall every morning. Then from there another employee would drive me out to a jobsite where I'd work for the entire day. Then I'd have to depend on finding a ride back home at the end of the day. Sometimes I had to hitchhike or walk carrying my tools.

Although Mike Baxter was happy to see me when I first got back, getting back together with him on an everyday basis didn't go so well.

We did go out to Geno's a few times. And we finally got another chance to see The Ramones in concert—this time with no ID check—with the group rocking another great show at Bowdoin College.

But tension between Mike and I quickly got bad, then worse.

My own attitude had changed. I would break out in angry rages. Mike used to depend on me to drive him everywhere. Now I had to have him drive me around. So, I would start arguments with him just to just get even by making him angry. I would say things like, "Just think. If you go to hell when you die, everything you've ever done will have been just a waste of time."

Mike would answer back in his freaking-out tone of voice, "AND IT SCAAAAAAARRRESSS MEEE!!"

"Not me," I'd always say in a very calm and confident tone. "I'm not scared. I've already been there. I *know* where I'm going when I die and I ain't gonna be scared. Don't believe all that crap they taught us at the Nazarene Church. It ain't as bad as what they tell ya'. There ain't no fire there, but you'll be wishing you were on fire when you do get there. It's just a little bit worse."

Mike started freaking out like before, screaming, "GET OUT! GET THE HELL OUT OF MY CAR NOW!"

I got out of his car that one last time and walked the rest of the way home.

Without any friends, all I really had left in my life was my job at Wagner Drywall. I was able to save a bit of money in my first few weeks back, and Dad helped me find a decent car for just $600.00. It was a beautiful red 1979 Mustang with over 140,000 miles on it. It was a good-running car even though it had a lot of miles. With an am/fm cassette player, it was all I needed.

From that point in time, I started taking my job more seriously. I folded the backseat down and opened the hatchback so I could load all my sanding tools inside. I took a black magic marker and wrote my name on all my tools. I loaded a big lamppost with three light sockets so I could work late at night. My only concern now was to make money the only way I knew how, working hard. Having my own vehicle and a job but no friends gave me that opportunity.

And that was what I really wanted, money.

I'd heard it said that money couldn't bring happiness. But I wasn't looking for happiness. I was simply working towards my own independence. As long I had money, I would never have to be at the mercy of someone else. There was no one else I could count on to feed me or provide housing for me, so I had to get out and earn my own.

By late April of 1987, I went all out, taking on as much work as I could. If I wasn't working overtime for Wagner Drywall, I was out working a side job making cash under the table. I'd start early every morning, working late into the night seven days a week.

And suddenly, the low self-image I'd felt just a month before was replaced by a new, motivated drive and determination. Listening to the radio while riding in my car to deposit more money in the bank, I heard a song by Huey Lewis and the News.

"*Step by step, one by one, higher and higher climbing Jacob's Ladder.*"

That song kept me motivated for the next several months.

Other songs I played on my cassette player that kept me thinking positively were, "I Must Not Think Bad Thoughts" by X, and "Running Fast" by Greg Graffin & Greg Hetson. Music was my only escape the many times I'd work late into the night, losing track of time while music played. I'd come home after midnight then get up early the next morning and do it all again. I was determined to earn as much money as I could so I would never be at the mercy of someone else again.

Those old sayings, '*Money doesn't buy happiness*' and '*Money doesn't solve your problem's*'? They had been proven false. I had already learned the hard way that without money I had to depend on someone else to feed me, someone else to provide housing for me, someone else to give me a ride when I needed one. I vowed to never let that happen to me again.

As far as I was concerned, money gave me my only real sense of security.

Not that I needed a lot of expensive things. I hated expensive things. I only wanted to keep my life as simple as possible.

By the end of May, all my hard work and positive attitude were beginning to pay off. I had almost $6,000 in the bank and was looking to move out of my parent's house. With the average cost of a one-bedroom apartment in Portland being over $600 a month and rising rapidly, I knew I would never be able to save money as fast as I had been saving it in the past few months. I needed to secure an affordable budget, and I wanted a clean place where I would never have to struggle to make payments.

That's when, looking through the real estate section of the Portland Press Herald, I saw just what I was looking for: One-bedroom condos starting at $45,000 in Old Orchard Beach. I wasted no time. I called the realtor's number and within the hour I was viewing a tiny one-bedroom apartment. The place was very clean, all newly constructed with new appliances.

This is it. I love it. It has everything I need to survive, I told myself.

I wasted no time putting $1,000 down. My realtor had me fill out a few papers and showed me the monthly payments of $287. Soon, I'd be hearing back from the bank if I was approved.

I left there feeling confident about myself. For the next couple of weeks, I was working with more enthusiasm than ever before, looking forward to owning my own home at a very affordable cost—one that would never increase over the next 30 years.

That was, until the bank informed me that my loan had not been approved.

At first, I was very upset. But then my realtor told me not to worry, she'd find another mortgage company for me.

So, I continued to work with enthusiasm, saving up as much money as I could. Soon, my bank account passed $9,000. And sure enough, my realtor called me back a few weeks later to tell me she had set up an appointment for me with another Mortgage Company.

Within a few weeks, I'd been approved.

Suddenly, though, after signing a stack of papers, I found out I'd be paying much a higher interest rate—over 13%—and the monthly payments would be

$402. This was much more than I had originally agreed to when I had first signed the contract.

But it was still much cheaper than most places were renting for, so I followed through with the contract.

By early August 1987, with a little help from Kevin Cates, a friend I worked with and often worked a lot of side jobs with, I had moved into my own tiny condo in Old Orchard Beach.

We used his pickup truck to transport the few things I owned. Most important were my queen-sized mattress to lay on the floor next to my brand-new Kenwood stereo system. I had just bought it with the money I had left over after closing costs, and it came complete with am/fm, CD, cassette and turntable.

So, along with a few boxes of clothes, I now had everything I needed to survive in my new home. With $1,500 left in my bank account, I planned to rebuild my savings and maybe refinance my condo loan to a lower monthly payment in the near future. For sure, I was a bit upset about the way I'd been swindled into a higher interest rate.

In fact, my anger over the situation lasted a few weeks. But then I just accepted it and continued to think positive and keep my new home clean.

My next goal was to buy as many records and CD's as I could afford. Music was my only freedom, the only happiness I'd ever known. Mine was the joy someone feels when they hear their favorite song come on the radio.

So, every week I'd stop at a used record store or flee market and buy as many records as I could carry out the door. I collected every type of music. I had records from Doris Day; Peter, Paul and Mary; Bob Dylan; Black Flag; The Ramones; The Dead Milkmen—every style of music for every mood I might be in.

But the one record I bought that I truly felt I wasted my money on was "The Smiths, Louder Than Bombs." I bought it because I liked the cover and wanted to try something new. It was a newly released double album set. It was one of the first records I'd bought after returning home. But I remember thinking just how corny the lyrics were on songs like "Half A Person" and "Girl Afraid." Who was this Morrissey? I couldn't even tell if the singer was a girl or a guy.

I set the record in with the rest of the stack, thinking that if I ever felt depressed enough, I'd listen to it again.

Apart from the few friends I worked with, after work I had no social life at all. Having gotten rid of all my former negative friends, I realized I only had one true friend left, Eric.

He was the only friend I'd kept in contact with, calling him once a week while he was still in Florida. I remembered all the good times we'd had at Geno's and the beautiful girls we'd met. Eric kept asking me whether I was still seeing "that beautiful red-haired girl."

"No way," I said. "She was just playing me. We need to meet some real women."

Eric was beginning to hate living in Florida and wanted to move back to Maine. I told him he should move up to stay at his father's house. But he was like me. He couldn't stand the thought of living in his parents' house after the age of twenty.

So, we made plans for him to stay with me.

Late one evening in the first week of October, Eric arrived at the Portland Jetport. His sister Tracy was there to pick him up and take him to their father's house. As soon as I heard he had arrived back in Maine, I drove out to see him.

He wasted no time gathering up the few things he had taken with him to Maine, so he could move in with me in my little condo.

"We gotta make some plans," I kept telling him during the ride down to Old Orchard Beach. "Plans to make some money, plans to keep everything simple, plans to not allow negative people to destroy our goals. And most of all, we gotta find us a couple of real girlfriends and never let another insecure bimbo set us up for a big letdown again."

And then I added some more good advice. "And whatever you do, don't ever sell your soul to the devil."

Eric just looked up at me. "Well, I wasn't planning on it.'"

I could tell he really was wondering what I was talking about.

But as he pretended to be with me, I continued, telling him about all the new bands I'd recently discovered.

After I'd shown Eric my tiny new condo, he selected a spot to roll out his little pad on the living room floor.

"This is it," I told him. "We have all the freedom we need. We can listen to records all night, stay out and party all night. But first we gotta get you a job."

Wagner Drywall was always looking for help. It was hard to find reliable people to do their dirty work. I used to say, "They're always hiring, always firing." So, when I mentioned my friend Eric to Frank the head foreman, he wanted to hire him immediately.

Eric started out as a truck driver at $6.00 an hour, with a lot of overtime. Having very little expenses and paying me just $25.00 a week to sleep on my floor, I expected he would be able to save up a lot of money fast.

And the first couple of weeks did work out great. We both rode to work together, worked all day, then rode home. On the weekends we were back at Geno's for some great music, a few beers, and the chance to dance with beautiful girls.

With Eric being the one friend that I believed I could trust and respect, I felt very confident sitting at a table and sharing a few drinks with him—along with a couple of pretty girls. I was really glad Eric was there with me one night. We all had a great time dancing, and I was hoping we'd see the two girls again the following weekend.

But after leaving Geno's that night, Eric had a big smile on his face for the ride home.

I said to him, "They were a couple of nice girls. I hope we see them again next week."

Eric said, "Yeah." The big grin was still on his face.

I added, "They were a little chubby. But I like 'em that way."

Eric quickly interrupted. "Yeah, I like 'em that way too. You can abuse 'em and they still stay with ya!" His grin got a little bigger as he let out a little chuckle.

Suddenly, my opinion of Eric dropped. I'd been thinking how genuine those girls were. Whatever gave Eric such a horrible idea that he would think it funny to abuse girls just because they're chubby?

A few more weeks passed before Eric got his own car. I was hoping he'd get his own apartment soon too. If he did, I could spend more time locked in my room listening to records by myself.

Eric, up to now, had only sat in front of his TV late into the night, snorting cocaine and watching porn videos. Plus, while I still kept most of my condo clean, there was Eric's little spot in the corner with a smelly ash tray and dirty laundry.

I'd been trying to move my life in a more positive direction, but everything Eric was doing brought me down.

The "Louder Than Bombs" album soon became my favorite album, and The Smiths became my favorite band. "The Queen is Dead" and "Meat is Murder" albums also became favorite albums to listen to, becoming a big influence on my life. The songs didn't sound so depressing anymore. I just wanted to escape the depressing world around me and indulge myself in the lyrics as though every song was written about me.

One afternoon in late November while listening to the "Meat is Murder" album, I was filled with excitement and said to Eric, "That does it. I'm going vegetarian."

Eric turned his head away from his TV, looking at me like I was some kind of lunatic. "Just because you listen to a song called 'Meat is Murder,' you think you gotta go vegetarian."

"Yup," I said. "I'm going vegetarian from now on and no one is going to stop me this time, I'm never gonna eat meat again."

CHAPTER 20

The Worst Best Friend

It was the first weekend in December. The Piranha Brothers and Stop Calling Me Frank were very disappointed in the low turnout at Geno's. The last time we'd seen these two bands play, the dance floor had been soaked with puddles of beer and broken glass. The crowd and I had a great time running and sliding across the dance floor, getting our clothes soaked with beer.

With all the empty seats tonight, though, Eric and I sat at the table closest to the stage. Eric had a beer and I decided I would just drink water and stay sober. A beautiful, petite dark-haired girl with deep blue eyes asked if she could sit with us. My heart began racing as soon as she sat down at our table.

She introduced herself as Miriam, and instantly I felt drawn to her, as if I had already known her from a previous life. She began telling me all about herself. She said she was from Boston and was studying to get her nurse's degree. She never stopped talking, and I took great interest in everything she said.

Eric had a big grin on his face, listening from across the table. When Miriam said she was a vegetarian, Eric smiled almost like he was rooting for her and me to get together.

When the band started to play, we had the whole floor to ourselves. We danced through almost every song. She was very good friends with several of the band members, and after the show she introduced me to all of them, showing me off like I was her newest lover.

I felt really good driving back home that night.

Eric even agreed. "She really likes you." He kept repeating this all the way home. I was lovestruck and he knew it.

But in the weeks to come, Eric's attitude changed, becoming even worse than before. Though Eric had a steady girlfriend of his own, he did everything he could to interfere with my relationship with Miriam.

Meanwhile, I saw Miriam as my only hope. Everyone else in my life was becoming increasingly negative. I came home from work every day and had to put up with Eric's constant complaining and arguing with me. So, I'd just go to my room and call Miriam just to hear her voice. I'd beg her to come see me, but she always used the same excuse. She had to study for exams.

One Saturday morning in early February, after staying up late on the phone with Miriam and pleading with her to let *me* come and see *her*, I couldn't take it anymore. Without any sure plans to follow, I decided I was simply going to leave and never come back.

I packed a small duffle bag with a few clothes and about $500 in my pocket, leaving everything else behind. I started walking. It wasn't long until the local city bus stopped right at the corner where I was ready to cross the street.

The door swung open and I asked the driver, "Where is this bus headed?"

"Biddeford," she answered.

"Good enough," I said, running up the steps and dropping my fare in the slot.

After walking around Biddeford for a while, I came to a small Greyhound Station near downtown. It had a ticket booth and an old wooden bench. I bought a one-way ticket to New York City.

Being the only person waiting, I laid down on that hard bench for over an hour, and finally a commuter bus that could take me up to Portland arrived. I waited there another hour, then left again later that afternoon. I had no real plan of where I was going, and I didn't know whether I would even return home. All I could think about was Miriam. She was the only reason I would even want to come back.

And for sure, I couldn't stand the thought of seeing Eric again or of listening to any of his constant negative insults. He'd only look at me and curse. "What would anybody see in you?" he'd ask, inferring that I wasn't good enough for Miriam or for anybody else.

Although I'd passed through New York many times before, this was my first time walking through the city. It was late in the evening by the time I arrived in downtown Manhattan. The streets and sidewalks were still very busy with traffic and people out walking. The noise and the lights were so bright that I could hardly tell it was near midnight. I wasn't sure if I should look for a place to sleep outside or spend money on an overpriced hotel. I looked around, seeing many homeless people sleeping on the sidewalk and using a few layers of cardboard for padding. The air was a bit chilly, though warm for an evening in February.

I'd brought one blanket with me. After attempting to bundle up for a nap on a sidewalk bench, the street noise and bright lights and chilly air were just too much for me. I walked around a little more and found a dumpy hotel with rooms starting at $69 per night. I decided it was worth it to be out of the cold and to have a quiet, safe room to sleep in.

But once I entered the room, I realized it wasn't much warmer there than out-doors, and the loud noise from the traffic only echoed louder at fifteen stories up. Also, there was a smell in the room. *Well*, I told myself, *at least this old mattress is softer than that sidewalk bench I tried to sleep on.*

I didn't dare get under the covers, though. I was afraid the sheets would be filthy. I just laid on top of the bed covers and watched a little black-and-white TV. When the only program on that late at night was Jimmy Swaggart, I kept it on just to keep myself from feeling so alone in that smelly old room.

I stayed awake with my head under my blanket for the rest of the night.

The next morning, I left that smelly hotel early. Wandering around the filthy sidewalks where lumps of dirty blankets covered the bodies of rejected beings, I began to wonder just how I was any different from any of them. The American flag hung high above us all, with filthy black soot covering its red, white, and blue.

In the midst of all the porn shops and other businesses that were closed on this Sunday morning, I found a kosher restaurant serving breakfast. Inside, most of the people seemed happy and cheerful. I just sat by myself in a corner booth and ordered an omelet. I hadn't come to New York looking for happiness. I'd come there to escape the misery that seemed to surround me wherever I went.

I finished my omelet and went back out to wander around the streets of Manhattan. I saw a white van stop to pass out sandwiches to the homeless. I thought about how close I was to becoming one of them. And I realized that anybody who knew me would never find me if I just stayed right there.

Ascending to the top of The Empire State Building, I looked down and wondered whether I should spend another night in that smelly hotel or save some money by sleeping on one of the hard sidewalk benches. Staring down at a forest of concrete and steel, I knew I could just disappear forever out there.

Instead, I decided to call Miriam from a phone booth. She pretended to sound worried about me, but I didn't think she really was.

Later that evening, I decided not to waste my money on a smelly hotel room. For the same price, I bought a ticket for a warm, soft seat on a Greyhound bus.

When I arrived home late Monday afternoon, Eric and his girlfriend seemed to only pretend that they'd been concerned for my whereabouts.

I went into work the next morning and had to explain why I hadn't shown up for work the day before. Given that I'd been screwing up the past two months, I'd also had to put up with increasing insults from Eric at home.

And now everybody at work knew I was going insane.

There was one good thing about paying the highest interest rate on my mortgage—the tax deduction. After using up a lot of my savings over the last few months, I was happy to receive over $1,800 on my tax return, which built my savings back up to nearly $4,000.

That amount of money really motivated me for a few days. I believed I was ready to get back into working overtime and setting new goals. Winter was almost past, and I thought a new motorcycle was just what I needed to boost my enthusiasm.

So, that last Saturday morning in February, Eric and I drove out to the Honda dealership to look at motorcycles. I saw many beautiful bikes, but the one that stood out was a White and Gray VFR700 Interceptor priced at $4,200.

"I want that one," I said to the salesman, pulling $1,000 cash out of my pocket.

He just smiled and said, "Well, that was an easy sale." Then he walked me to his office to sign a few papers. I had the bike delivered to my mother's house to store in the garage until the rest of the snow melted.

Returning home, I went back to my room and laid on my bed and tried to go back to sleep.

Eric started complaining. "You just bought a new motorcycle and now you go back to feeling depressed."

"Leave me alone," I said, keeping my head under the covers, then later trying to call Miriam.

When I found out she'd moved, I was devastated.

Mario had returned from Texas to Maine back in January after falling behind in his truck payments. In Texas, things had still been the same as when I'd decided not to stay there. There were no jobs anywhere.

Mario had been staying at his former neighbor's house while he took on as much work as he could until he paid off his truck. Mario, though, was very disappointed in me for my slacking off on my job. While he spent his overtime hours training Eric to become a great taper, I was going home early everyday feeling depressed and not wanting to do anything but mope and listen to music. This could have been an opportunity for me to learn the full trade of drywall and become more than just a sander, making a lot more money. But the only thing I had on my mind was building a relationship with Miriam.

In the meantime, the very person I trusted as my best friend was moving forward on the job that I helped him get. He'd come home and insult me, telling me nobody would ever want me.

"I want him out of here," I thought to myself.

Fortunately, I ran into a couple of old friends who both had just gotten out of the Cumberland County Jail after serving a year. Chuck was living with his girlfriend in a beautiful apartment above Paul's Food Center in downtown Portland. Doug sometimes slept on the floor of Chuck's apartment, other times he would stay at the homeless shelter.

But lately Doug had been sleeping on my floor.

At first Eric was okay with it when we all went out drinking together.

Those two guys would even smoke weed and watch porn together... until the day a little small change was missing from Eric's jar. Eric had a fit and blamed me for bringing Doug over. Then he threatened to move out if I brought Doug over again.

That's just what I wanted to hear. I started bringing Doug over every day. Eric finally moved out at the end of April.

I tried going to work after Eric moved out, but seeing him again at the worksite was only bringing me down.

Mario thought he could talk some sense into me by saying, "Stop hanging around with Doug."

He just didn't understand Doug was by far a better friend than Eric had been.

A few days later, I walked off the job at Wagner Drywall. I wouldn't have to look at Eric or listen to anybody anymore. When I got home, I shut myself in my room and tried to go to sleep, vowing never to come out of my room until something good happened. I'd closed all the shades and pulled the blankets over my head, falling into a deep sleep...

...until suddenly, I woke up from a terrible dream of hanging myself.

I got up to get something to eat but kept my vow to stay in my house until something good happened. I went back to bed praying for a better dream.

When I did dream again, I saw Miriam in a totally dark room, where she sat in a chair while I cried at her feet. She looked down on me like a tormentor who had control over my soul...

...then she disappeared, leaving me in total darkness.

Waking up from this dream that felt so real, I got up and looked out the window. It was just starting to get dark.

Well, that's good. It's dark, so I can go back to sleep, I thought. *Maybe I'll see her again in my next dream. I don't care if it's a nightmare just as long as she's there.*

I went back to sleep and she was there. I saw her beautiful smile...

...then all her teeth fell out.

The following day, I couldn't stand it any longer. I had to go out and find Miriam.

I searched all the places she used to go, walking through the Old Port then Geno's. I had no luck finding her. I hung out with Doug and slept on the floor in Chuck's apartment when I wasn't searching.

It had been about six months since I'd drunk any alcohol or smoked any weed. But Chuck's house was always flowing with both. I took just one small sip of a rum and coke, and that was enough to give me a good buzz.

Doug and I stayed up late laughing and enjoying the evening. It was the first time I'd laughed in a long time. But deep down inside, I still hurt. Hanging out with Doug helped me through the pain. Doug smoked a lot of weed, and he would steal money to get drugs. I knew he was even stealing from me at times. But the one thing that made him a better friend than Eric was, Doug stood by his friends. At a time when I felt I didn't have a friend in the world, Doug was there.

Eric wasn't the worst friend I'd ever had, but he certainly was the *worst best friend* I'd ever had.

And this was at a time when I didn't care about anything. I'd let Doug use my motorcycle anytime he wanted. I'd sleep all day and stay up drinking all night. Sometimes Doug and I would stay at my place in Old Orchard Beach, then at other times we were on the floor at Chuck's apartment. We even spent one night at the homeless shelter where the drunk next to my cot stunk so bad and snored so loudly I couldn't sleep at all.

My life was deteriorating, and fast.

All my positive thinking and hard work to make my life easier had gone to waste. *But my situation is only temporary*, I kept telling myself. *Everything will get better soon as soon as I find Miriam.*

Doug and I raced my Interceptor everywhere we went. It's a wonder we didn't get killed. Doug bragged he hit 145 mph on the Interstate 295. I only reached 140mph on that same stretch, riding alone.

Another time, while Doug was driving, I held on tight when we hit 140 mph. Looking back now, it sends shivers down my spine.

Every person around me was so negative in those days, I did not want to live anymore. I was truly hoping to die in an accident or find something or someone worth living for.

But after a few weeks of searching, I finally found Miriam. She was coming out of one of her classes at Maine Medical Center. At first, she seemed to be happy to see me, and I was overwhelmed with joy. I'd found the one person who could make my life worth living. So, I met up with her every day to walk her home. I didn't care about anything else. Doug could just take my motorcycle anytime he wanted, as long as I could see Miriam for that brief time every day.

Every day would end after a short walk and a hug. Then I'd go back to Chuck's apartment and go back to sleep. Still, I was happier during that short time Miriam and I spent together than at any time I'd ever remembered…

…until the day she told me she didn't want to see me anymore.

I buckled over and started to cry. It was the first time I'd cried like this since I hadn't made my junior high school baseball team, and it was the *hardest* I'd ever cried. I'd never seen anyone else cry so hard, not since I'd seen a boy cry this way back in fifth grade.

Miriam sat in her chair, shouting, "Go home!"

I looked up with blurry vision, but I couldn't move. My whole body was shivering as fluids flowed from my face. I looked up again, barely seeing through my tears. But I heard the faint sound of her voice as she pointed to the door. "Go home." I still couldn't move.

Finally, she changed her tone and asked me if I wanted a towel.

"Yes," I mumbled, choking back my tears.

She handed me a few paper towels, and within seconds those towels were soaked. She handed me a few more. I sat up in her chair trying to catch my breath.

After a few minutes, I was able to stand up. But I was still dizzy. I nearly passed out.

Then she told me to go home again.

I nearly passed out again.

At last, she reached out to give me a hug. And she told me everything was going to be alright.

But I knew it wasn't.

I ignored her demands not to stop by her house anymore.

And sometimes, she even pretended to be nice to me.

Other times, I had to listen to her lecturing me about serious relationships. With a curse in her angry tone, she ended it. "THAT'S HOW PEOPLE GET HURT!"

Like I really cared about getting hurt at this point in my life.

CHAPTER 21

Chuck's Refrigerator

The partying never ended at Chuck's apartment. Even as I slept on the floor in the corner, the music continued to play. There were always people coming and going, sharing joints and drinking beer.

One morning, I woke up early. Feeling hungry, I looked through Chuck's refrigerator. "There's nothing in here but beer. There's nothing to eat?"

"You want a fur burger?" a skinny blonde girl asked me from the couch. She'd just woke up.

"No thanks, I'm a vegetarian," I answered, still searching through the cabinets, unable to find anything at all to eat.

Bobbie, a pencil thin blonde, and her lesbian lover Denise had come to spend the night after Bobbie had had a bad breakup with her boyfriend. Bobbie moved over on the couch so I could take a place between them. Denise had dark brown hair and, frequently, a bitchy attitude, though at times she actually seemed to get along well with me. She sat still rolled up in a blanket, leaning on the other side of the couch.

The two of them started ranting on about how abusive Mark had been to Bobbie. I only sat between them, quietly listening, the two of them searching through ashtrays for cigarette butts. They were so desperate for a smoke that they relit each butt, smoking it to the filter.

Chuck himself had left early for work, having just a cigarette and a beer for breakfast. How anybody could survive on just cigarettes and beer was beyond me. I woke up starving every morning and couldn't imagine going to work all day without eating real food.

I ran downstairs to Paul's Food Center and came back with a couple of cheese pizzas, a mushroom, and an onion. Cutting up the veggies and decking out the pizzas, I popped them in the oven. We cranked up the music while we waited for our pizzas to bake.

I'd become very skinny and weak from lying on the floor, hardly eating or exercising. I knew I looked very ill. It was no wonder Miriam would have nothing to do with me. The girls today, though, didn't care how ill I looked. They were there to talk to me, and I was there to listen.

After the three of us ate our first decent amount of food in a long time, I started washing the dishes and planned on lying back down in my little corner like I'd been doing for the past week. But with Bobbie and Denise dancing around the apartment and lots of beer in the fridge, it wasn't worth it to lay around feeling sorry for myself.

Doug came in with a few other friends and soon we had a little party started. The music was cranked up loud enough to disturb the neighbors. Denise and I started dancing to Def Leppard's "Pour Some Sugar On Me." Suddenly she grabbed me, wrapping one leg around my ass, and laid a big sloppy kiss on my lips. She clung to me for about half a minute.

"Go for it, Smitty!" Doug said, rooting me on as he chugged down another beer.

I only stood there with a stupid grin, flattered that Denise had taken interest in me. But I had no interest in responding. I just continued dancing around the apartment.

Meanwhile, Doug was trying to make a move on Bobbie, but Bobbie wasn't interested. Doug turned to me, pleading for me to defend him. "Smitty, tell her I'm not that bad. Tell her I'm not always this drunk. Come on, tell her I'm not that bad." Almost in tears, he added, "I'm blowing my chance with a beautiful girl."

Bobbie kept repeating, "Doug, I'm not interested in you."

Doug kept on whining. "I'm blowing my chance with a beautiful girl." And he was blaming me for it because I wouldn't tell Bobbie what a great guy he was.

"Doug, she's not interested." I felt a little guilty having to tell him. I knew how bad I'd always felt when my friends didn't come to my defense.

Later that evening, Chuck came home. The party was still going strong and another party was going on down the hall. Denise was running around topless back and forth between the two parties.

I was bored, though, and wanted to go to sleep. I pulled a couple of heavy blankets over my head and fell asleep in my little corner on the floor.

The next morning, Denise was passed out with Doug on the couch. I got up to get something to eat and there was nothing in the refrigerator, not even beer this time.

How much longer could I go on living like this?

A few more days passed. We heard a knock on the door. It was the landlord and his wife. They were angry, demanding to know who we all were. They had rented the apartment to Chuck and his girlfriend, but Chuck's girlfriend had moved out weeks ago, and I'd been paying Chuck $50 a week to sleep on his floor. Chuck had never said anything to me about moving out, and he had stopped paying the rent.

Just as quick as we could all get dressed, we were evicted.

Suddenly Bobbie and Denise were depending on me. We all rode down to my little condo in Old Orchard Beach, and they loved my place. We all worked together to clean up the mess that Eric and Doug had left behind. It was the first time in three months that the place had been clean, and I was starting to feel good about myself, living here with my two new roommates.

Bobbie picked some dandelions from the lawn and said, "These are for my boyfriend." She kissed me on the check and gave them to me. I just smiled and said thank you.

I had no intentions of being her boyfriend.

It was the second week of May and I hadn't worked in over six weeks. Now that I had new friends, I felt a lot better about myself and was ready to get back to work.

It was much harder for me to go back to work this time, though. I wasn't just "broke," I was deeply in debt. On top of that, my car had broken down along the stretch of Route 1 near the Scarborough Saco line. Leaving my car on the side of the road, I'd hitchhiked a few miles down the road to a car dealership.

I had no choice but to buy a brand-new car from the crookedest car dealer in the state, Jolly John.

Jolly John was well known for his sly slogan, "No Money Down." And that was my deal for a brand-new Ford Escort.

After meeting a salesman, I told him my situation. He walked me through the lot full of Ford Escorts and asked me what color I wanted. Not really enthused about the idea of putting myself further in debt, I said, "I guess I'll take the red one."

Within an hour of signing papers and transferring my insurance, I was driving a brand new 1988 Ford Escort with a full tank of gas. It rode so smoothly and smelled so clean. I supposed most people would have been excited to have a new car. But not me. I hated it before I got home.

I hated the color I picked, I hated the increase of my insurance rate, and I hated the fact that I was in debt for a car I never wanted to buy in the first place.

But I decided I would make the best of things, now that I had reliable transportation and could get to work without worrying about my car breaking down.

Fortunately for me, I was in great demand at Wagner Drywall. After skipping work for six straight weeks, most any other employee would have been fired.

Eric and Packy had both quit Wagner so that they could make more money working for Metropolitan Drywall, a startup company that took nearly half of Wagner's employees with them.

This situation left me in great demand and gave me a lot of overtime.

I was beginning to feel good about myself again. Even though I was far in debt, I was able to keep up the payments on everything and had two wonderful new roommates. Coming home every day to two girls who were happy to see me made my life a lot easier. We always had fun out walking around town in the evenings. Bobbie attracted a lot of attention from guys and I enjoyed being seen with two girls on my arms.

At home, we covered the walls with graffiti using crayons and magic markers and turning my little condo into the most unique art exhibit in town.

Also, given access to all my equipment I'd collected over the past few months in my many attempts to start a band, Bobbie and Denise decided they wanted to learn how to play guitar. I told them I didn't know much but I would teach them what I knew. They learned quickly and soon Bobbie took up the guitar, while Denise took up the bass.

I said to them, "Keep practicing. We're going to start a band."

Denise was drawing an interesting picture of a human head with a bunch of little figures going in and out of the brain. Up above the picture she wrote, "Life in One Thought."

"That's it," I said. "That's the name of our band, Life in One Thought."

At first, Denise thought it was a dumb idea. But after thinking about it, she agreed it would be a great name for a band.

Even though Mark had been quite violent with Bobbie, she would still call him daily, running up my phone bill. One evening, she asked me to give her a ride out to see him. She told me she wanted to pick up the rest of her clothes and then come straight back home.

But as soon as she walked into his apartment, an argument broke out. I waited in the car, wondering if I should go in to defend her. But then they both came back out, and she said she'd decided to stay.

As I was getting ready to go, I heard them break out in screaming at each other again. Bobbie came running out of his apartment screaming, "No, don't go! Take me with you!"

I waited for her to get back in the car, but Mark stopped her. They were both screaming at each other again.

I waited for her to get back in the car.

A few minutes later they were both hugging and kissing, and Bobbie decided to stay.

When I got home, Denise was sitting on the floor with her back against the wall crying. She was upset at Bobbie for going back to Mark, and she started spilling out her whole life of drama to me. I sat listening to what her life was like growing up in foster care. She'd been raped, molested, and abused at every home she'd stayed in, then left to fend for herself after her eighteenth birthday.

Prostitution was the only way she knew how to survive. She sat with her knees up to her chest, I pretended not to notice her crotch hairs showing under that short skirt she was wearing.

Denise went on whimpering about how Doug took advantage of her when she was passed out on Chuck's couch. I sat staring out the window, not saying a word. I couldn't tell whether she was leaving herself open for me or if I was supposed to be the strong shoulder she could lean on.

Somehow, this 18-year-old girl I'd only known for two weeks, the only friend I had left in the world, was spilling her whole life of drama on me and I had to learn to be the strong one.

She talked about suicide and truly believed she'd committed suicide in her previous life and knew she would die of a suicide at the end of this life. She went on talking about Bobbie and her bisexuality and how much she hated Mark for all the times he'd beat her.

I interrupted with a stupid question. "Why did she go back to him after all that abuse?"

"Duh!" She looked at me like I'd asked the stupidest question she ever heard. "Duh, duh, duuuuuhhh!"

Then she screamed, "BECAUSE SHE LIKES THE WAY HE FUCKS!!"

This made me feel like a real idiot for asking.

A few days later, Bobbie was back to my condo after she'd had another violent breakup with Mark. Denise was much happier with Bobbie back with us, and it looked like everything was going well for the three of us. I kept encouraging them to practice on the guitar and bass. I had big plans.

We really were going to start a band. And we all agreed we'd call it "Life in One Thought."

Bobbie had plenty of the young good-looking guys in Old Orchard Beach interested in her. Some were willing to spend all their money trying to impress her. Other guys would break out in a fist fight, believing they were her one and only.

With so many guys taking so much interest in her, it brought a lot of trouble in the neighborhood.

But I never could figure out what any of these guys saw in this pencil thin blonde with no sense of commitment. Still, I did everything I could to encourage her to choose the guy she liked best and keep him for her steady boyfriend.

She'd go on with excuses like, "I don't want to be in a steady relationship right now, because that's how people get hurt."

Those were the same exact words that someone had used on me just a few weeks before. And now I was hearing them again from a girl who'd been through so much abuse in her life but now had a chance to choose any one of the many nice guys who are willing to treat her like a princess.

She just played them all and talked about getting back together with Mark.

I was working most of the time and had no idea what was going in my home while I was gone. Every day, I'd come home with a bag of groceries and try to keep the refrigerator well stocked with good food. But with all the guys the girls had coming and going during the day, there would be nothing left in the fridge but a few cans of beer when I came home.

I tried not to show it, but tension and anger were beginning to build up in me towards them. They had both been offered jobs at Kentucky Fried Chicken the very first week they'd moved in with me, but they'd never showed up for even their first day on the job.

I encouraged them to find a job someplace else.

Bobbie tried to explain to me that they didn't work.

"What do you mean, you don't work?" I was sounding stupid for asking. "How do you make any money if you don't work?"

She explained, "We see people. We get paid to see people."

That's what she liked to call it. *Get paid to see people.* Not a hooker, they had a little more class than that.

The final blow came the day when I came home from work and both my guitar and bass were gone. Bobbie and Denise were there just staring out the window.

I asked them, "Where is my guitar and where is my bass?!"

They both looked ready to cry and afraid to look at me.

Bobbie turned and said, "We'll buy you a new one."

I asked, "WHAT HAPPENED TO THEM?!"

Bobbie and Denise just sat there, staring out the window as if feeling really bad.

Then they confessed that the two guys they'd spent the night with were gone in the morning, along with my guitar and bass.

That's when I lost it. I started screaming, "How are we going to start a band now? If you keep bringing all these creepy guys in here who steal all our equipment, we ain't never gonna have a band!"

Then I started laying down the new rules in my household. "As long as you both are living under my roof you are only allowed one boyfriend. And you both have to start looking for a real job and start paying rent. I want you to start cleaning up behind yourselves, and no more smoking in here!"

"No Smoking?!" Bobbie had lost it. "That's it! I'll move out if I can't smoke in here. I'm moving out!"

"That was going to be my next suggestion," I replied. "I want you both to start looking for a new place to live."

After that argument, we did try to all get along again for the next few weeks. The girls both went outside to smoke, and they stopped bringing strange guys in the house.

But with all our goals of starting a band gone down the drain, stress and tension were taking over.

There was one annoying girl none of us could stand. She was a chubby, loud-mouthed girl with big frizzy blonde hair who thought herself beautiful. She would usually invite herself up to our little apartment after the girls were done "seeing people." Even though we didn't like her, no one really wanted to say anything until after she'd leave.

Then Bobbie would start up, "I can't stand that fat ugly Heather."

And Denise would tell stories about the time they were all invited to a party to do a strip tease and some of the guys were spittin' on her.

"She made us look bad. I hate her," Bobbie said.

In a way, I felt sorry for Heather. If she had been in my elementary school class, I certainly would have been bullying her. She was every bit as ugly as Bobbie and Denise described her. And her personality was even worse.

Still, with all the tension growing between the three of us, I would make the mistake of being nice to Heather when no one else would.

By midsummer, things had gotten really bad between the three of us. One day, I came home, and my apartment was cleaned out. Bobbie and Denise had taken everything, including the shower curtains, towels, and everything in the refrigerator.

Denise had always worn my Sex Pistols, Dead Kennedy's, or other punk rock tee-shirts I'd collected. Now she actually *had* them all, leaving me with just a few ratty shirts for work. I had to take a shower without a curtain, drying myself off with the same dirty shirt I wore to work.

My apartment was empty. All I had was a mattress, without sheets or blankets.

But for the first time in a long time, there was peace in my home.

I laid down and went to sleep.

CHAPTER 22

The Big Announcement

The one good thing about living on my own again was keeping my life simple.

I could stock my refrigerator with enough food for the week, plan my meals for each day, and not have to worry about someone else eating it. I saved money on my utility bills by keeping all the lights out and making no long-distance phone calls.

The simple life was all I'd really wanted when I'd bought this tiny condo, and by the end of the summer I realized that I had everything I truly wanted—after many months of chaos. I could finally come home after working all day and just relax in my own home.

It was late September. The weather was foggy and drizzly. I was feeling lonely, sad that nobody ever came to see me anymore. Ever since Bobbie and Denise had left, I'd had no friends at all.

Suddenly the door buzzer woke me from my state of depression.

I jumped up, excited. "Who is it?"

I was hoping to hear some good news from the intercom downstairs.

"It's Heather. Can I come up?"

Her voice almost put me back in my state of depression. "Oh, I guess so."

The very sound of her annoying voice was enough to bring anybody down. But I was already down, and I didn't think my life could sink any lower than it already was. Heather's very presence attracted extreme negative energy, and I could feel creepiness as soon as she walked in the door.

I pretended to be happy to see her since she was at present my only friend. I figured the situation would just be temporary, until I found some new friends.

After spending a first day hanging out together with Heather, I actually didn't mind driving her around and shopping at the Goodwill Store. It was my first time ever shopping at Goodwill, and I learned I could save a lot of money by buying second hand stuff. Heather knew of an even better way of saving money. She'd try on as many clothes as she could, then walk out the door wearing layers of clothing and a few extra shirts in her purse.

Heather came to visit more and more often, and my depression at home got worse and worse. I guess she must have thought she was doing me a favor every time she stopped by to cheer me up.

I felt a lot happier when I was at work, where I stayed busy sanding drywall and listening to music. Best of all, I was earning money and rebuilding my savings account.

It seemed like I was getting my life back in order—until I received my property tax bill in the mail. It had my name at the top, but the address for the property was not the property I owned. Plus, the amount of tax due was far beyond what I was shown when I purchased my little place.

I was upset when I first read the bill, but after a few days I decided to leave work early and take the bill to city hall so I could explain to them that they'd made a mistake. When I walked in to see the town clerk and explain my situation, I very calmly said, "I own 6 Imperial Street, Unit 12. You sent me this bill for 12 Imperial Street."

I went on to explain that the tax bill was charging me for an entire building, and for land which I did not own.

"I only own one small unit of a building at 6 Imperial Street. Could you please correct my tax bill?"

I'd spoken very politely, but the woman behind the desk answered back rudely. "There's no mistake on the amount due. They are your taxes, and you are required to pay them!"

We got into a bit of a rude argument and when I left, I believed the lady was just too stupid to argue with.

I set the paper aside when I got home, thinking I should try and get the problem straightened out another time. But after a few days, I got tired of looking at it and sent it to the mortgage company hoping maybe they might see the problem and get it straightened out.

I was in no mood for worrying about problems. I'd dealt with enough problems in past ten months. It was time for my life to move forward.

By the end of October, a red and black Chevy pickup truck with Wisconsin license plates pulled up and parked in front of Wagner Drywalls office.

"Who's that?" I asked Frank, watching a big guy with long blonde hair look a bit lost as he got out of his truck.

"That's your helper," Frank answered quickly, rushing over to introduce himself to the fellow.

Then Frank turned back to me and said, "This is Dave Olson. He drove here all the way from Wisconsin. He's going to be working with you today. I want you to teach him everything you know."

Dave spoke with a strong mid-western accent, smoked Marlboro cigarettes, and drank Pepsi for breakfast and lunch—and sometimes nothing but beer for dinner. What amazed me was, this guy was as strong as a bull. He could stay out drinking till 3:00 AM and still be up and ready for work at 6:30 every morning.

Since his truck broke down within his very first week on the job, Dave had to rely on me to pick him up every morning. I learned that in many ways we were complete opposites. I was a vegetarian, while Dave enjoyed hunting and fishing. But in many other ways, we were the same.

We both liked to work hard, and Dave also had a strong Christian upbringing. His recent divorce, though, had led him to heavy drinking. He'd met his girlfriend Lori back in Minnesota just a few weeks before her big job promotion relocated her here to Portland, Maine. Dave had thought he'd never see her again, but she'd continued to write him letters inviting him to come live with her.

With no intentions on leaving Wisconsin, Dave's heavy drinking had gotten him fired from his job. Feeling that he had nowhere else he could go, he decided to take her up on her offer and moved out to be with her. He himself had no intentions of marrying her, but he knew she was expecting a lot more out of their relationship.

I enjoyed working together with Dave late into the night on many jobs, and we began to build a friendship. Neither one of us felt like we had a whole lot to go home to, so we usually just kept working till late in the day.

By the spring of 1989, I had built up my bank account and thought maybe it might be a good idea to lower my monthly bills by paying off my car. When I made the call to Ford Motor Credit, I started out speaking very politely, asking how much the remaining balance on my car was. But when I heard the answer, my temper exploded.

"WHAT DO YOU MEAN $9,000!! IF I PAY IT OFF NOW, I SHOULDN'T HAVE TO PAY ANY MORE INTEREST!!!"

The stupid lady on the phone just kept arguing, "Sir, you've only made nine payments."

"WELL, WHAT DID YOU DO WITH THOSE NINE PAYMENTS??!!! YOU'RE SUPPOSED TO SUBTRACT THEM FROM THE BALANCE, NOT ADD THEM TO IT!!"

The argument got quite loud and went on for about twenty minutes. Finally, I realized the lady on the phone was just too stupid to argue with.

But what I'd found most disturbing was that Ford Motor Credit would hire somebody that stupid to handle all their phone calls. She'd probably had a college degree but couldn't figure out if a car cost $7,200 to start, before subtracting the $300 factory rebate and the nine monthly payments of $202. My balance owed *had* to be less than the $7,200 I'd started with.

As it turned out, though, my slippery salesman had slipped a lot of paper in front of me when I was signing my name. He'd sold me tire insurance, life insurance, extra warrantees for parts I hadn't needed—and who knew what else?—when I'd been signing that stack of papers he'd slipped under my pen.

I regret to this day that I did not stop making payments until they threatened to repossess the car, after which I would have removed every piece of it, leaving just the body and frame in the parking lot for them to come and take.

But with all the work we had ahead of us, it was just easier to keep paying the $202 each month than it would have been to spend time looking for another car and having to deal with registering another vehicle all over again.

The one I'd bought ended up costing me over $12,000 after all the interest was paid, for a car I'd never wanted in the first place. I tried not to get upset about it, but it was a major setback when I was trying to set my goal of lowering my monthly expenses.

Shortly after my financial setback, my mother called to inform me that her house was going to be foreclosed on by the end of the week. When my father had left her the house, my mother hadn't understood that that meant she was to assume the remaining payments as well.

I had to think up something quick.

Knowing I had just enough money in my savings to get her all caught up on her house payments, I came to the rescue, leaving myself flat broke again—with heavy debt for a car I didn't even want.

Denise had called me several times since she'd left my condo on bad terms. She'd been wanting us to get back together as friends, but I knew she wanted us to be a lot more than just good friends.

We met up a few times and talked on the phone a lot over the winter months. By the summer, we were spending nearly every weekend together riding around on my motorcycle and enjoying amusement park rides at Fun Town. I was really enjoying our friendship and wish we could have kept it that way. Over the summer of '89, she asked me a few times to marry her. But I couldn't think of her as anything more than a friend.

Bobbie came over one warm summer night, and we all enjoyed one last weekend together. Bobbie had quit drinking alcohol and smoking weed, and she was even working on quitting cigarettes. She said it was my influence that made her decide to quit.

I didn't know what I'd done to make her decide all that, but I was glad she'd made some positive changes.

The next morning, I gave Bobbie a ride to her new boyfriend's house. She was only living a few miles down the road, and when she got out of the car, I had to sit and wait with Denise hanging out the passenger side window. Bobbie bent down to kiss her passionately. They slipped their tongues deep down each other throats. I thought it was like long-lost lovers kissing after being separated for many years.

They cried and shouted, "I love you!"

I finally drove away.

Denise sat in the car looking lovestruck as I drove us back to my place.

I never thought of Denise as anything more than a close friend. She would often be upset with me for not feeling any sexual attraction to her. She had a few other lesbian relationships, so I could never understand why she was so interested in marrying me.

I saw Denise a few more times during that summer of '89. She'd found a new friend named Crystal, with beautiful light brown hair and dark brown eyes. When Denise introduced her to me, she knew I was taken to her beauty and Crystal showed a lot of interest in me.

I was really hoping we were all going to be good friends.

The girls came over to my place one last time, all excited about an apartment they liked. They wanted to borrow money for a security deposit, and I gave it to them.

But our friendship turned out short-lived. After lending them the money, I never saw either of them again.

Meanwhile, Heather was coming over more and more frequently. Soon she was living on my couch. I told her to start looking for a job if she wanted to stay at my house, knowing very well nobody in their right mind would hire her.

I let her stay there, anyway. She was somebody to talk to when I came home from work. With nothing else to do and having no friends, I found that Heather was my only hope for any form of social life outside of work. She knew a lot of people between Old Orchard Beach and Biddeford.

I really had no interest, though, in making friends with any of her friends. It was from pure boredom that I drove her around, meeting a lot of new people. And soon I actually became a part of her social group, finding myself socializing with people I would have never in my most desperate days chosen to be friends with. I felt out of place no matter where we went.

Some of her friends actually looked up to me. I wasn't sure why. Maybe it was because I was the only one in their group of friends who could actually keep a full-time job. One of Heather's closest friends, an 18-year-old single mother of two who had no idea who the father of her 2nd child was, once shouted out across the room during a party, "Relationships are stupid and a waste of time!"

Then she looked over at me and added, "Right, Smitty?"

She was clearly hoping to get my approval, but I didn't know where anyone ever got the idea that I was against relationships. They thought that just because I wasn't in one or because I choose not to hug anyone?

I didn't like the idea that these people were looking up to me for all the wrong reasons. These were not the type of people I would want a hug from or ever be in a relationship with. I often asked myself why I even knew people like these.

Heather was leaning on me for everything. She used my address to receive her food stamps. And she'd invite her friends over and talk about me like I was her best friend. I certainly didn't see us that way. I only thought of her as my one friend and hoped she would move on soon...

...although there were a few times I felt there was a good reason I was there with her, such as on the one night I gave her a ride to Biddeford to meet up with her friend Tammy. Heather went up to Tammy's apartment while I waited at the bottom of the stairs. Music was blaring and a baby was crying.

Suddenly, Heather came running down the stairs carrying a screaming baby. "Come on let's go!" she demanded, running back towards the car and freaking out as she struggled to tell me what was going on in the apartment. "Everybody in there was tripping on acid and nobody even cared that the baby was crying."

We drove back home, where Heather opened the still screaming baby's diaper. It looked like it hadn't been changed in several days and was leaking out the sides. The baby herself had diaper rash so bad that I felt sick to my stomach from what I saw. I quickly ran back out to the drug store to buy some new diapers and cream for the rash.

When I got back, Heather had already given the baby a bath and began putting on the cream, the baby still crying. I went back out to get some baby food, and we stayed up most of the night feeding her and worrying about her serious diaper rash.

We took care of that baby for the next two days.

Tammy finally called in a panic. She thought somebody had stolen her baby. But Heather told Tammy to calm down, that we had taken care of her baby. Tammy let us know she felt relieved that Heather had come to the rescue. Tammy seemed to understand that she could always count on Heather. Tammy looked up to her and respected her, because she'd trusted Heather to take care of her baby many times before.

At the same time, Heather and Tammy both looked up to me and thought of me as their only true trustworthy friend.

It's a shame I couldn't feel the same about them. They were simply the only friends I had at that time.

By Christmas of 1989, Heather wanted to get me something special. She knew I really wanted a cat, but during that time I did not think I was ready to take on the responsibility of caring for a cat.

About a week before Christmas day, I came home from work, and Heather said to me, "Go look in your room. There's a surprise for you in there."

She was a beautiful white and gray kitten with a beautiful red bow around her neck. She was a thoroughbred Manx with no tail, and my first thought was, *Oh, no. I can't take care of a cat right now. I've got so much chaos in my life, and I'm always working overtime. I'm never home.*

But after a few minutes of watching my beautiful new kitten, I knew I had to keep her. I decided to name her MARi, a name I liked from a girl I once met back in the days when I was still friends with Eric.

A few years later, I would actually contact Mari and tell her all about my beautiful cat. But she wasn't impressed with my cat. I was a little confused that she didn't like cats at all.

I asked if she liked dogs.

She sounded confused, as if she never thought anything at all about dogs or cats. *What a wasted conversation that was!* I thought.

Any person who had any sense of kindness in them loved dogs and cats, I believed. So, from then on, I never showed any interest in a girl who didn't like cats.

I made my big announcement when Heather and all her friends were sitting around my living room. "I love this cat more than anything else in this world!"

And keeping MARi happy was the most important thing to me.

Every day, I hurried home from work to feed her, make sure she had clean water in her dish and scoop her litter box. She was my one and only reason to live.

I even painted a large mural of MARi on the wall over my bed.

CHAPTER 23

Heather's Apartment

By the spring of 1990, Heather had somehow managed to convince the owner of an apartment downstairs that she would be a responsible tenant willing to faithfully pay rent for his vacant apartment. This arrangement gave me back my freedom, living with my beautiful cat MARi, while Heather lived down on the first floor, with all her girlfriends coming and going.

One rainy Sunday morning, she invited me down to see her little apartment when a few of her friends were spending the weekend. When I walked in, Georgia, a tall blonde with a tint of orange-colored hair, sat on the couch next to Allison, a pretty red-haired girl visiting from Bangor. There was also Kerry, Heather's roommate. I was sure *she* was paying all the rent while Heather continued to act as the boss in *her* apartment.

Anyway, the girls needed someone who was old enough to buy alcohol. So, after hanging out with them for a few hours—waiting until noon, which was the legal time for the sale of alcohol on Sundays—I took a ride with Allison up to Radley's Market to buy a 12-pack of the cheapest beer we could find. When we returned to Heather's apartment, Georgia was putting makeup on Heather and showing her different shades of makeup. She turned and said, "I think Heather's pretty. If I was a guy, I'd Fuck her."

I thought that was the stupidest thing I'd ever heard a girl say. I answered back, "Well, it's a good thing you're not a guy."

When Georgia was finished putting makeup on Heather, she looked over at me. "Okay, who's next?"

"Well, I guess that's me," I said. "I'm next."

"Well, come sit right here."

So, I sat in the chair and she proceeded to put makeup on me. Starting with nail coloring for my eye liner, she made my eyelids stick open and formed hard crusty layers of red and blue on my eyebrows.

We all laughed.

I wasn't yet thinking how it wouldn't be so funny when it would take several days of scrubbing in the shower for all that color to come off.

Anyway, with all my makeup on and a few more beers inside us, we were all dancing around the living room. I was probably asking for it by the way I was dancing, and suddenly Georgia moved the dancing into the bedroom, where we started jumping on the bed. I had absolutely no interest in Georgia. I was just having a little fun dancing.

Suddenly, though, she pulled both of my legs out, knocking me down on the bed. With Kerry and Allison looking on, Georgia jumped on top of me, sitting up on my chest. "You want me, you want me." She kept repeating this, bouncing her butt up and down and sliding closer to my face.

"No, I don't!" I said, not feeling the least bit intimidated.

"Oh, yes, you do! No guy has ever turned me down!" She shouted in my face as she bounced a little harder, reaching behind herself to unbuckle my pants.

Kerry and Allison grabbed and pulled on each pant leg, and my pants slipped right out from under my butt. Now I was lying on the bed in my underwear, with one girl pinning my shoulders with her knees and holding my arms out straight over my head.

Georgia turned and ordered the other two girls, "Okay, hold his legs."

I felt Allison and Kerry grab my legs and I thought, "Uh-oh. This is getting serious. Are these girls really going to try to rape me? Should I just lay here and let them? No! I can't let this happen!"

I squirmed loose then broke free, grabbing my pants and running to the kitchen in my underwear.

Heather sat at the kitchen table as I stood pulling my pants up.

And suddenly, I noticed my wallet didn't line up with the curve of my butt. I reached in my back pocket, where my wallet had been reset backwards, and I immediately knew the other two girls had cleaned out my wallet.

Luckily, I hadn't left a whole lot of money in it.

Heather sat there at the table, laughing. "I had nothing to do with this one."

"All right! Who stole all my money?" I demanded to know.

Georgia went into an *acting-surprised* voice. "Oh, I can't believe somebody here would steal your money. But I guess I better check my wallet too…Uh, oh! No! Somebody stole my money too! Can you believe that?"

I didn't care who it was that stole my money that day. I never felt any shame or guilt. Still, I was glad I broke free from whatever they were planning to do to me. Anyone else might have thought it was a sexual assault. But for me it was just another average day of play with a group of friends, the only friends I had.

So, I let the matter go.

Dave and I had been riding to work together every morning and working late almost every night for over a year and a half. Now he was dropping everything he owned—just a duffle bag with a few ratty work clothes—on my living room floor. Dave had had enough of pretending love for Lori, and he'd finally moved out of her place. With all the overtime we'd worked together, I thought Dave would have saved a little money. But he was flat broke, with no place else to go.

It was clear, Dave was going to be staying on my couch every night until whenever. So, I warned him about *that girl* downstairs.

But Dave wasn't about taking warnings seriously, even though he was a very smart, good-looking, hardworking guy. He'd had a lot of bad breaks in life and he'd taken to heavy drinking and smoked like a chimney after his first marriage failed. He'd already met Heather on brief occasions and didn't think she was as much trouble as I warned him about.

Neither of us had friends anywhere else, though, so, Dave and I were downstairs drinking beer almost every weekend at Heather's. Dave often stayed there a lot later than I did, and soon he started sleeping on her couch instead of mine. But he did this with no interest in Heather, because he had a lot more class than that.

And there were always other girls coming over to hang out and smoke some weed every night.

Mornings, Dave was always up early for work and ready to ride in with me. One morning, while Dave and I were on the way to work, I made the comment about Heather, "She's absolutely disgusting, isn't she?"

"Oh, yeah," Dave said shaking his head. "Yah she's disgusting alright. But she had some friends over last night, and I met her beautiful friend with brown hair. She's really short, with big tits and a pretty face."

I said, "What? That sounds like her friend Tammy."

Dave had a big smile on his face. "Tammy. Yes, that was her name." He sounded love-struck.

I didn't like it when my friends interfered with my taking interest in Miriam, so I was in no way going to interfere with Dave taking interest in Tammy.

I just kept my thoughts to myself, letting Dave find out the truth about Tammy on his own.

The following week, Tammy invited her friend Melissa to come stay for a week. Melissa was a thin blonde with light brown eyes and a bitchy attitude. She smoked and drank a lot and seemed to be more into herself than anything else.

But for some reason, she was drawn to me and I was drawn to her.

One evening, we were all sitting around the coffee table in Heather's living room playing a game of quarters. We took turns trying to bounce a quarter into an empty glass, and if the quarter landed in the glass you pointed to someone around the table and they had to take a drink. We usually made the drinks pretty strong.

Anyway, Melissa and I were sitting close together when the game started. When it came my turn, I bounced the quarter in on my first try. I turned and moved a little closer to Melissa and asked, "Would you like to share this with me?"

Heather snapped, "That's not how you play!"

But Melissa and I crossed our glasses around each other's arms, holding our glasses up close to our lips, and drank together. I was feeling really good that night sitting close to Melissa and ignoring all the negativity that was coming from across the table.

Meanwhile, Dave was sitting close to Tammy, and Heather began to throw a temper tantrum about it. As for Melissa and me, we were forced—by the negative energy coming from everyone else in the room—to stick close together. However, though Melissa was very pretty, we were in no way drawn together by any *physical* attraction.

Melissa actually lived in the small town of Perry, Maine, four and a half hours away. Tammy had recently relocated there to stay with the family of her first child. Both Melissa and Tammy had to return to Perry by the end of the week, with no one else willing to take the trip. I was more than happy to spend another four and a half hours sitting in the front seat next to Melissa.

It was cold and damp that Easter Sunday. We had to squeeze two large duffle bags beside Tammy in the back seat of my little Ford Escort. I was looking forward to the long ride, even allowing Melissa to take the driver's seat.

Tammy soon fell asleep after we got on the highway, leaving Melissa and me alone together in the front seat for the next four hours. Melissa drove pretty radical and too fast for the mood I was in, and her selection of music was far beyond my taste. Listening to bands like Skid Row and Aerosmith, for which I wasn't in the mood, I still felt a positive energy sitting close to Mellissa. I eventually tried to get her to like some of the music I liked by slipping in a Smiths tape playing the song, "There is a Light That Never Goes Out." The lyrics to the song were perfect for the mood I was feeling.

But I could tell Melissa just wasn't into it. For some reason, though, I still liked her and, so that I could be more like her, I asked if I should start smoking.

She turned and looked at me with an almost angry expression, laughing at the same time. "Don't you dare start smoking just because of me."

I lit one up, anyway. Melissa and I were such complete opposites, yet I felt such a strong desire to be with her. I was praying the ride would never end.

But with her kind of radical driving and music playing, the time passed too quickly, and we were very close to her home when we dropped Tammy off. Then Melissa gave me a quick tour of the small town of Calais before we crossed over the border to St. Stephens, New Brunswick, the place she was born. Although she'd lived in the United States for most of her life, she was still a Canadian citizen.

The ride was over with a long hug and an empty feeling like something had been torn from my heart. I had to face that four and a half hours of driving back home by myself.

I had a deep fear that I might never see Melissa again.

A few weeks had passed when Tammy had had enough of living so far away from the rest of her friends and family. She called Heather, begging her to find someone willing to give her a ride back home to Biddeford.

That's when Dave volunteered *us*.

We left work as early as we could, and I let Dave do all the driving. It was late at night by the time we arrived to pick up Tammy. I had kept a silent hope that Melissa would be riding along with us, but no such luck. I climbed in the back seat and left the two alone in the front.

I tried to snuggle under a blanket and maybe get a little sleep, knowing we had to get up early for work the next morning. But no sooner did we get a few miles down the road than Tammy turned around and asked me if I had Melissa's phone number.

"No, I forgot to ask her."

Tammy passed me a tiny piece of paper with Melissa's phone number written on it.

"Thank you," I said, a bit of excitement in my voice, my hopes of seeing Melissa again possibly to be realized soon.

I waited for a good excuse to call her. When I heard the news that Aerosmith was coming to Old Orchard Beach I knew the concert could be my opportunity. I called Melissa up with the exciting news, and she was as excited about seeing Aerosmith as I was as excited about seeing her again.

I completed my work ahead of schedule the week of the concert and left immediately after work on Thursday for the long ride up to see Melissa. It was a lonely ride. But when I saw her waiting for me at a little corner store, she looked so beautiful sitting on the front steps smoking a cigarette that I stepped out of the car and ran to embrace her, feeling happiness again after months of negativity. It was truly good medicine for me.

I let Melissa drive while I sat in the passenger's seat next to her, knowing she was going to be with me for all of the next two days.

The following morning, I took Melissa for a motorcycle ride. She wasn't impressed with downtown Portland or any of the other places I showed her. But she did enjoy riding with me.

When we returned back to Old Orchard Beach, she wanted to hang out with Tammy and Heather for a few hours before the concert. I stayed up in my apartment, cooking up a big vegetarian dinner and hoping Melissa would come up and join me. I only ate by myself, though, worried she never ate enough. She'd hardly eaten anything at all since she'd been here with me, and what little she had eaten was junk food.

And now she was downstairs drinking with Heather and Tammy.

This didn't look good.

We all walked up to the stadium together. I stayed close to Melissa but noticed her eyes where already checking out other guys. The Black Crows were already finishing up preparations for their opening act when we arrived at the front gate. Leaving Heather, Tammy, and Dave outside, Melissa and I had our tickets in hand, while they had to listen and peek through the gate.

Melissa wasn't satisfied with the front row bleacher seats we had, though, and a crowd of fans up behind us weren't satisfied either. Many were jumping the rail to get a better seat, but the security guards would catch them and bring them back.

Then a group of 20 decided that on the count of 3—1-2-3!—they would all jump the rail all at once. But the security personnel rushed to stop them, and that's when Melissa and I just stepped over the rail and walked to the front.

As soon as Aerosmith took the stage, the pushing and shoving for the front row moved us in separate directions. Suddenly, I had no idea where Melissa was. Watching Steven Tyler sing like a wild man from about three rows back, and pushed further to the side, it was hard for me to enjoy the show. I was worried about Melissa. Maybe the security guys dragged her away, or she'd gotten crushed in the crowd.

After the concert was over, I went searching for her but ended up walking home alone.

When I got there, she was there waiting for me.

I ran to her arms like an insecure child who'd lost their mother. "I was so worried about you when I couldn't find you!"

But she just went on and on, excited to tell me how close she'd been to the stage. She'd actually managed to squeeze herself up to the front. And now she sounded completely love-struck as she told me she'd been able to see straight into the eyes of Joe Perry. She'd had a crush on lead guitarist Joe Perry for a long time, but on this night, she'd been able to see into his eyes and was overjoyed.

"He was so close, he looked right at me! Oh, I can't believe he looked right into my eyes."

It was obvious that Melissa had had a really great time without me.

But I'd had enough for the evening and went upstairs to my room where I felt safe, snuggled up in bed with MARi, while Melissa stayed out a little longer to party down in Heather's apartment.

Melissa must have come in very late in the evening. When I woke up, I found her asleep on my couch.

I tried eating breakfast but was feeling depressed and didn't have much of an appetite. Melissa didn't eat much either and we got ready to take that one last journey back to Perry, Maine. I knew I would never see her again and should have been glad. She'd never really been very nice to me.

It was a long ride ahead of us and we made sure we brought a large selection of music to listen to. Melissa kept pretty quiet until we got few miles down the road and she started cursing about Heather.

"Heather was doing her thing last night. I hate what she does, I hate it!

I don't ever want to be associated with anyone like that." She went on to tell about all the disgusting old men paying Heather money for sex. "I hate it, I hate it!" she repeated.

"I hate it too," I said, staring out the side window while Melissa kept driving. She had Eagles' Greatest Hits in the tape deck but rewound it every time the song Desperado ended.

She played that song eleven more times, then I started to cry.

Melissa really knew how to torment a guy, but it wasn't the thought of never seeing her again that was tormenting me. I didn't think I ever really loved Melissa, anyway, and I didn't think we even liked each other. It was just that I had tremendous fear of negative energy coming from the only friend I would have left when Melissa was gone.

I hung on to our moment together before saying our last goodbye.

And after we had hugged, an empty feeling came over me and I drove away from Melissa listening to my own music for moping to the song. "I Know It's Over," by The Smiths, and it set the mood for my long ride home.

Heather was inviting just about anybody passing by on the street to come to her parties. Sometimes her place became pretty crowded with total strangers just joining in for the beer or to share a joint. Heather loved being the popular host.

"Hey, I love this place I sucked a lot of cock to get all this." she bragged proudly out loud in front of all her guests. Most of her guests thought she was a little strange but showed up regularly at her parties, anyway, seeing that there were far more interesting people there than any place else. A small group of friends from Biddeford had also started coming almost every night. Maybe it was because they were too young to get into bars, or it was that there was plenty of beer and weed at Heather's house that kept them coming.

In those days, Dave and I had been working a lot of overtime, Dave being the truck driver and traveling back and forth. I had to stay all six weeks up in Bangor while I left Dave in charge of feeding MARi at home. I worked in constant worry about her but knew I could count on Dave to feed her. I worked over seventy hours per week until that job was completed just before September 1st.

Even though I had plenty of money in the bank after that, serious financial difficulties were just the beginning of the problems to come. For instance, I received notification in the mail of an over $200 increase in my monthly mortgage payments due to the short fall in my escrow account. When I first read the notice, I got on the phone and started screaming the demanding they fix the problem, or I would never make another payment again.

I truly believed at the time that those harsh words were enough to make any banker reexamine the mistake they had made and correct the problem. I went back to relaxing on the couch with my kitty every evening, not giving it another thought.

One evening, Dave came upstairs to pour himself a glass of Jack Daniels. With a little anger in his voice he mumbled, "I can't wait till this life is over!"

I sat holding MARi on my couch, watching him pour his drink. I asked, "Where's Dave gonna go when this life is over?"

He just slammed his fist down on the counter top, swallowed his Jack Daniels, shook his head a few times, and blurted out, "I'm going to Hell!"

"That's right," I said. "You know it's a better place than you are now."

Then he stormed out the door.

Everything changed quickly the first weekend of September. Heather's partying had gotten so out of control she never told Dave or anyone else about her eviction notice that she had received a few months earlier. She simply kept collecting Dave's $50 a week to sleep on her couch, never giving it one thought that the day would come when the Sheriff's Department would actually have her physically removed.

This all happened after she sold all the kitchen appliances.

Dave went back to sleeping on my couch and a few girls from his small circle of friends began to gather in my little apartment. We shut Heather completely out of our circle of friends.

I sat quietly holding MARi while listening to all the disgusting stories about Heather. I knew everything they were saying about her was true, but I felt a bit guilty laughing while the girls continued talking behind her back. There had been a time when Heather was the only friend I had in this world. And this small group of new friends I had now would never have met if we had not known Heather.

One evening, we all went out for a walk together, enjoying the close bond of friendships we hoped would never end. The air was feeling colder now that the summer was over, but anyone could see that this was one happy group of friends.

Suddenly, a car pulled up to the curb near us. Heather shouted out the back window, "Hey, thanks for stealing all my friends!"

CHAPTER 24

Circumstances

With the colder nights settling in, a group of my closely bonding new friends gathered around my couch and living room floor. Couples began pairing up.

Dave had just started dating Lynn, a tall, thin 19-year-old girl with a pretty face, brown hair, and light blue eyes. Then there was Mary and Kato, a couple who had been going together through most of the summer but were now taking their relationship more seriously.

With this closeness of friends, I felt very relaxed at home, sharing lots of laughter and good times. We all enjoyed pigging out while watching Gilligan's Island on TV, then cranking up some music and drinking beer. It was a place to feel free and at home for anyone who needed a place to sleep.

Ann sat across the room sipping her wine cooler while I sat by myself looking out the window and trying not to be seen noticing if Ann showed a slight bit of interest in me. I didn't want her to think I did. Ann was very pretty with beautiful brown eyes and dark hair. But for some reason, I tried to keep my distance from her. I never understood why she even hung out with us. She was totally different from the rest of us. She always wore short skirts, high-heeled shoes, and way too much makeup.

Instead of drinking beer like the rest of us, she drank wine. If I said anything to her at all, she just rolled her eyes back like she'd just heard something stupid. She constantly complained every time a guy looked at her, but she complained even more when she got no looks at all. The only guy Ann ever took seriously was a married man who took her to his hotel room every time he was in town for business. The guy had promised her he would leave his wife and kids to marry her one day, filling her head with a lot of false hope.

Anyway, the circumstances were, she was at my house every night with no place else to go. Lynn and Dave had pretty much taken over my living room couch, so, the first few nights Ann slept on my living room floor… until she just couldn't take it anymore, and she made a demand of me.

"Come on Smitty," she said, "let's get out. Let's go for a ride somewhere, anywhere. We gotta get out for a while."

I agreed we'd spent way too much time cramped up in my little apartment. I really didn't want to waste any money on gas, but it was a spur-of-the-moment thing. I let her take over and drive, and she drove us late into the night, telling me her life story. She also complained about Lynn and Dave always making out on my couch like a couple of insecure 16-year-olds who just couldn't keep away from each other.

"Those two make me sick," Ann kept repeating.

We rode to a small town in New Hampshire, the place where she lived through most of her high school years. We stopped to visit one of her old high school friends who shared an apartment with her boyfriend. We all sat around the kitchen table while the two girls babbled on for hours. The boyfriend and I sat quietly watching and enduring all the babble about absolutely nothing.

Finally, they stopped, and Ann's friend asked, "So, how did you two meet?"

It was embarrassing that she clearly assumed we were already a couple. We just looked at each other, wondering what to say.

"Well, we…ah, just kinda, ah …. ended up together because no one could stand either one of us… so we just kinda got stuck with each other," I said.

Ann and I both knew very well we couldn't stand each other. It was merely circumstances that kept us together. We had been spending so much time together, people had actually started thinking of us as a couple. But we argued everywhere we went. Lynn had even made the comment, "You two fight like you're married."

Sometimes, I even thought that an evil fate had brought Ann and me together. So, in some ways, I found it quite amusing that people thought of us the way they did. Because most of the time, Ann was just as annoying to me as I was to her.

One rainy evening we were out riding in my car, listening to an oldies station. When the song "Rainy Night in Georgia" by Brook Benton came over the airwaves, it was a beautiful moment to reminisce to the song and the lyrics. I sat gazing out the window, rain pouring down on the roof of the car.

But suddenly my moment was interrupted.

"What the hell is this crap?!" Ann said, quickly changing the station.

"Everybody Dance Now" by C+C Music Factory was the most annoying song I'd ever heard. But this chick cranked it up as if it was the best song she'd ever heard.

"What the hell did you do that for?" I asked. "I was get'n into that other song and you changed it to *this* crap!" I tried tuning the radio back to the other song, but now that Ann was arguing with me, I couldn't recapture the former beautiful feeling the song had at first given me.

Ann and I might have argued a lot, but there were times we stayed up late into the night playing gin rummy and sipping wine. That was about as happy as it ever got, though, when we were together. I didn't mind washing all her laundry, doing all the cooking for us, and washing all the dishes, while she pretty much laid around watching TV through most of the day. I even gave her my shoulder to cry on.

And most of the time, I was able to hide my depression from Ann. But one night we were sitting alone together on my couch, and I asked her if she would be willing to take care of MARi if I killed myself. I told her I'd give her $10,000 to buy 10,000 boxes of cat food for the rest of her life.

Her eyes lit up with excitement.

And I imagined her going on a shopping spree. I envisioned all the clothes she would have bought. I really didn't think she'd have cared if my cat was fed or not.

So, I decided to hang in there just for the sake of my cat.

Tension was growing between me and the mortgage company that was threatening to raise my monthly payments. Using a lot of curse words, I made it clear to them that I was not going to pay one penny more. I had already been ripped off by their high interest rates when I bought my place. My whole purpose in buying it had been to keep my living expenses low. But then I'd also gotten ripped off buying my motorcycle and my car.

Frustration and anger had been building up inside of me as I saw all my plans for an easy life getting extremely difficult. And to make matters worse, work came almost to a standstill after I lost my temper on a jobsite. I was terminated from the only major construction project going on at that time, which was just before an approaching recession.

At first, I didn't let my job loss bother me. I had plenty of money in the bank and I needed the break from work. But then Dave and Lynn found a very affordable cozy little apartment for just $75 per week, leaving me stuck living with Ann.

And Ann wasted no time at all redecorating the place and making it her own. I tried my best to get along with Ann and make the best of what we had. Plus, I was running out of money fast, jobs were hard to find, and the few small drywall jobs I did find offered pay so low we barely made enough to cover the utilities and food for both of us.

One afternoon when the telephone rang, I answered, hearing a familiar voice asking for Ann. I knew right away whose voice it was, although I'd never met the guy. I'd heard his voice many times before when Bobbie and Denise had lived with me, and I knew exactly what this guy was looking for.

He was always looking for young girls who would do anything for money.

When I first confronted Ann about it, she tried to deny the voice I heard was of the same man. But I knew. And slamming a rack of dishes on the floor, I demanded to know why that man was calling.

She blurted out, "BECAUSE WE NEED THE MONEY!"

"WE DON'T NEED THAT KIND OF MONEY!" I shouted back. "I THOUGHT YOU HAD MORE CLASS THAN THAT!"

The arguing got pretty ugly.

Ann kept insisting it was none of my business.

But if she was living under my roof and eating my food, I had the right to say how I felt about it.

She threatened to leave.

But then she realized she had nowhere else she could go.

By January of 1991, the weather outside was bitterly cold, with no jobs for either of us. We spent a lot of time together in my cozy little condo. We still didn't like each other, but we tried to keep ourselves occupied. We often stayed up late into the night writing letters to our wanna-fall- in-love-with significant one that we wished we could be with. I wrote a two-page letter to Angela, a girl I had only met through an agency I found advertising British/American pen pals in the back pages of Spin Magazine. Angela and I were both big fans of the music groups The SMITHS and Morrissey, and as for me, I was in love after the first letter I received from Angela. I was hoping with each letter that she felt the same about me.

Ann wrote to her married man. She had already written over twenty pages before I finished writing my two. She continued to write long into the night.

I continued to wake up early every morning. Even if I wasn't working, I was out looking every chance a got. But I usually came home feeling depressed because there just wasn't enough work anywhere.

I drove Ann to a few job interviews, but because of the way she dressed—with a short skirt and showing a lot of cleavage—I thought she looked a little provocative for a job interviews. I was surprised she got any offers at all and was upset when she stormed out of an interview angry that they had only offered her five dollars an hour.

"But that's more than you're making sitting on my couch doing nothing," I argued in the car, driving Ann back home. I didn't get it. All that time we wasted, bored out of our minds, and she wouldn't take a $5.00/ hour job. I would have done it for fifty cents an hour just to have something to do with my time.

We were definitely wasting too much time together doing nothing.

Ann and I shared a few more lonely nights in my apartment.

Then I got a phone call from Carlene, a friend of a friend, crying on the phone because her boyfriend had just broken up with her. She was gasping for breath and sounding hysterically out of control, telling me all her drama.

She screamed into the phone, "HE HAD ME ALL SET UP JUST SO HE COULD LET ME DOWN!"

I tried to calm her down, and knowing she needed a shoulder to cry on, I invited her over to hang out with us.

Carlene got along really well with Ann. The two of them stayed up late into the night talking about sex, guys, and all the times they'd been all set up, just to be let down. I knew it hadn't been very long before this that Carlene had one of my friends all set up just so she could let *him* down.

But now everything was different because it had happened to her.

While I was always there for Ann, or anybody else, to lean on during emotionally unstable times, nobody was ever there to help me, and nobody cared about my situation with the mortgage company. I was getting more and more frustrated, calling all over Southern Maine and not finding even one lawyer who would listen to me. Most of them, I was sure, would jump at the chance to represent a criminal. But as for me, I had to deal with city hall sending me the wrong tax bill and my mortgage company raising my monthly rate to cover the short fall in my escrow account. On top of these things, they wanted to bill me for insurance on this property that I didn't even own.

I never really wanted to raise my voice or use profane words, but many of those lawyers I tried to explain my situation to were very disrespectful and rude to me. Plus, the mortgage company had rejected every payment since October of 1990 and were now threatening to foreclose.

I was getting extremely angry. Things weren't supposed to be this way, and I thought I had done everything right. I had always paid my bills at least a month in advance. I had always planned ahead to always make life easy. Now everything I'd worked for had gone wrong. What was I going to do? Nobody was there to help me.

I got down on my knees and asked God to help me, and for the first time in nearly three years I cried. Then I picked myself up and came up with a new plan.

"Ann," I said, "we gotta start looking for a new place to live. The bank wants to foreclose on this place, so we need to find a place fast. I have some money reserved in 10-year savings certificates, and I could cash them in, eight years early. I'll have to pay a large fee, but that's the only money we have, and we've got to get out of this place."

Ann was with me on this and I was glad. If I was to go out on my own looking for an apartment, nobody would take me seriously, no matter how much money

I showed them. With Ann by my side, we looked like a happy couple as we drove around viewing every available apartment in Old Orchard Beach. I was hoping to find a cozy, affordable place like Lynn and Dave had.

But Ann had better ideas. She did all the talking, and I followed close behind holding my checkbook. We looked at many beautiful apartments. Some were not available right away. Some were way too expensive. Some places didn't allow cats. Some were cheap, but Ann said *no way* to them.

Then we viewed a beautiful penthouse at the top of The Brunswick Hotel.

"I want this one," Ann insisted with confidence, walking through the spacious living room and stepping out through the large glass doors looking down on the beach from the balcony.

"I don't know," I said, shaking my head. "I'm not sure if we can afford it."

Ann walked up the stairs where the landlord showed us another two bedrooms, another balcony, and two more bathrooms—which made three bathrooms total. All this was available for just $600 per month.

But then the landlord dropped a bomb. "Oh, but I'll have to charge $1,000 for the months of July and August. This place rents for a lot more during the tourist season."

"No way. We can't afford it." My pulse was rising as I turned to Ann. "There's just no way we can afford this place."

"Oh, but we'll both be working by then," she countered. "We can easily afford it if we both have jobs."

Like Ann, I was getting tired of searching. I also feared not finding a place before being forced to leave my old condo by foreclosure. And this apartment was a great deal for the price. I had enough money to pay three months in advance.

With Ann's persistence, I gave in and signed the lease. I immediately wrote out a check to cover the rent for the next three months, leaving us plenty of time to figure out how we were going to pay the rent three months from now.

Ann and I were pretty excited about our new place. We moved in just one week after signing the lease. Mary and Kato showed up to help us move some of the larger furniture. It took about a day and a half before I had everything out of my little condo.

In some ways, I was happy to be finally leaving that tiny place, it had so many bad memories. But I also had a lot of anger because I'd put so much money into it, and now I had to give it all up. Many people told me I was stupid for giving up my home after paying three and a half years on it, but they really didn't know the circumstances.

The truth was, I'd tried to get help. I'd tried talking to city hall. I'd tried to find a lawyer. I'd prayed.

But each and every time I'd tried to solve my problems, I'd been treated like I didn't count. It was finally time to move forward and not look back.

The first night in our new apartment, we invited all our friends. Ann couldn't wait to show Lynn, Dave, Mary, and Kato how well we were living. The first words that came out of Dave's mouth after seeing our new place were, "I'm glad I'm not paying for all this."

I pretended I loved our new apartment. But deep down inside, I worried. *Neither one of us has a full-time job. What are we gonna do three months from now when the rent is due?*

Ann laughed after everybody left and said, "They're all so jealous of us. We have all this, and all they have is their little piece of shit apartment."

I really didn't think anyone was jealous of us. I certainly didn't feel like we had anything at all. With money being so tight, there was no telling how soon it would be before we lost everything.

We continued inviting friends over every night, and I continued to pretend to be happy living with Ann.

In early April of 1991, going into our second month of living in the penthouse, the place was beginning to feel like home. I took a huge cut in pay to just $8.50 per hour in order to regain my fulltime job at Wagner Drywall. I didn't complain about the pay. I knew there were a lot of people out of work, and I felt lucky to find any job at all during the recession. I set everything I made aside. I wanted to make sure we stayed at least one month ahead on the rent.

Plus, it was beginning to seem that Ann and I were getting along well. Ann found a job waiting tables. She even helped pay some of the rent as she promised. We made a few new friends when Ann's brother Aaron brought a few of his friends over. Ryan was a blonde-haired guy who always a had big smile. Ann really liked Ryan, and for the two of them, it was almost love at first sight—for a few weeks, anyway. Then he dumped her.

And there was Sandy, a thin, dark-haired 24-year-old mother of two. It didn't concern Aaron that she was still married. He kept commenting about her legs and about how he couldn't wait till she had them wrapped around him.

And then there was Sandy's best friend Michelle, a beautiful, dark- skinned 19-year-old with a pretty face and a beautiful smile. She always carried a big plastic cup with a straw filled with coffee brandy. She had a very interesting taste in music. She reminded me a lot of myself when I was her age.

And her eyes lit up when she found out from Ann that we were not at all the couple we appeared to be.

At that instant, I knew Michelle was planning to make a move on me.

CHAPTER 25

That Haunting Feeling

Michelle sat on the living room floor giving Tarot Card readings. I sat in the circle with Sandy, Aaron, Ryan, and Ann. Dave sat on the couch with his arm around Lynn, looking on in disbelief. He'd been raised in a Pentecostal church and believed Tarot Cards were only of use in attracting evil spirits.

Sandy, though, said she wanted to know if there was any way she could contact her ex-boyfriend who had died in a motorcycle accident a few years ago.

"Well, I've got a Ouija Board upstairs," I said, excitement in my voice. "I've had it for a few years and never used it because I never had the right group of people together willing to try it out."

This was my chance. Michelle was an experienced Ouija Board leader.

So, while Dave and Lynn stayed downstairs, the rest of us went upstairs. But Ann got scared and left the room as soon as we laid the board out on the floor, and Aaron and Ryan left the room shortly after the lights went out.

It was just Sandy and I, then, we sat quietly in the dimly lit room as Michelle set her hands softly over the planchette, speaking in a very strange voice. I began to feel very fidgety. As the excitement wore off, I felt a strange spirit come over me. The planchette moved slowly, and my whole body was shaking. I tried to sit still and relax. But I couldn't, and we heard strange noises all around us.

I suddenly stood up and said, "The reason he's upset with you is because you married this other man so quickly after his death."

Instantly, all the sound around us quieted. The planchette stopped moving.

Michelle stood up and said, "That's it, there's your answer."

I felt a little confused. We had gone through all these spirits just to find an answer to something I'd known all along. Sandy's boyfriend had died in a motorcycle accident, and she'd married another man less than two months later. Sandy's former boyfriend must have been wondering if she'd really felt anything for him at all.

Anyway, when the game was over, I didn't think much of it. We all went back downstairs and drank a few more glasses of coffee brandy, laughing and enjoying the rest of our evening. I said to Dave, "How come you and Lynn didn't want to join in on it? You missed out. We could feel spirits moving all around us."

Dave shook his head. "No way. I won't have anything to do with that thing. Keep that Ouija board away from me."

I'd thought of it as a truly interesting experience, though, and wanted to go deeper into the spirit world.

But after that night, Michelle insisted she never wanted to see another Ouija Board again.

I couldn't figure out why.

Dave and Lynn were truly happy together and I was happy for them. Though Ann kept insisting that they were extremely jealous of us, I knew those two were truly made for each other. Dave had cut back on his drinking, had started dressing in nicer clothes, and was keeping their apartment clean. Everything about him and Lynn showed a real love for each other.

Meanwhile, Ann continued to show our apartment off to every guy she met. Most of them were scared away by her high-maintenance lifestyle. At times, I'd answer the phone in the middle of the night and have to listen to another story about how gorgeous Ann was and how she'd had a guy all set up just to let him down. One guy even threatened to slash the tires on her car after what she did to him.

I said, "Wait a minute. That's *my* car she drives."

I'd suddenly found myself caught in the middle of approaching trouble. But mostly, I didn't let it bother me. In fact, I kept to myself most of the time. Except for nights when Sandy and Michelle were in the apartment, I stayed in my room writing letters to Angela.

My heart was still set on Angela. I ignored all the looming trouble that Ann was bringing into this place. I was determined that when I found the opportunity to save some money, I was going to pay for Angela's flight to America and we were going to escape from this place to find happiness together.

So, I worked as much overtime as I could, whenever I could. Given my low wages and the cost of living in Ann's and my apartment, though, I was struggling just to pay the rent each month, leaving barely enough money for anything else.

And since I had my heart set on Angela, no one else was going to come between me and my plan to fall in love with her. That was, until one night that I had thought would be just another night of coffee brandy and listening to music…

We all sat on the floor in front of my stereo, a selection of CD's scattered before us. Michelle was sitting so close to me that I could feel the energy drawing us together. There was nothing that could have stopped us.

She leaned forward and kissed me.

I felt her soft lips, then the taste of coffee brandy as her tongue slipped through my lips. I lay on the floor, paralyzed, as she laid herself on top of me. The feeling was so good that I asked myself, *Should I give up on Angela and give all of my love to Michelle?*

I felt torn. This unexpected new thing had happened so suddenly. I was still in love with Angela, a girl I hadn't even met yet, and now I was falling for Michelle, whose kiss felt so good. *I must surrender all of my love to Michelle now!* I thought.

Suddenly, Ann walked through the door. But she quickly turned around and left, seeing what was going on. So, Michelle and I quickly resumed our kissing— passionately, non-stop, late into the night—until she passed out on my living room floor.

I quietly ran up to my room and laid on my bed thinking about both Angela and Michelle. I ended up staying awake all night trying to decide.

I really liked Michelle, but I hadn't even met Angela yet.

Michelle was beautiful, but so was my picture of Angela.

I could have Michelle now. I would have to wait for Angela.

Angela could help me get out of the country, and we could move to England or Scotland, which is what I really wanted—to get out of the country after the foreclosure on my condo. I'd never be able to buy a house or establish credit to buy anything in this country again.

Yes, I wanted to be with Angela and move to Scotland to start life over.

But Michelle…her kisses felt so good.

I just couldn't decide.

The next morning, I was downstairs. Michelle had left sometime in the night. I had thought she would wait to see me.

When I returned home from work that evening, I called Michelle and told her how worried about her I'd been. I hadn't wanted her to drive herself home, drunk as she was. And I told her that I really loved her, even though I'd had my heart set on Angela, which left me with a tough decision.

In the end, though, I did know what I truly wanted.

When I lay in my bed that night, I felt the presence of spirits moving about my room. I didn't think much of them. They were just there, nothing more than visitors. I'd lain awake at night before, battling thoughts of Angela or Michelle. Praying for a sign from God to help me make the right decision, I could hear those spirits laughing at me and flying about the room.

Their laughter made me angry when I tried to fall asleep, those same spirits waking me with fear many times during the night. But finally, I chose not to let them bother me. I spoke out loud to them, "I'm not scared of you! Get out! You don't scare me one bit."

The spirits kept coming back to bother me once in a while, though, and most of the time I had to make myself ignore them.

Before the start of the summer, Ann's brother Aaron needed a place to stay for a while. Ann suggested he could sleep on our couch for $100 a week. This arrangement helped us out a great deal just before the summer's rent jumped to $1,000 for the months of July and August. We easily covered all the bills over the summer, then, and I was even able to save a lot more money with all the overtime I was working.

So, knowing this would be my only opportunity to do so, I let Angela know in my next letter that I was willing to pay for her flight if she was willing to come and stay for a two-week visit. She agreed, and we set a date. We would meet at Boston's Logan Airport on October 2, 1991.

Over the next several weeks our letters crossed in the mail. Our anticipation and excitement grew with each letter.

When our big day came, I arrived at the airport early, giving myself plenty of time to find the right terminal and be ready when I finally met Angela. Feeling very nervous and excited at the same time, I waited, the moment of her arrival just a few minutes away.

But when I watched her flight number light up, I started to panic! Her plane would be landing in just a few minutes and I'd been waiting at the wrong terminal!

I ran to find the nearest information booth. The woman there told me all incoming flights were on the other side of the airport.

"Oh, no!!!" I freaked out.

The lady quickly advised me to take the shuttle bus.

But I had no time to wait around for the shuttle bus. I ran, franticly searching... searching...till I *finally* found the right terminal.

Out of breath, I watched for Angela, my excitement reaching its peak. I shifted nervously as I looked for a beautiful young lady with auburn hair and brown eyes and wearing a Smiths T-shirt. My eyes sifted feverishly through the crowd of arriving passengers.

Then I saw her.

But...she appeared to be tired, maybe from jetlag.

She looked up and right away noticed me wearing my own Smiths T-shirt.

A wave of disappointment swept over me. Maybe I'd expected too much. Angela wasn't at all what I'd thought she would be.

Anyway, she was finally here, and I had to make the best of it.

I approached her and said, "Hi, are you Angela?"

She looked at me and smiled. "Yes," she answered with her British accent.

We didn't have a whole lot more to say to each other as I helped carry her luggage to my car. I wasn't sure if she was feeling as disappointed in meeting me as I was in meeting her, but she kept quiet for the first half-hour of our two-hour ride up to Maine.

When she finally broke the silence again with her British accent, she asked, "Do you mind if I smoke?"

My disappointment fell to another level. "They're your lungs, you do what you want."

"Well, some people don't allow smoking in their car." She'd lashed back at me quickly, starting up our first argument.

"If you wanna smoke, then go ahead and smoke. I don't care."

I knew very well I hated the smell of cigarette smoke, but I'd let her do whatever she wanted.

I tried to make the best of the next two weeks, taking Angela to all the places I'd promised in my letters. First, we went to New York City to see the Statue of Liberty. Surprisingly, we got along very well on the trip, and I allowed her to do most of the driving. She wasn't impressed with the filthy streets of New York, but we both enjoyed each other's company, singing along whenever we heard a good song on the radio. I even found myself singing along to George Michael's "One More Try" and sharing cigarettes with Angela on the way back.

What's happening to me? I asked myself. *Am I becoming more like this girl? Or am I pretending I like George Michael and smoking cigarettes to impress her? Do I have to let my standards down to make this relationship work out? I've waited too long, invested too much time and money into bringing her here. We've got to make this work out!*

That was all I was thinking in the short time we spent together.

Dave and Lynn got along fine with Angela. They came over to meet her and enjoyed playing board games, drinking beer, and laughing late into the night.

Lynn pulled me aside. "She's really nice, Smitty. Don't blow it."

Yeah, I know.

And she seemed to be very nice to most of my other friends.

But she was also embarrassing at times when we were out together—like the time she decided to light up a cigarette in a coffee shop, flicking the ashes on a spread-out newspaper and demanding to know why our table didn't have an ashtray.

I noticed everybody was staring at our table.

The manager came out to ask her kindly to please extinguish her cigarette. Smoking was prohibited in his coffee shop.

She argued with the man, saying it was ridiculous that she was not allowed to smoke while drinking her coffee.

I felt that, since she was my date, I should have been defending her.

But she was clearly in the wrong.

The final blow came when Angela was cleaning out the inside of my car as we rode down the highway. She tossed all the trash out the window.

"WHAT DID YOU DO THAT FOR?!" I shouted, watching through the rearview mirror as the paper bag broke open and trash blew everywhere.

She looked at me. "Well, I was trying to clean out your car."

"You didn't have to throw all that trash out the window! You remember how much you hated those filthy streets in New York City?"

I tried to talk some sense into her, but she kept insisting that one small bag of trash wouldn't make a difference. We got into a pretty heated argument that ended in no talking between us.

The following day, she called the airline and found out she could trade her flight ticket for an immediate flight back home. This shortened her two-week visit to just ten days.

And I was more than glad to take her back to the airport later that evening.

We hugged each other good-bye one last time, but with a cold lack of sympathy. I felt sad, but when I got back to my car, the first words I mumbled to myself were, "Yuck! She was disgusting. I'm glad she's gone."

She was gone and I didn't have to listen to her constant complaining or put up with her annoying smoking and heavy drinking. I should have been feeling relieved.

But driving away from the airport, that old familiar empty feeling of being alone began to haunt me again. I missed having Angela next to me. I missed her constant whining and complaining.

Severe depression overtook me for the next several weeks. I tried taking up many of Angela's habits, like smoking and drinking coffee. She'd left behind for me a cassette tape by Right Said Fred. "I'm too sexy for my shirt, so sexy it hurts." I hated it. I thought it had the stupidest lyrics.

But suddenly, I couldn't stop thinking of Angela, listening to anything and doing everything to make me feel like she was still there with me.

By mid-November, Ann found herself a steady boyfriend.

Meanwhile, I was still moping, trying to recover from the emptiness I'd been feeling.

And after having spent a whole year living on false hope, I found myself flat broke again. Feeling weak and emotionally drained, I went to bed early every night, feeling the return of those former haunting spirits. I felt their presence as they flew around the ceiling, and again I tried not to let them bother me.

But each night they kept returning. And I could tell that MARi sensed something evil in my room. She clearly felt scared and ran out every time those spirits returned. This last time, they let their presence be known with fierce anger and I could feel those haunting spirits coming at me, then through me, then back up to the ceiling. I heard laughter like they were laughing at my soul. They knew I was feeling weak, and they were ready to destroy me.

Still, I tried to show no fear. "GET OUT, I AINT SCARED OF YOU!" I demanded.

But with more fierce anger, those spirits returned. I couldn't stand it anymore. The fear was so overwhelming that I crawled out of bed and knelt down on the side of my bed to pray. "Please, God, in the name of Jesus, forgive me for all my sins, and please drive these evil spirits away."

Instantly, there was silence. The spirits were gone.

I crawled back in my bed, still feeling a little shaken. And I was finally able to get some sleep.

Those spirits never returned.

By the end of December, Ann and I celebrated Christmas with a beautiful decorated tree set up in front of the big windows overlooking the ocean. MARi slept on top of a beautifully wrapped box. Ann's boyfriend smiled, and with a pretending-to-be-friendly look about him, he reached down and tried to pet MARi.

But MARi could always sense trouble, even before it arrived. She hissed and ran upstairs to hide.

It wasn't long after that that the police were knocking on our door, looking for a guy named Scott Simpson and showing us a mugshot of a guy that looked just like Ann's boyfriend.

I said, "He's not here right now."

But the police seemed ready to force their way in.

"I SAID HE'S NOT HERE!"

They clearly knew that they could come no further without a warrant.

When Ann returned home later that night, I informed her that the police had been there just a few hours ago looking for Scott.

She didn't seem surprised at all. She said she already knew the police were out looking for him. She told me about the story he'd given her of how he was being falsely accused of rape, forgery, and credit card theft.

I raised my voice and said, "ANN, WHAT THE HELL DOES THIS GUY DO FOR WORK?! HE SPENDS MONEY LIKE HE DOESN'T CARE WHERE IT'S COMING FROM! DOES HE EVEN HAVE A JOB? HE'S WITH YOU EVERY

DAY AND EVERY NIGHT AND I'VE NEVER SEEN HIM GOING TO WORK! HOW DOES HE MAKE HIS MONEY?!"

Ann tried to defend him, saying, "He said he owns some apartment buildings."

"And you believe him?" I said, shaking my head. "I don't want you bringing that guy back here anymore."

We were into a pretty heated argument and Ann kept insisting she could bring anybody she wanted into our apartment as long as her name was on the lease.

In the days following, the police knocked on the door a few more times looking for Scott Simpson and becoming very annoyed, insisting that I knew where he was.

At that time, money was tight, and I had such a fear of creditors seizing my money that I kept very little of it in the bank. I had to hide what little money I earned where I thought it was safe to hide—behind a picture, inside the frame.

And I did this until the day I was planning to use the money to pay the rent. But I was shocked as I opened up the frame and there was no money there.

I burst out in anger, "ANN!!! WHERE THE HELL IS SCOTT?!" I screamed, coming down the stairs.

Ann was sitting calmly on the couch, as if wondering what I was so upset about. "He's not here," she said. "He had to leave for a few weeks on a business trip."

"HE STOLE OUR RENT MONEY!"

"What? He couldn't have." Ann insisted he didn't do it. "There's no way he could have gone in your room. I was with him the entire time. It wasn't him! No way! He would never do that."

"WE HAVE NO MONEY TO PAY THE RENT, ANN! THE RENT IS DUE NEXT WEEK AND WE HAVE NO MONEY!"

We were into another heated argument.

But suddenly the phone rang. It was Scott.

Ann sat up crying, listening on the phone. When she hung up, she insisted, "He said he didn't do it. But he can't come back because the police are looking for him."

Sure enough, the police continued to knock on the door over the next several days, insisting we knew Scott's whereabouts.

It wasn't until my credit card statement came in the mail a few weeks later that Ann *really* broke down and cried. Scott had done all his Christmas shopping, bought expensive gifts, stayed with Ann in expensive hotels, and eaten at expensive restaurants—all using my American Express Gold Card.

Ann sat sobbing on the couch for days. "He said that he loved me and wanted to marry me!" she blurted out between tears.

But she'd finally realized that this guy she felt so certain truly loved her was nothing but a con artist with a long criminal record.

It had been a struggle just to keep up with the rent. But Ann had quit her job, thinking that her guy was going to take care of her for the rest of her life.

Meanwhile, the country had fallen even deeper into the recession.

What little work I can find will never be enough to get caught up for the month behind we are, I told myself.

By the middle of January 1992, we got a phone call from the landlord. He was wondering why he hadn't received a rent check from us yet. It was heartbreaking. We had to tell him how much we really loved it there, but somebody had stolen our rent money and there was just no way we could recover.

We promised him we'd have everything out by the end of January, and he agreed to let us stay till the end of the month to avoid eviction.

By this time, Ann and I really despised each other. But we tried getting along for those last two weeks before we had to move out. And we decided to have one last party before having to give up our home.

Meanwhile, Ann made arrangements to move in with her best friend Linda, who'd been living in Boston with her boyfriend. I had not yet figured out where I would be moving to, and there was just one week left till the end of the month.

On the night of the party, Linda and her boyfriend Guy drove up from Boston planning to attend our party then spend the night and drive back down to Boston with a carload of Ann's belongings. But Ann herself didn't stay in our apartment for long, temporarily leaving me alone with her friends while she took off somewhere with her new boyfriend.

Lynn and Dave showed up a little later, though, and helped start up some good conversations. Guy sat quietly while Lynn and Linda got to know each other. I selected some good party music, cranking up The B52's, and soon we were all dancing around the apartment.

Later, Ann returned for a short time but went back out again, and we were all having a much better time without her. Meanwhile, Guy and Linda seemed like a happy couple, considering their eleven-year age difference. Guy was thirty-one years old, had a college degree in psychology, and came from a very wealthy family from San Diego, California. Wearing a sports coat and tie, along with his dark curly hair and good looks, he could usually talk his way through any situation. Linda was just twenty years old, a tall thin blonde who sat close to Guy as we all sat down on the floor around the coffee table.

Guy was quite impressed with our beautiful apartment and the view of the ocean. He couldn't understand why Ann wanted to move out of the place. When I told him how much the rent was, and that it was Ann's boyfriend who had stolen our rent money, he spoke up in sudden surprise.

"That's all that you pay? $600 per month for all this?"

He'd been paying a lot more to live in the run-down building they'd been renting in Boston, and he quickly came up with an idea. "How much do you need the save this place?"

I said, "Well, we just need the $600 for the month of January, and then the month of February is due next week."

Guy's face lit up. "What if we came up with the money and started paying half the rent? Would you be able to keep this place?"

It sounded like a good idea, right at the time when I'd become desperate and had no clue as to where I would be living at the end of the week if I didn't agree to Guy's proposal.

Linda, though, was totally against the idea—at least, at first she was, when we said that she and Guy were going to be taking over Ann's room and Ann would have to stay on the couch downstairs.

But Guy insisted he was taking over half the apartment, whether Ann was staying or not. He was tired of paying high rents for a dumpy apartment in Boston.

So as quick as that, we had a new plan and I didn't have to worry where I was going to move to. The next morning, I called the landlord to tell him our new plan, and he agreed to it and arranged to meet with us the following week to sign the new lease.

But Ann was furious when she heard about our plan. "No way! I'm not sleeping on the couch! I'm moving out!"

And she did.

Of course, she was back to reconsider her place on the couch in less than two weeks.

CHAPTER 26

I'm Gettin' Outta Here

In the spring of '92, I turned 27, joined a gym, and started working out again. I was beginning to feel good about myself and the friends I had. With Linda and Guy both working and paying their fair share of the bills, we didn't have to work so hard just to cover all our household expenses. We all got along well. Even with Ann sleeping on the couch, there was very little complaining during those first three months of living together.

Linda and I got along especially well, and we usually did most of the cleaning, while Guy had a habit of talking his way out of doing any physical work. During the daytime, Linda actually spent a lot more time grocery shopping and riding around in her car with me than she spent time doing anything with Guy. Whenever Linda and Guy started to argue, I would hear Linda say, "Why can't you be more like Steve?"

Guy just laughed it off every time. Nothing seemed to worry him. I don't think he would've even cared if I *did* try to steal Linda away from him. Guy's life was built on his good looks, nice clothes, and smooth talking. Coming from a wealthy family, he'd never experienced any real financial struggles, and he seemed to always find an easier way to make money. Even during the recession, he quickly found a job selling Electrolux Vacuum Cleaners and quickly became the top salesman in his first two months on the job.

So, with summer approaching, Guy's ego was on the rise and getting out of control. He decided he only needed to work two days a week and could still make enough sales to keep up with the other top salesmen. Using his smooth-talking sales pitch, he met with a few motel managers around Old Orchard Beach and set up gigs to shampoo the carpets before the summer tourist season began. He took me along with him to make sure each job was complete.

I didn't mind doing Guy's dirty work to make a little extra money by shampooing carpets. The work was much easier than drywall, and there wasn't much work anywhere else.

On the side, Guy was still collecting unemployment checks from The State of Massachusetts. He'd once worked for a collection agency there, and that had given him access to many social security numbers. So, after he'd been laid off, he'd also made sure to take advantage of an unused social security number when he'd started working for Electrolux. He had extra income backing him up and didn't see the need to work so hard.

But while Guy was becoming more and more confident that he could talk his way through any situation, the confidence I'd been feeling in this new group of friends, was beginning to wear off. Back in February, Dave and Lynn had moved to Florida hoping to find fulltime work. Michelle had already found herself a steady boyfriend and had no use for me anymore. Linda and Ann moved out as soon as Guy started to show a darker side of himself.

All this left me living in the apartment alone with Guy.

And not even Linda had known of his past addiction to crack cocaine.

It was something we never saw coming, since we'd never seen Guy use any other drugs, not even weed. He was always very active, playing sports and loved surfing. He drank a few beers, and that's all we'd ever seen him do.

But after four months of living in our big beautiful apartment, he'd gone back to his old habit of locking himself in the bathroom with the overhead fan on, sitting on the can for hours holding his lighter and a crackpipe.

Once again, then, I was feeling trapped. With negativity taking over our once happy home, I had no real friends and spent most of my free time hiding in my room, listening to music, writing letters, and cuddling up with MARi to create my own little isolated world.

The only thing I truly cared about at that time was keeping my cat safe.

Then I came across an ad in the classified pages of Cat Fancy Magazine. Someone was looking for a live-in caretaker for a cat sanctuary in Cambria, California. They needed someone who loved cats and was able to lift heavy bags of cat litter and cat food.

I didn't think I stood a chance at hearing anything back, since thousands of people around the world might be reading the same ad. I decided to write a letter, anyway, because I was feeling bored and trapped in my own little world. I needed somebody to spill my life story to.

I ended up writing a four-page letter, including a little about myself and a whole lot more about MARi and my love for cats. After mailing the letter, I didn't think much of it, and I almost forgot I had even written it.

The following week, though, to my surprise I received a call from a couple in Cambria, California. I felt the odds of that happening were like winning the lottery. Out of the hundreds of letters they'd received from all over the world, mine, they said, made me sound like I was the most qualified for the job. I wasn't sure what they expected of me, though, since I'd never really thought the letter I'd written would have been considered but only looked over then tossed away.

Suddenly, I was faced with a big decision to make. I'd been invited to come for a personal interview and visit what could soon become my new home. I had to pay for my own airline ticket, which was extremely hard on my budget, especially if I decided in the end not to take the job.

But I did book the flight for the Memorial Day weekend, scheduled to arrive at the San Luis Obispo Airport on the Saturday afternoon of May 23, 1992, and it was a beautiful sunny day when I met Gerry and Lisa Shacter, the couple who ran The Warm Hearth Foundation.

They were waiting to pick me up, and right away they seemed like a pretty easy-going couple, completely opposite each other but open-minded and accepting to just about anyone. They made me feel very welcome, stopping in a restaurant along the way where they introduced me to Lynn Grizzard and her partner. I liked them both and thought to myself, *these two ladies will be my new friends if I decide to take this job.*

Lynn was a 37-year old lesbian woman who worked in the computer store owned by Gerry and Lisa. After lunch we all went for a little ride and stopped to take a tour of the big house Lynn lived in with her partner—along with a few cats, dogs, geese and other rescued animals. These animals were all well taken care of and the house was remarkably clean, considering all the animals running free throughout the house and yard.

I was hoping the house they had planned for me to stay in was at least half as beautiful as the house Lynn lived in.

The next place we drove to was up a long, dusty dirt road with a lot of sharp turns high up in the mountains. We stopped at a beautiful little cabin at the end of the long driveway far from any neighbors. The newly constructed cabin had a beautiful loft and big windows looking out through the front. A little stream rippled down along the side of the steep driveway. Six dirty litter boxes were lined up along the side wall and surrounded by the clutter and filthy cat beds. I assumed it would be my job to keep this place clean.

It seemed like an easy enough job, just 10 cats for me to clean up behind. That day, we all pitched in and scooped out the litter boxes and shook out the cat beds before leaving the cabin.

After taking another long dusty ride back down the mountain, we finally reach the paved road, and it took us down another long curvy road to the town of Cambria. Looking through from my backseat window, I saw many beautiful houses built on steep hills overlooking the Pacific Ocean.

When we stopped in the driveway of an older neglected house that almost looked abandoned, we all stepped out of the van. I heard the sound of cats scrambling behind the lattice enclosed porch, and a few came to greet us when we opened the gate. I was disappointed, though, that the rest of them went into hiding, fearing a stranger in the house.

Lisa told me not to worry. They would come out once they got to know me.

The smell of urine was overwhelming when we entered the house, cobwebs along the ceiling, cat hair and flee eggs covering the floors. I could see why they needed someone to clean up and maintain a daily clean-up operation.

The job, though, only paid $800 per month with free housing, and after seeing the inside, I wasn't sure I really wanted the job at all. There were 38 cats living in the house, and the ladies knew each of them by name. How was I ever going to remember all the cats' names?

They showed me a clean bedroom downstairs, where I'd be staying the night. But feeling a wave of disappointment at everything else I'd seen, I almost made up my mind right then and there. *I'm not living like this! No way! I'm not taking this job. I wasted my time and money coming out here.*

After spending the night in that very strange room, I kept quiet about my decision not to take the job. I wanted to wait until I returned home to make up some excuse why I couldn't take the job, to avoid any hurt feelings. Gerry and Lisa drove me back to the airport, and I led them on by saying I'd give the job some serious thought.

But I knew damn well I had no intentions of returning to take the job. I'd wasted over $400 on a plane ticket just to stay less than twenty-four hours in California. I truly felt that the whole trip was a waste of my time and money.

It looked like everything was getting back to normal when I returned home. Guy was acting friendly towards me again, as if he'd totally forgotten the way he was acting just a few days before. Linda was even making plans to get back together with him.

With the rent for the month of June due in just a few days, I told Guy, "I'm getting ready to pay the rent. Do you have your half ready?"

Guy looked up at me and said, "I already sent my half in. You can just send in your half."

I thought it a bit strange that he did it like that. We had always put our money together and sent in one check. But I didn't question Guy at the time. I just wrote out a check for my half of the rent and sent it to the landlord.

Guy spent the first week of June surfing during the day, playing volley ball in the late afternoon, and socializing at the bar downstairs during the evening. With the summer approaching, it didn't look like he had any intentions of working.

As for me, I was also out on the beach, allowing the cold waves to rush around me and sinking my legs deep into the sand. I was trying to convince myself that everything was getting back to normal. But a creepy feeling came over me: I *knew* Guy hadn't send in his half of the rent.

How much longer was this going to go on?

If Guy thinks I'm going to cover his half of the rent while he pays nothing, he's crazy.

I suddenly started thinking more seriously about taking the cat job in California. I could clean up that filthy house and live worry-free in regard to paying rent. $800 a month salary was all I would need. I would be safe there in California, away from all the negativity, and I could make new friends, positive friends.

A few days later, I was still only *thinking* about the cat job.

But then I discovered money was missing from my room.

And I made up my mind. *I'm gettin' outta here!*

Of course, Guy made up a quick excuse by saying somebody must have broken into the apartment. I just pretended I didn't care if it was somebody else who had broken in. I knew it was him and said, "I'm gettin' outta here. I'm out of money, out of friends, I've got all this stuff in here, and the only thing in this world I care about is my cat MARi."

I made a phone call to let Gerry and Lisa know I'd decided I was going to take the job and I would be driving out there with my cat soon. I started selling everything I had as cheaply as I could, as fast as it could sell. I sold my motorcycle for just $1,000, less than half its worth. I sold two guitars for $100 each. I gave away my entire vinyl record collection, over 500 records, some of which were very rare recordings which could never be replaced.

I didn't care about anything else but keeping my cat MARi safe and having enough money for the long journey across the country. I called Michelle to tell her I was leaving, and I wanted to give her my tarot cards, the Ouija board, and as many records as she wanted. She came over with her boyfriend (making me feel a bit jealous) and chose The Cure's Kiss Me Kiss Me Kiss Me album and The Repo Man sound track. I was disappointed they didn't take more records.

I gave the rest to Guy, and he later sold them to a used record store. I didn't care how much he got for them. I just wanted to get rid of everything as soon as possible.

I stored a few of my larger items at my mother's house. She was quite upset about my short notice for leaving to go to California. I told her it was a big job promotion. I was going to be rescuing animals and doing environmental research, whatever that meant, just to make it sound like a really important job. But I didn't want her to know the living conditions I'd be in and the fact that I'd only be making $800 a month rescuing stray cats.

She suggested we pray together before I go. I sat on the couch next to Mom and she prayed a long sincere prayer.

Then I said a short prayer before letting mom hug me good-bye. It was one of the few times I'd ever let my mom hug me.

"I'll be all right, Mom. We prayed," I assured her one last time before quickly heading out the door.

I drove back down to the apartment to finish packing a few boxes of clothes, CD's, and a few other items I could fit in the back seat of my little Ford Escort.

Guy, with his smooth talking, had pretended to be a friendly person and had already found a couple of roommates to help pay the rent after I left. (I would later find out that they were *all* evicted by the end of the summer. Guy's two roommates were paying him the rent money, but he was spending it on crack cocaine.) They allowed me to spend one last night sleeping on the couch so I could leave early the next morning.

I felt a little sad when I woke up, hearing the waves crash on the beach, looking out over the balcony one last time. I wondered if I was truly making the right decision to leave all this behind.

First, I set the litter box on the floor behind my car's passenger seat. Then I placed MARi's food and water dish up on the back-window ledge. At last, with everything ready to go in the car, I took MARi in her carrier and carried her from the apartment out to the car. The cool morning air would soon make way for hotter weather as the day wore on, and I had to be extremely careful not to let the sun overheat the car. I worried what might happen if MARi tried to escape while I was driving.

So, I was also extremely careful as I let her out of her carrier after the car got moving down the highway. I kept the windows open no more than a few inches for fear that MARi might get scared and jump out.

Driving along, an empty feeling came over me again.

But I thought, *this time I'm really leaving, this time I may never come back. I have a place to go, a new home. And a new job is waiting for me there.*

CHAPTER 27

Cambria California

It was Sunday, July 12, 1992, and our trip had been going well, so far. A cloud-covered sky seemed to follow us up until we reached the California State line, and then the hot sun began to glare bright on my windshield.

I had to open the windows a little more to allow the air to flow through better and keep us cool. MARi had been hiding under the seat, but now she jumped up on the back-window ledge to look around. I could tell she was scared and didn't know what was going on as we travelled down California Highway 101 at about 60 miles per hour.

Suddenly, the line of cars in front of us slowed down quickly, almost to a stop. I hit the brakes and MARi flew from the back of the car to the front, landing all four paws on the dashboard.

Oh, My God that scared me! I thought. *She could have flown out the window!*

We were approaching the town of Paso Robles, just a little over thirty miles from Cambria. *Looks like we're going to make it, we're almost there.*

But suddenly, the car lost all its power and I had to coast us to the side of the road. We were stranded. "Oh, no! Not now! Please, God, don't leave us stranded here in the hot sun!" I pleaded and prayed.

For a while, I sat with the windows open, waiting for the engine to cool down. I knew that climbing all those steep mountains behind us had been too much for my car's little 4-cylinder engine. When I tried to restart it again, it wouldn't.

I tried again and again… till the battery died.

I prayed, "Please, just one last run."

But it was no use. The engine was dead. I even looked and saw radiator fluid dripping from the exhaust pipe. It probably had a cracked engine block, but I didn't know for sure. I put MARi in her carrier and walked several blocks, searching for a phone booth.

Fortunately, before nearly dying of heat stroke I found one in a shaded area. And luckily, Gerry was in his office to answer the phone. But I had to sit and wait for another half hour for Gerry and Lisa to drive out and find me.

When their air-conditioned Dodge Caravan showed up, MARi and I finally had relief from the heat. I loaded MARi in first, then we backed the van up to my car to load up all my clothes and the few things I'd brought with me.

This is it. I'm stranded here, I thought. *I couldn't go back home to Maine now even if I wanted to.*

My 1988 Ford Escort, with just a little over 90,000 miles on it, was towed to the junk yard the very next day. I had just finished paying for it before making this trip. And now I was flat broke again. Everything I'd worked for over the past five years was gone—my condo, my motorcycle, my stereo, my guitars, my records…and now my car.

Plus, once again I was at the mercy of someone else to provide my food and shelter. My cat job had to work out for me, or I would be left stranded completely.

But quickly, Gerry and Lisa made me feel very welcome at my new home. Exhausted from all the driving on my road trip, I went straight to my new room and went to sleep.

I woke up the next morning to start my job with a positive attitude. Gerry and Lisa left for work at their computer store, leaving me by myself at the house. Before they went, though, Gerry recommended for me to relax and spend my first day simply getting to know all the cats.

I insisted, though, on giving the house a thorough cleaning, starting with all the litter boxes then mopping the floors and vacuuming the carpets. A cool breeze blew through the open windows and soon the bad odor was gone. When I began to fill all the freshly cleaned food bowls, most of the cats gathered around, purring and rubbing up against me. This was easy. Those cats knew who was going to be feeding them from then on.

Later that afternoon, the house smelled much better. I felt pretty good about my new job and the house I would be living in. I decided to go out for a walk to explore the Town of Cambria, knowing the weather was always pleasant along the central coast of California. High temps would usually only reach the low 70's, even when nearby towns had temps in the 90's. Cambria was a place to escape the summer heat.

Being a little town with a lot of gift shops to attract tourists, plus a couple of gas stations, one library, two banks, a post office, and a small grocery store called The Cookie Crock, Cambria had everything a small town needed for a person like me to survive, right within walking distance.

Gerry and Lisa, though, had also left me with a 1982 Toyota Celica for running errands and commuting back and forth to their cabin in the mountains. What I liked best about it was, they took care of all the maintenance and gave me a gas card, so that I had no vehicle expenses. I could live almost responsibility-free, with no rent to pay or utilities expenses, and no car payments. All I had to do was just wake up every morning to scoop the cat boxes and fill their food dishes and maybe even have time to relax and enjoy life.

My first official day on the job, I already had everything organized from the day before. I felt no need to get out of bed before 7 o'clock. I decided that every morning I would enjoy my breakfast and never have to start working until I'd finished watching the Flintstones on TV at 8 o'clock. Too much of my life I'd spent waking up at 4:30 am and working late into the night, always being under constant stress. But now, I no longer had to deal with those long stressful workdays. I could start out each day by enjoying my breakfast with MARi purring on my lap.

Later that evening, I had to drive down to meet up with Gerry and Lisa at their computer store in San Luis Obispo about 40 miles away. I was looking forward to this short trip because our plans were to go to a building supply store, and I was anxious to get started on some of the projects they had planned for me.

But even more than that, I was anxious to meet up with Lynn Grizzard, who was going to be there as well. I was hoping she would become my first close friend since I'd moved.

I followed the map Gerry had drawn out for me to find Witco Computers, a place I would become very familiar with in the months to come. But this being my first day there, everything looked very strange. We all met up in the parking lot in front of their store, but I was still feeling a bit confused about where we were going next. To my relief, Gerry suggested that Lynn should ride in the car with me and follow them in the van.

This is great, I thought, *an opportunity to talk to Lynn and hopefully start becoming good friends.* I smiled, showing a little of my excitement.

"Okay, let's go!" I said as I started to take the driver's seat.

Lynn suggested, "Oh, can I drive?"

"Yeah, that would be great. I hate driving and I don't know where we're going, anyway." I ran back around to the passenger's side and jumped in while Lynn took the driver's seat.

I wanted to start off the conversation by asking why I was chosen out of the hundreds of responses they'd received?

But as soon as we started cruising down the highway, she quickly changed the subject and asked me with a bit of enthusiasm in her voice, "So, are you straight or are you gay?"

I wasn't expecting this to be the first question she'd ask me and wasn't sure why it was so important. But she turned her eyes away from the road to look over at me for a quick answer.

"Well, I just consider myself asexual. I don't really like to be identified by any sexual orientation."

"No way!" she said, a puzzled look on her face, as if she wasn't satisfied with my answer.

I was hoping for a more interesting topic to talk about, but she went on asking more questions like, "Well, haven't you ever tried homosexuality?"

"No, not really, although a lot of men have tried to force themselves on me. Each time, I just pulled away from them."

She shot back quickly, with a demanding tone and a still-confused look on her face. "But you're not giving it a chance. How can you say you don't like something if you don't give it a chance?"

Suddenly, I felt like jumping out of the car even as it was moving at 60 miles per hour. I tried to tune the radio to find a good song, hoping to change the subject and maybe talk about music.

But Lynn didn't seem to take much interest in anything else I had to say after that. As far as she was concerned, I was homophobic and of no interest to her, no matter what I had to say.

We didn't have a whole lot more to say to each other for the rest of the ride, nor did she even have anything to say to me any time thereafter unless it was work-related.

The following Saturday I was anxious to get started on some of the construction projects up at the cabin. Gerry and Lisa were there to explain to me just how they wanted everything to look. They pointed to the steep embankment behind the back deck. "We want these 10x10-inch wood beams laid in place for 4-foot wide steps up to the top. Then make a level surface at the top."

I looked at everything, not really knowing exactly what I was to start doing or how to do it. I said, "Okay, I can do that. No problem."

Figuring it out, I started with a pick and shovel, loosening all the dirt at the bottom. Then I tried laying the 4-foot beams, leveling each one and driving stakes in the ground to hold them in place. Then I filled gravel in behind them to start the next level. If it wasn't for the scorching heat, I might have been enjoying myself. I was covered in sweat and mud by the time I set the fourth step in.

Gerry and Lisa came outside to tell me to take a break and make sure I was drinking enough water. We all sat on the deck where Lisa prepared a plate of carrots, celery, and cucumber sticks for me while they sat and ate hamburgers.

I was in the middle of enjoying my vegetables when Gerry decided to inspect my little project, walking up and down the little steps I'd made.

"These steps look fantastic!" he said with a big smile.

"You're doing a great job, Steve," Lisa added.

To my surprise, the work *was* coming along much better than I at first had thought it would, considering I didn't know what I was doing before I started. I'd just taken it one step at a time.

By the end of the day, the whole project looked fantastic.

Most of the time, I had the whole house in Cambria to myself. Gerry usually came by once a week with a list of chores for me to do. I had the freedom to set my own hours and come and go as I pleased, without any stress or pressure to meet any great demands.

So, I should have been happy. I had everything I'd ever wanted, a house full of cats and a worry-free life.

But in reality, I was bored out of my mind.

After just a few weeks of going through the same routine every morning, I had all my chores done by 10:00 am. *Well, this is great! I have all the rest of the day to do anything I want!* Maybe I'd walk down the hill and sit by the ocean or go hang out at the library, or just walk around downtown.

Or no, maybe not.

I decided to go back to my bed, put my head under the covers, and fall back asleep.

And this started happening more and more frequently as depression became my only state of existence.

I did, though, have an enjoyable time of day with my job—between 6:30 and 7:30 PM every evening. This was the time I looked forward to carrying a backpack filled with cat food and a bottle of water. Putting on my stereo headphones set with some of my most favorite depressing songs, I'd listen to Morrissey's "Every Day is Like Sunday," R.E.M.'s "Don't Go Back to Rockville" or The Sunday's "Here's Where the Story Ends." These were all songs that drove me into a deeper depression, which is where I wanted to stay.

I felt no real reason to feel any other way. I had everything I wanted, very little responsibility, and the freedom to feel the way I felt—angry about my past, cheated out of life, and having lost everything I'd worked so hard for.

Also, I lived in fear of creditors who might be trying to find me, meanwhile worried too that life would never give me the opportunity to own my own house again. *But I feel safe here. Nobody really knows me here. I'm completely invisible to the world. I don't exist to anyone else. I'm just a lost soul. Still, I am free. I am so free. I have nobody to talk to, so I talk to a house full of cats. I have nobody to argue with, so I argue with the voice inside my head.*

Sometimes I envisioned myself punching out the lawyer who hadn't listened to me. I begged God's forgiveness every time this anger overtook me, but it kept coming back. So, walking and indulging in depressing music were my only relief. Plus, there was pleasure for me in simply watching all the stray cats run towards me when I filled their dish behind the bushes of The Cookie Crock parking lot. That made my day. Sometimes five, sometimes ten, sometimes twenty or more cats came running and purring, all gathered around a large plate of food.

A life in the wild still had its moments, it seemed, with free food for a gathering of my friends. I felt very fortunate to be the one who brought each moment of happiness to those lonely, helpless stray cats.

After feeding the cats, I'd buy a few items at The Cookie Crock before making my journey back to the house, carrying in my backpack full of frozen burritos, bananas, milk and Cheerios. I pretty much ate the same quick and easy meals every day without noticing my weight loss and other ill effects all my depression had on my health.

A few of the cats had leukemia and had to stay in the front section of the house. Another group lived in the section at the back of the house, and every morning I'd open the back gate so they could play outside. Then every evening, I'd have to call them all in for the night, checking off a list to make sure they were all accounted for. Another cat with diabetes lived by herself in a small room, and I had to inject her with insulin twice a day.

As I walked through my daily routine, depending on which section of the house I was working in, one or two cats would follow close behind me. At the front of the house, it was always Woody, a beautiful dark striped tabby. Woody looked healthy, was full of energy, and loved attention. He would often dash towards the door, and I had to be extremely careful not to allow any leukemic cats in with the other heathy cats.

Also, I had to thoroughly wash my hands after touching any of the leukemic cats.

MARi usually sat up on the windowsill, guarding her territory. I opened the window every morning so she could go outside and enjoy climbing trees and hopefully make some friends with some of the other cats. But she enjoyed sitting out in the sunshine by herself and had no interest in making friends with any other cats. She hissed and growled if any cat came near her.

Then there was Rusty, a big orange tabby who was usually gentle and purred when I picked him up. But over the other cats, he ruled the outdoors and they feared him. I'd never seen him lose a fight. When I brought him in at night, he had to stay in a caged-in section to prevent him from fighting with the others.

One day, Rusty decided to jump in my window while MARi was napping on my bed. I was sitting up writing a letter when suddenly I heard a loud "ROOOUUURRROOUUUWW!!!!!" as the two cats scrambled across the floor.

I quickly jumped up and Rusty jumped back on the windowsill and beat it out of there. I looked at all the orange fur on the floor, and MARi looked up at me with her beautiful eyes and said "Meow" like she was very proud of herself. I felt proud of her too. Rusty was one of the toughest cats I'd ever seen, and MARi was able to defend her own territory against Rusty.

I started attending a Baptist Church, hoping to meet positive people and make some new friends, which I did. Andrew Hull was a really nice guy who attended college and wore a suit and tie almost everywhere he went. Andrew became the only friend I had who wasn't a cat for those first six months of living in Cambria. He carried his Bible with him just about everywhere. I could usually keep up a pretty intelligent conversation with him, and sometimes he'd have me over to his grandmother's house for Sunday dinner.

He also invited me to a lot of Christian gatherings that usually met at the Cal Poly University auditorium. I never felt like I fit in with this group of college-age Christians. They seemed too interested in politics and being a part of the Right Wing Christian Conservative movement. I've never taken interest in politics and thought Christians should have nothing to do with it.

Gerry soon realized that the chores he had set for me in Cambria were not enough to keep me busy for an entire day. He decided to have me work one day a week cleaning windows and vacuuming the carpets at the computer store. This I hated, even more than I hated the boredom and depression I felt staying home in Cambria. I felt very out of place among the computer geeks and diehard Star Trek fans.

I tolerated the fact that I was a total misfit cleaning the office, though having to follow orders from Lynn Grizzard was enough to make me feel as useless and out of place as a vegetarian in a butcher shop.

The worst day was election day. Gerry and Lisa were encouraging everybody to vote for Bill Clinton, giving each employee a chance to leave the office to cast their vote. *What a waste of time*, I thought.

And Gerry was disappointed in me for not taking the time to vote. He said to me, "I wish you would vote—just to get one more vote in to help us get Bush out of there."

I wasn't planning on losing any sleep over the results of a stupid election, but Clinton was the last person I wanted to see win it. In Gerry and Lisa's opinion, though, by not taking the time off work to go vote, I was getting in the way of their plans to gain as many votes as possible for the candidate who wanted to keep abortion legal. They made it very clear that they supported gay rights and government funded abortions.

203

My personal opinion was, I hated the government. And I believed it was only insecure people who would get together every election year to cast their vote to elect another power-hungry evil ruler to control our lives.

I would have nothing to do with it.

By the start of the new year, Gerry decided to put me on the company payroll. This meant they were going to start taking taxes out of my paycheck. Not only was it less money for me, but it also meant creditors could find me if I gave out my social security number.

Now I had reason to worry.

But I remembered a good plan that I'd learned from my former friend and roommate Guy Singer. I could change just one digit of my social security number, making it look accidental that I made the number six look like an eight. That way I could still remain invisible to creditors and the government.

It seemed like a good idea at the time.

Less than two years later, though, it would cost me big.

Meanwhile, after my first year of living in the house full of cats, I had become quite comfortable with my living situation. I won the war on fleas by combing each cat daily and keeping the house clean. I organized my schedule so that I could finish my chores and spend time every day out walking or relaxing near the ocean.

I'd decided that I was where I'd stay for as long as I felt content, having everything I needed.

CHAPTER 28

Love at First Sight

I had come to terms with my living situation, but Gerry's demands and expectations quickly became almost unreasonable.

First, he started expecting me to provide my own transportation. So, I bought myself a 1983 Nissan Pulsar for $1,500, draining me of all my savings. And what a piece of junk! It had over 180,000 miles on it. Back in Maine, a piece of junk like that Pulsar would sell for no more than $400. But the people of California seemed to think a rusty old clunker was worth $2,000 or even $3,000. Based on what I had to choose from, then, I simply bought what I could afford.

Gerry and Lisa had bought a huge piece of real estate up in the mountains, which took over an hour and a half of driving upward along dusty roads through sharp turns and steep climbs to get there. This put a lot of wear and tear on my already worn-out Nissan. I got frustrated trying to keep up with the repairs. The situation made it almost impossible for me to save much money, but I managed to set aside a few hundred dollars from each paycheck while using my credit card to take care of most of the car repairs.

On top of this, with big plans to renovate the property, Gerry and Lisa gave me a long list of projects to do every day. These were added to my daily routine of cleaning all the litter boxes and filling food dishes. Their goal was to bring all their cats, over a hundred cats in all, to one farm. They seemed excited about all the building projects and their plans to rescue more cats. But they never seemed to take notice of the tremendous amount of additional stress and responsibility they were putting on me. At first, I thought all the extra work was only temporary and I'd be back to my regular routine after a few weeks. But with each passing week, more hours of hard labor were added.

I did the best I could to keep up with all the extra work. I could usually tolerate a long and heavy workload, but this was getting to be too much for me. They never seemed to consider the amount of driving time I had to put in in addition to all the regular work of scooping all the litter boxes and filling all the food dishes in Cambria before starting any of the building projects.

Tension slowly started building up between Gerry and me.

Then, Gerry suddenly snapped and threatened to fire me because I had missed a few important details on one of his lists of daily chores, which were becoming long and monotonous. Each time, I read through them quickly, and one time I skipped over the details of an antibiotic I was supposed to give to two cats who had been sneezing. No harm was done, the cats were fine.

But it gave me an excuse to snap back and tell him I was planning on quitting soon, anyway. I had seen this coming for a long time.

They wanted me to stick around for just a little longer, though, to finish up a few more construction projects. Then they planned to fire me. It actually worked out well for all of us, and I had no hard feelings towards them. In fact, I felt a great relief and we agreed that I'd be leaving as soon as I finished all the drywall in the barn.

The last place I wanted to go was back to Maine. But I didn't have much choice considering the circumstances. I needed to find another job and a place to live.

I knew I could rely on my good buddy Packy to have some drywall jobs lined up for me. All it took was one quick call and I was hired. Then I called Dave, who had just moved back from Florida and was in the middle of a breakup with Lynn. It was good timing because he needed a roommate and money to make a security deposit for a very clean, newly renovated two-bedroom apartment in Biddeford. Money was going to be tight, but I knew this opportunity was my only hope of having a place lined up for me. I sent Dave a $500 check overnight express mail. He would be moving in on March 1st with an extra room for me when I arrived.

I felt a lot better about working for Gerry and Lisa, knowing it would all be over soon. They were on much more friendly terms with me as well, almost showing regret about the way they'd been overworking me.

It was the last week of February, and I was still hanging sheetrock in the barn. Gerry called to tell me a woman was coming to bring some bunnies to keep at the farm. He told me to listen for the phone to ring, so I would know when to drive down to the bottom of the mountain to let her through the gate.

I instantly had a feeling come over me like I couldn't wait to meet this woman. "OK, I'll stay near and listen for the phone to ring," I said. Then setting the phone down, I went back to work for a few more hours, wondering as time went by why the phone didn't ring. I was really anxious to meet this woman. I had no idea who she was but felt a strong desire to meet her. *Why hasn't that phone rung yet?* I kept thinking to myself.

Finally, I set my tools down and walked over to the workbench where the receiver sat crookedly on the phone. "No wonder she hasn't been able to reach me yet!" I set the receiver down straight and the phone rang immediately.

It was Gerry. "I told you to wait for her to call! She's been down there trying to call, but the lines been busy for over an hour!"

"I don't know what happened," I said. "Maybe one of the cats knocked the phone off the hook."

"I don't care what happened! You drive down to the gate and let her in! She's been waiting for over an hour."

I hung up the phone and got in my car and drove a little over two miles to the gate, and she was waiting in a white Toyota Tacoma. Before I even got a good look at her, I opened the gate and she followed me up to the farm.

"I love it here!" she said, already falling in love with the beautiful landscape around us. "I love it here! It's such a beautiful view of the mountains."

While she was captivated by the beautiful scenery all around us, there was something about *her* that fascinated *me*. She was much older than I was, but there was something about the way she'd aged and kept her beauty that made me feel so drawn to her. Her long blonde beautiful hair, her blue eyes, and the way she smiled when all the cats gathered around us—it was love at first sight.

I helped her unload the eight bunnies in carriers from the back of her truck.

"This is perfect," she said. "I'll be bringing more bunnies up next week and then I have about thirty cats I need to find homes for." She clearly felt a lot of relief that she had finally found a good home where all her rescued animals would be well taken care of.

"Oh, we've got lots of room here," I said, showing her the back of the house where a lattice-enclosed section was built to keep all the bunnies safe.

She said she was running late and had to leave very quickly after setting her bunnies in their new home. She left me a long letter to pass on to Gerry and Lisa, having signed her full name, address, and phone number in big letters at the bottom of the page.

Maris Jordan. I just stared at her name and phone number.

And for the next several days, I felt the urge to call her. But I couldn't get up the nerve. She was way too old for me, way out of my league, and I couldn't think up a good excuse to call her.

The following Saturday I was enjoying one of my first full weekends off in a long time, relaxing in my room in Cambria and spending time petting MARi and listening to music. Keeping my phone close beside me, I tried to get the nerve up or think up an excuse to call that beautiful woman with all the bunnies.

Oh, what's the use? She couldn't possibly have any reason to want to talk to me, and I'll be leaving this place in less than two weeks anyway, I thought to myself. *This is crazy. Why should I ever think she'd be interested in me?*

Suddenly, the phone rang.

"Hello?" I said, picking it up on the first ring.

"Stevie, is that you? Oh, I've been trying to call you all week!"

Her beautiful voice on the phone—how did she know my number? She seemed to know everything about me. And she started asking all kinds of questions about working for Gerry and Lisa and who else would be working there at the farm taking care of all those cats and bunnies.

"Well, I work there by myself most of the time. But I'll be leaving in about two weeks, and they are looking for someone else to take my place."

She suddenly sounded very interested in replacing me when I left. I told her that she could have my job, and that I was sure Gerry and Lisa would be thrilled to hire her as soon as I was gone. As I did this, I was overjoyed that this beautiful woman was calling me. I wanted to ask her if I could see her again before I left.

But before I could think up the right words to say, she invited herself to come see me later that evening.

Hanging up the phone, I started cleaning up around the house. I wanted it to look extra clean before Maris saw it. I filled my backpack and walked with a spring in my step to the Cookie Crock to feed the stays. I thought of her all the while I was walking. This was the first time since I'd come here that I'd met someone with such positive energy. Who was she? Why did I feel so drawn to her?

Maybe I should stay here in California a little longer, I thought. *I've finally met someone I truly feel connected to. But is she really interested in me? What does she see in me? Maybe it's just in my head. I'll try not to get my hopes up too high.*

When she'd said she'd stop by later that evening, I'd thought she meant at seven o'clock, maybe eight, at the latest. So, by 9:30 PM that evening, I was already in bed, ready to give up hope.

But suddenly, headlights lit up my window.

I quickly jumped out of bed, pulled on a pair of sweatpants, and opened the window. MARi jumped up to the windowsill to see what was going on, and since

I wanted to make a good impression on my guest, showing her my beautiful cat, so clean and healthy, I held MARi in my arms as beautiful Maris Jordan approached my window.

"Oh, she's beautiful!" she said, standing outside my window and reaching out to pet MARi.

I didn't have to do much to impress her. She started telling me her whole life story, or at least the parts of her life she wanted me to know about without my asking. She'd grown up in Connecticut and moved to California in the early 1970's. She'd liked being called Marsi (pronounced Mar-see) in her younger years when she'd worked as an actress and model. But she'd left Hollywood in the early 1980's and rented a ranch in the nearby Town of Harmony to rescue and shelter animals. Now she was running out of money, facing eviction, and needed to find homes for all the many animals she had staying at her ranch.

I just stared quietly, listening to this beautiful woman tell me everything about herself. I'd loved it all so far.

But she absolutely refused to tell me her age.

And it would be many years before I would learn that she was 17 years and 8 months older than I was, which made her 46 on this day that we met.

Marsi kept me up half the night as she talked on and on. We agreed to get together again on Sunday afternoon. Marsi was a night owl and liked to sleep in until noon, but I was an early morning riser and looked forward to seeing her again that afternoon.

So, when she finally did arrive at about 4:30 PM, it was much later than I'd expected. And I was hoping we could ride in her Toyota, but she insisted on me driving her around in my little beat-up Nissan. I had no idea where we were going, I just turned right when she said to turn right and turned left when she said to turn left.

We stopped at a few houses and knocked on doors, hoping to find good homes for a few of her dogs. Then we took a short ride up to San Simeon where we parked the car and just sat and talked. She did most of the talking, making plans for us to get together the following weekend. She'd bring one of her dogs along so we could play with a Frisbee in the park.

This all sounded like a great idea to me, and I suddenly wished I wasn't leaving so soon. I had to say, "I can't. This will be my last weekend before leaving for Maine. I have so much work I need to get finished. Maybe if Gerry and Lisa want to hire you to take my place, we could work together during my final week."

This too sounded like a great idea to both Marsi and me. But when I suggested the idea to Gerry and Lisa, they flipped out.

"OH, NO! WE AIN'T HIRING THAT MARSI JORDAN!!!"

"NO WAY! SHE'S CRAZY!!!!"

"But, why?" I asked them, thinking Marsi would be the best person to take my place after I left. "You still haven't found anyone else yet, right?" I kept insisting to know why they didn't want to hire her.

"BECAUSE SHE'S CRAZY!!!

Lisa kept insisting, "She's not all there. She's crazy! I can't stand her."

Gerry went on to explain how they'd offered to take her cats and rabbits off her hands and help her find a home for her horse. But that's all they could do for her. She was just too crazy.

I couldn't understand why they kept telling me that.

A few days before I left, Gerry looked at my car shaking his head.

"You really think that car's going to make it to Maine?" he asked me.

"Yup, I know it will. I'm gonna pray during my entire trip."

The night before I left, I said good-bye to Marsi, feeling a bit of sadness over leaving her so soon after we'd just met. I also said my good-byes to Gerry and Lisa, noticing a bit of sadness in them too.

But I felt no regrets. I was finally "gettin' outta here."

I woke up early on the morning of March 10, 1994, packing all my clothes, MARi and her litter box, and few other items into my little Nissan Pulsar. With barely enough space to see out the back window, I said a quick prayer then began my journey down highway 46.

But 10 miles from Bakersfield, I felt something dragging under the car. I pulled over to the side of the road to take a look underneath.

Oh, no! I couldn't believe it. The bracket that held the engine up from the bottom was dragging on the road. What was I to do, just keep driving and drag it all the rest of the way, praying the two engine mounts on the top would hold up long enough to make it to Maine?

I got back in the car and kept driving until I made it to Bakersfield, where I found a garage that didn't look too busy. And fortunately, there was a mechanic there who was willing to help me. He gave me a choice: to either pay a high cost of labor and have to wait another day for the new part to come in, or he could simply remove the dragging part for $5 and I could be on my way, hoping the engine didn't fall out.

I didn't have much money or time. I chose to have him remove the dragging part. I wouldn't have worried the slightest bit if MARi hadn't been in the car with me. If I broke down, I could just hitchhike or take a Greyhound Bus. But with MARi, there was no way they'd let me bring a cat on the bus.

So, I worried and prayed, constantly driving through freezing cold weather in the mid-west. Finally reaching the Northeast and coming up Interstate 95, places began looking familiar to me as I drove northward.

Turning my radio to WBLM about midway through New Hampshire, I had a familiar feeling as I heard the familiar sound of the Rock'n Roll Blimp. *I just know it. I'm gonna make it.*

"We're almost there, MARi. It's gonna be alright."

MARi had been hiding under the seat, scared and worried the entire trip. But now that it was almost over, after four days of driving, the nightmare was over.

We finally arrived. "Thank you, God. We made it."

We had one last steep hill to climb on Hill Street in Biddeford before reaching Granite Street, where our apartment was all ready for us to move in. I waited for the light to turn green about halfway to the top of the hill. Then I slowly let out the clutch.

Suddenly, the shifter slipped right out of my hand, almost through the floor, stuck in first gear. I continued to climb to the top of the hill then straight up Granite Street and into the parking lot.

We made it! The only thing that held the car together through that entire trip was prayer.

Then…the bolts from the top of the engine broke loose, letting the engine drop down to within inches of the road. The transmission dropped too, with the weight of the engine.

If these things had happened on the highway, I might have had a really big problem.

Thank God, I'd prayed all the way.

CHAPTER 29

Am I Wasting My Time?

On December 23, 1994, I stopped at my Dad's house to drop off a few Christmas presents. Dad sat at the kitchen table smoking a cigarette and drinking his coffee while reading the morning paper. I sat across the table from him, looking through the classifieds. My eyes skimmed across the real estate section and suddenly I saw a three-bedroom Cape with a large garage for just $57,000.

"This can't be the full price for a house in Portland," I said. "No way! You can't even buy a house lot for that price. There's no way, it just can't be so."

Dad was a bit doubtful too, but he said, "Go ahead, give 'em a call. You've got nothing to lose."

So, I made a quick phone call and talked to the realtor.

"Oh, yes, that's the full price. And you're welcome to take a look at it." He gave me the address on Riverside Street, and we set up a time later that afternoon to meet at the property.

I drove to the address he had given me. I looked at it from the outside. It was a very solid house that looked like it had been abandoned for a few years and had a newly constructed garage on half an acre of land. I parked in the driveway and waited a few more minutes for the realtor to show up.

I liked what I saw, but the price on the property was almost too good to be true. So, I had my doubts. Plus, there was no way I could even get financing after what had happened to my condo just three years ago.

I kept sitting there waiting and wondering if I was just wasting my time. But finally, a dark colored BMW drove up behind me in the driveway and I met Dan Patry, owner of Patry Family Realty. We shook hands and he took me inside for a tour.

The basement had flood damage. Although all the water had been pumped out and completely dried, the furnace, the hot water heater, and the oil tank were all destroyed and had to be hauled away. Other than that, the rest of the house had new floors and kitchen cabinets. The bathroom floor was peeling and cracking, but that wouldn't cost too much to replace. Upstairs it had beautiful hardwood floors and walls. The house was beautiful, and having a big garage on an industrial lot, the property was perfect for someone in the drywall business.

"This place is a steal. Why is it so cheap?" I asked.

Dan explained that the house had been foreclosed on about five years previous. It had been on the market for much too long, and they'd lowered the price in order to attract more buyers.

"Well, how many people have shown interest in it so far?"

Dan smiled and said "You're the only one, so far. And to tell you the truth, I don't think anyone else is interested. Christmas time is the best time to shop for a house, because it's the slowest time of year for real estate sales."

He suggested I place a very low bid and see what happened.

I figured I had nothing to lose. I wrote a check out for a $1,000 deposit and a bid of $53,000.

I followed Dan back to his office in Old Orchard Beach, feeling excited that by a slim chance that I could actually be approved for the financing. But the haunted feeling from my past foreclosure gave me a lot of doubt too.

While Dan continued to fill out the contract—along with a stack of papers for me to sign—questions came up.

"Have you ever owned a house in the past three years?"

"Have you ever had a foreclosure or lawsuit against you?"

That's when I knew I was wasting my time. There was no use going any further. I felt a great disappointment come over me, and I hung my head, explaining my situation to Dan. I expected him to discontinue any further paperwork and return my check.

But he just looked up at me and said, "No problem, I think I can get that taken off your credit report."

Really? I thought.

Overwhelming doubt still hung over me.

Over the next several days, I waited anxiously for the phone call that would break bad news to me—that I'd been denied and they were refunding my deposit.

I was ready to accept it, and there was no use feeling stressed about it anymore. I'd wasted my time and Dan's.

But suddenly, the call came, and Dan sounded excited. "Steve, I've got great news! They've accepted your bid!"

My heart jumped. "*WHAT?!*"

I was shocked but thought the nightmare was over. I would finally be able to move my life forward, repair my credit, gain instant equity, and own my own home. At that moment, Dan had really boosted my confidence, and I was so excited that I called Marsi to tell her the good news. I felt so confident about everything, I even asked her to marry me.

"We can have a happy home with lots of room in the yard for our kitties and bunnies!" I said.

At first, she sounded as excited as I was and made lots of plans to come out and live with me.

My excitement came to an end a few days later. I wasn't out of the ditch just yet. Dan called to tell me that I needed to fill out more paper work—this time, actual mortgage applications.

"What? I thought you already said my loan was approved! Why are we filling out more loan applications?" Clearly, I was quite confused.

Dan explained to me the owners had accepted my bid of $53,000, and that was *all* that had happened.

A sharp pain shot through my chest, worry and stress attacking me all over again.

But Dan kept insisting, "Don't worry! We will find a bank that will approve you."

Over the next several weeks, I became extremely stressed, having stacks of papers to sign and being turned down by several different banks. My doubts increased with each passing day.

I was at last ready to give up hope, ready to tell Dan not to waste any more of my time. My credit was bad, and I didn't make much money. Who was I fooling, to think any bank was going to finance a house for me?

But Dan insisted we give it one more try, and he set me up for an interview with GMAC Mortgage Corporation.

I walked into that interview feeling it was hopeless and a waste of time. But unlike all the other banks, they actually took me seriously. They listened to what I had to say. And after I'd filled out another stack of papers, they shook my hand and treated me like a serious client.

After I left the office, though, I still had to wait for their approval. Once again, doubt was overtaking my confidence.

I didn't expect to hear back from GMAC. But after a few days, they called to tell me they had more paperwork for me to fill out. So, okay, I'd fill out more paperwork.

Then, they called again for me to do more paperwork.

And for several weeks I had to keep answering questions.

Then they asked me to explain, *in detail*, what had happened when I'd failed to make payments on my condo.

By that time, I was feeling very frustrated and used every curse word I could to explain that I had made every payment on time. I'd never missed a payment, and it was their mistake, not mine.

I thought that would be the last I would hear from GMAC Mortgage Corporation. I had to set this illusion behind me and get on with my life.

But just a few days later, to my surprise, Dan Patry called to tell me the good news that I had been approved! They had a closing date set for the second week of April, and all I had to bring was my ID and a check for $314.56.

I was absolutely stunned by this news.

After four months of constant stress, the nightmare would finally be over.

I met up with Dan one last time, in the office of Granite Title Company, on April 11, 1995, to sign another stack of papers.

I felt a great relief this time. My ordeal was truly over, and the bad credit which had haunted me for the past three years—and the fear of wasting my money paying rent for the rest of my life—was a thing of the past.

I actually now owned my own house, with instant equity.

I stood up from my seat feeling a lot lighter, as if a heavy load had been lifted from me.

Dan looked up at me, smiled, and asked me if I'd had any doubts.

"Well," I said, "maybe just a little."

But he said, "Nope, not me! I knew we could make it happen."

It had to be a miracle from God that everything worked out the way it did. And I could never thank Patry Family Realty enough for all their dedication and hard work in helping me buy that house on Riverside Street. They had saved me from financial ruin, and this gave me overwhelming opportunities in the years to come.

Within the next two weeks, I had completely moved into my new home. I wasted no time, cleaning out the basement, scrubbing the walls clean from mildew, and installing a new furnace and hot water heater. Upstairs, I used Murphy's Oil Soap and opened the windows to allow fresh air to flow through. For a house that had been neglected for nearly five years, it looked surprisingly like a home again.

I also borrowed my mother's lawnmower to mow the lawn. Then I planted perennials along the side porch. Before summer had even begun, my house was looking beautiful both inside and out.

When I met my new neighbor, Mr. Skinner, who was a grey, thin-haired man in his late sixties, he was very interested in renting space in my garage. He was always smiling and working on projects around his house, whether he was digging up the ground to build proper water drainage behind his house to keep his basement dry or inside laying down floor tiles. He was a jack of all trades, and he was always there to help me with any projects I needed help on. We worked out a deal. In exchange for a rented space in my garage, he helped remodel my bathroom.

So, I was finally feeling good about my life and the direction I was heading. The only thing missing in my life was a good woman. I had been calling Marsi every week and sending pictures and letters along with my proposal to marry her. We had only met during my last two weeks of living in California, and we hadn't seen each other since. My imagination had grown beyond her domineering beauty. I called her in the middle of the night.

"Marsi, will you marry me?"

"Oh, how cute!" was her first response.

But then it took some persuading. "Marsi, I have this beautiful house, and we can have a few kitties and bunnies to play in the back yard."

I also said, "You are so beautiful. I love you, Marsi."

And she finally said *yes!*

So, on October 5, 1995, I took on her name for what was a very short- lived arrangement. We talked on the phone and wrote letters every week, making plans to live together soon.

I would not see her again for the next 11 years.

But I carried her name from that day on. My legal name became Steven M. Jordan.

1996 proved to be a year of prosperity for me. While rents in Portland were increasing to nearly $800 per month for small one-bedroom apartments, I had it made. My budget was easy to meet, with only $569 per month for a mortgage on a 3-bedroom home. So, I didn't *have* to work so hard anymore. But sometimes I did, just to keep a little extra money in the bank.

With extra money, extra time, and a new name, I needed to get out and find something new to do. I needed to join new groups where people never knew me as Stephen Smith. First, I tried taking karate classes. But after a few weeks, I realized it was taking up too much of my time. And I tried getting into network marketing, but I just wasn't really into it and failed to make a single sale.

I did, though, think it would be a lot of fun just to get my name out to a lot of places to start receiving mail with my new name.

The one class that changed my life forever was a vegetarian cooking class. After nearly 10 years without eating meat, I thought I knew everything about eating vegetarian. My philosophy was, *if it ain't got no meat in it, then it's okay to be eat'n it.*

To my surprise, though, I didn't know *anything at all* about eating a healthy vegetarian diet. I had been nothing but a junk food vegetarian for the past ten years, consuming nothing but processed soy products, cheese, and sugary snacks. Where were all the vegetables in my diet?

I joined the class hoping simply to meet other vegetarians. But I actually started learning more and more each week. And I became great friends with Larry Fleming, the class instructor, a devout Seventh Day Adventist who had been setting up vegetarian restaurants all over the world for nearly twenty years.

To my surprise, when I asked Larry if it had been him passing out business cards for free vegetarian dinners in Hollywood back in 1987, he said, "Oh, yes!" He had been in Hollywood promoting a new restaurant back then.

Now that upset me just a little. I could have learned all this stuff many years earlier. I could have saved myself from a lot of headaches, tiredness, and other health issues if only I'd started eating a total vegan diet many years before.

Over the next several years, I became very close friends with Larry and his wife Maria. By the end of 1997, I was excited to be a part-time employee in the first of their many-to-come Little Lads Vegan Restaurants. Larry's plan was to start the very first vegan fast food restaurant franchise. At its peak he had, I think, six or seven active restaurants in different locations in Maine, plus one large restaurant in New York City. His goal was to serve fast, affordable, healthy vegan food.

His restaurants served an all-you-can-eat vegan buffet for just $2.99.

But, of course, none of these restaurants ever turned a profit. Most of them barely paid the rent. Their only mission was to promote and educate about the vegan lifestyle.

Working at the Portland Little Lads gave me the opportunity to meet new friends. Rick was a big guy at 37 years old and bound to his wheelchair with cerebral palsy when we met. He overheard me preaching the healthy benefits of eating a lot of vegetables and keeping a strict vegan diet.

Rick decided he wanted to give this vegan lifestyle a try, and we became instant friends. When he invited me to his apartment that same day, he dragged a big trash can up to his refrigerator, opened the door, and started tossing all the meat into the trash.

"Wow, you're really serious about going vegan," I said, smiling as I helped take his trash out to the dumpster.

And for the next two years, we were the absolute best of friends. We went everywhere together, cooked up vegan meals, and invited our friends over for dinner. Rick's health and strength in his legs improved rapidly. He was able to stand on his own after just a few days. Within six months, he was able to walk across a room on his own. His doctors were very impressed with his rapid improvement but refused to believe it had anything to do with his change in diet.

After just one year of staying on a totally vegan diet, though, Rick was able to walk an entire mile. I sat in his wheelchair while he pushed me along The Baxter Boulevard from one mile-marker to the next. He fell once but got up on his own and finished the mile. I felt it was a great accomplishment and truly believe to this day that if he had continued to eat a healthy vegan diet, he would have had no use for that wheelchair ever again.

But we'll never know just how much strength he could have gained in his legs. With all the persuasion from his doctors and social workers to start eating meat again, he finally gave in to his old eating habits. When he went on an all-out binge of eating Big Mac's, Bacon Double Cheeseburgers, Twinkies, doughnuts and other junk food, it instantly set him back worse than he was before, after having made a whole year of progress as a vegan.

Along with the loss of strength in his legs, his anger grew out of control. And our friendship began to fall apart soon after. I blamed his social workers and doctors 100% for the condition he was in. That also held true for the millions of other patients out there who could have been cured if only their doctors had told them to stop eating junk food and start eating more fruits and vegetables.

By 2002, I felt almost guilty for having a 3-bedroom home of my own, while other people couldn't even afford a one-bedroom apartment. I had a beautiful garden in which I grew a lot of my own vegetables and knew I'd accomplished a lot for a single guy. Whenever I thought back to what my life had been like before I was given the great opportunity to own my own house, I truly felt a great responsibility to help others.

When I first saw Camille, I thought she was creepy, disgusting, and lazy. She was a tall black woman, a single mother of two, who dressed very provocatively and looked a lot older than her twenty-something age. In my younger years, I would have avoided coming anywhere near this creepy-looking lady. But as in the days when I'd met Heather, Camille was the only friend who came to see me. Being a Christian, I knew it was wrong of me to prejudge anyone, no matter what their appearance might be. You never knew what their situation might be. Maybe she'd never had the same opportunities I'd had.

Camille had been raised in The Seventh Day Adventist Church. But she was a heavy drug user, lived in a filthy apartment, and fed her kids nothing but junk food. Her lifestyle was far from the church teachings of living a clean and healthy lifestyle. She attended church occasionally, but usually it was when she was looking for help or a handout, sometimes seeking attention and adding a lot of drama to a long prayer.

For some reason, after helping her out once, I became the person she called every time she needed someone to talk to. I was there for her calls many times in the middle of the night. I'd listen to the drama about her life as a prostitute and how badly she wanted to change her life. I talked her out of many suicide attempts, and we prayed together on the phone. I was always there to help her in any way I could.

And I always thought that one day, when she finally got her life together, she would come back and thank me for all the times I'd helped her.

One cold November evening, Camille stopped by and came knocking on my door. It was urgent, she said. She had been evicted from her apartment. It was cold and she had nowhere else to go. Plus, the Department of Human Services had been threatening to take her kids away, and she had lost her Section 8 housing welfare checks. She'd come to me as her last resort.

I couldn't just leave her out in the cold. So, I let her stay in a spare room that she had stayed in a few times before. I'd never had a problem with her spending the night before. We'd usually stayed up late listening to music or watching a movie together. But this time she had nowhere else to go and she would be staying a little longer.

After about a week of her staying at my place, I was getting pretty sick and tired of cleaning up behind her. I thought this was supposed to be a temporary stay, but it seemed to drag on. I remembered, though, what it had been like for me when I'd had no place to live. I remember how hard it had been to find a job when I didn't even have an address for that first section of a job application. I knew I had to be there to keep helping her out.

So, when I noticed Hannaford's Super Market was accepting applications for several available positions, I hurried home to tell her the good news. "Camille! Camille! Guess what? I've got some great news! They're hiring down at Hannaford's. You've got to hurry and go down there and fill out an application!"

I'd thought she would be as excited as I was, but she just looked at me like, *so what?* It didn't concern her in the slightest.

Another week passed, and she still made no attempt to find a job or clean up behind herself. I had to get out for work every day, while she stayed at my house making a mess. The house had become unbearable with the cigarette smoke and filthy dishes. And when I asked her to start cleaning up behind herself, she became very angry and violent. I couldn't take it any longer. I began to fear for my own life and for what she might do to my cat.

I packed up a few clothes and put MARi in her carrier box then snuck out of the house. Even though my friendship with Rick was on shaky terms at the time, he let me stay in his apartment during the two weeks it took to legally have Camille evicted from my house. It was a long, stressful two weeks. She turned up the heat, opened the windows, and kept all the lights on just to run the utility bills as high as she could. She did everything she could to make herself a big cost to me. The legal fees were costly too, but she finally left.

And what a mess she left behind.

Rick and I still remained friends of a sort, but our relationship would never be as close as it had been before.

Still, I'd helped a lot of mentally ill people during that time of close friendship with Rick. And one thing I'd noticed was, they were all much smarter than they believed they were. Evidently, a long time ago somebody had told them they were stupid. And for some reason, these people had never tried to prove them wrong. So, that's what they believed.

And then there were those useless doctors and social workers who did everything they could to keep them believing *that was what they were*. As for Camille, she was gone, and I didn't care what happened to her. She'd had every opportunity to do something with her life, yet she'd done nothing to help herself. For years I'd felt sorry for *all* the homeless people, thinking life was just unfair to them...

But I'd finally come to realize that I was wasting my time helping people who'd had even more opportunity than me but had done nothing with it.

CHAPTER 30

Stop and Smell the Flowers

In the spring of 2006, after many years of postcards and letters, Marsi finally came to see me. I was overjoyed to see her, but I knew that we were not the same two people who had met many years before. I'd realized just how crazy she truly was by reading her postcards and letters.

We did have a few enjoyable days together finding an isolated beach along the Biddeford Pool Road or going on nature hikes. Most of her craziness would show, though, whenever we were out in public, like the time we ate a Chinese restaurant and she argued with the man behind the serving line. She told the man she didn't want any rice on her plate, and the man served her a half plate of vegetables. She immediately snapped. "LOOK AT THAT PLATE! THERE'S HARDLY ANYTHING ON IT! WHEN I SAID I DIDN'T WANT ANY RICE, YOU SHOULD HAVE GIVEN ME MORE VEGETABLES!!!"

I tried to calm her down while the man went back to fill her plate with more vegetables. But she continued to curse and complain the whole time we were eating our dinner. Then, after eating just a small portion of her vegetables, she'd had enough, and I ate the rest.

I said to her, "See, you didn't even eat half the amount he gave to you the first time. Why did you have to argue over food you couldn't even finish anyway?"

She snapped back, "IT DIDN'T MATTER! WE PAID FOR A FULL PLATE AND I EXPECTED A FULL PLATE!!"

Then there were weekend drives up the coast and lots of talk about buying a big house overlooking the ocean. I was happy with a small house and yard— simple, easy to maintain, and affordable. But she wanted to look at million-dollar homes in Boothby Harbor.

I told her, "I hate big houses, I don't like anything to be complicated."

I'd thought I could tolerate her domineering personality and quick temper. But she was getting out of control, and she would start an argument even if I agreed with her. Whatever I once had felt for her was certainly not based on much more than my imagination. I had been living in such extremely negative circumstances, I'd actually thought she was a positive energy drawing me near to her.

Although we remained close friends, her attitude only worsened in the years to come.

When I first met Renee in November of 2007, we were on our way to an archeology seminar at The University of Maine. I had to listen to a lot of criticism from Marsi. "There must be something wrong with this woman you met, because she's going with you."

But criticism like that didn't bother me at all. I'd heard it so many times before. Renee was the first woman to really take interest in me— despite the insults I had to take from Marsi. She said, "The only reason she is staying with you is because she is insecure."

Those insults didn't tell the truth. Renee was very intelligent, very easy going, and open minded. And she took care of herself.

I can say today, Renee and I have learned so much from each other over the years. Most importantly, she's been a savior to me. For the first time in my life, at age 42, I feel safe in a relationship without all the worry of quick mood swings or the threat of her leaving me just when we get to feeling good.

Renee has taught me how to relax, whereas before my life was full of stress. I'd known that I'd carried enough stress for it to have serious effects on my health. No matter how many fruits and vegetables I'd eaten or how much I'd exercised, stress alone could have been a killer.

Somehow I Survived... all those years under constant stress.

It was Jesus who saved me from my sins, but it was Renee who made my life worth living. Renee was, and still is, far different from any other woman I've met. She's never tried to pin me down on the floor after few drinks. She's never kept asking me to buy her things or pay her bills. She's never told me I was stupid or insecure.

Renee, the complete opposite of Marsi, with beautiful brown eyes and dark hair, is truly like no other woman I've ever met, and she actually helps me in any way she can. We work together preparing dinner and washing dishes. We spend